ANDROID DREAMS

TOBY WALSH

Hurst and Company, London

ANDROID

DREAMS

The Past, Present
and Future of Artificial
Intelligence

TOBY WALSH

First published in the United Kingdom in 2017 by
C. Hurst & Co. (Publishers) Ltd.,
41 Great Russell Street, London, WC1B 3PL
© Toby Walsh, 2017
All rights reserved.
First published in Australia by LaTrobe University Press
in conjunction with Black Inc.

A Cataloguing-in-Publication data record for this book
is available from the British Library.

ISBN: 9781849048712

This book is printed using paper from registered sustainable
and managed sources.

www.hurstpublishers.com

Printed and bound in Great Britain by Bell and Bain Ltd, Glasgow

To A and B
who make my life so interesting

Contents

Prologue

I begin with a quotation from 1950. The world was a much simpler place back then. Television was in black and white. Jet planes were still to enter passenger service. The silicon transistor was yet to be invented. And there were fewer than a dozen computers in existence worldwide.[1] Each was a glorious combination of vacuum tubes, relays, plug boards and capacitors that filled a room.

It therefore took a bold person to predict: 'I believe that at the end of the [twentieth] century the use of words and general educated opinion will have altered so much that one will be able to speak of machines thinking without expecting to be contradicted.'[2] What an idea! Thinking machines. Will machines really be able to think in the near future? And if they can, how long before they are better at it than us?

But first—who made this bold prediction? Should their prediction carry much weight? Well, the person who made it was ranked by *Time* magazine in 1999 as one of the '100 Most Important People of the 20th Century'.[3] He was, without a doubt, one of the century's more enigmatic thinkers. A mathematician. A wartime hero. Above all, a dreamer. And his dreams continue to influence us today, long past his early death.

An Oscar-winning movie has told the story of how pivotal he was in the breaking of the Germans' Enigma code during World

War II. Winston Churchill described how he and his fellow code-breakers were 'the geese that laid the golden egg—but never cackled'. By the reckoning of most historians, breaking Enigma shortened the war by at least two years. And that undoubtedly saved millions of lives. But come the end of the twenty-first century, I doubt that code-breaking is what the author of our quotation will be *most* remembered for.

En route to breaking Enigma, he laid down the theoretical foundations of computing and helped build one of the first practical computing devices, the bombe, which was used to decode the Germans' messages.[4] His ideas permeate computer science today. He proposed a fundamental and completely general model of the computer, a model he dreamed up before we even had the first computer.[5] In recognition of his contributions, the most prestigious prize in computing is named after him. But despite the immense impact that computers have on every aspect of our lives, I doubt he will be most remembered for having laid many of the foundation stones of computer science.

He also had a large impact on a branch of biology called morphogenesis. This impact stems from a single paper, 'The Chemical Basis of Morphogenesis', which he published in one of the world's oldest scientific journals.[6] Previous authors in the journal include iconic figures such as Charles Darwin (whose theory of evolution changed the way we think about ourselves), Alexander Fleming (whose discovery of penicillin has saved tens of millions of lives), and James Watson, Francis Crick and Dorothy Hodgkin (whose discovery of the structure of DNA kick-started the genetic revolution). His paper put forth a theory of pattern formation in nature, explaining how stripes, spots and spirals are created in plants and animals. The paper is now his most highly cited. However, I doubt that pattern formation is what he will be most remembered for come the end of the twenty-first century.

He is also a significant figure for the gay community. In the 1950s homosexuality was illegal in the United Kingdom. Many view his prosecution for homosexual acts in 1952 and his subsequent chemical castration as having contributed to his untimely death, and as an abandonment by the British establishment that he had so helped in World War II.[7] In 2009, following a public petition, Prime Minister Gordon Brown formally apologised for his treatment. Four years later, the Queen signed a rare royal pardon. Unsurprisingly, some in the gay community view him as a martyr. But I doubt that he will be most remembered for these issues at the end of the twenty-first century.

So for what will he be most remembered? I suspect it will be for a paper he published in *Mind*, a rather obscure philosophical journal. The quotation at the start of this chapter is taken from this paper. Up to that point, the journal had perhaps been most famous for publishing 'What the Tortoise Said to Achilles', a paper written by Lewis Carroll on the logic of Zeno's paradox.[8] The paper from which our quotation is taken is today recognised as one of the most seminal in the history of Artificial Intelligence.[9] It envisages a future in which machines think. When our author wrote this paper, the dozen or so computers in existence around the world were large and very expensive. They were also much less powerful than the smartphone that likely sits in your pocket today. It must have been hard to imagine then what an impact computers would have on our lives. And even harder to imagine that, one day, they might *think* for themselves. Yet the paper anticipates and attempts to refute all the major arguments that have subsequently been raised against the possibility of thinking machines. Many view the author of this paper as one of the fathers of the field of AI.

He is, of course, Alan Mathison Turing, Fellow of the Royal Society, born 1912, died 1954, by his own hand.

I predict that, when the twenty-first century ends, Alan Turing will be most remembered for laying the foundations to this field that is trying to build thinking machines. These machines are set to alter our lives just as dramatically as the steam engine did at the start of the industrial age. They will change how we work, how we play, how we educate our children, how we treat the sick and elderly, and ultimately how human-kind is remembered. They are likely our most transformative creations. Science fiction is full of robots that think. Science fact is set shortly to follow this lead.

Our lives are racing towards the future dreamed of in science fiction. The pocket computers we carry with us every day can answer the strangest questions, entertain us with games and movies, guide us home when we get lost, find us a job or a life-long partner, play a love song, and connect us instantly to friends around the world. Indeed, being a phone is one of their least remarkable features.

Of course, my prediction that Turing's greatest legacy will be helping to start the field of Artificial Intelligence raises several questions. Will Turing be remembered at the turn of the next century by these machines that think? Will this be a good future? Will robots take over all the hard and dangerous work? Will our economies prosper? Will we able to work less and enjoy more leisure? Or will Hollywood be right, and will the future be difficult? Will the rich get richer and the rest of us get poorer? Will many of us be put out of work? Worse still, will the robots ultimately take over? Are we currently sowing the seeds of our own destruction?

This book will explore such questions, and will predict where AI is taking us. In Part One, I look at what we can learn from the past. You can perhaps best understand where a technology is taking us if you know where it came from. In Part Two, I con-sider where AI is today, and examine the risks and benefits of building thinking machines. I try to assess realistically what this great endeavour might achieve. The idea of building thinking machines is undoubtedly a bold and ambitious endeavour that, if it succeeds, will have a huge impact on society. Finally, in Part Three, I discuss the future of AI in more detail. Are some of the wild predictions found in books and films likely to come to pass? Are they fanciful enough? And I'll put some 'skin in the game' by making ten predictions about what AI will have achieved by 2050. Some may surprise you.

These are heady days for the field. In the last five years, billions of dollars of venture capital have poured into companies working on Artificial Intelligence.[10] Some very large bets are being made. The computing giant IBM is betting $1 billion on its cognitive computing platform, Watson.[11] Toyota is spending $1 billion on a lab to study autonomy. OpenAI, an initiative to build safe and general-purpose Artificial Intelligence, is being backed with another $1 billion. The Saudi-backed SoftBank Vision Fund, launched in October 2015, has around $100 billion to invest in technology companies, with a focus on AI and the 'internet of things'. And many other tech players, including Google, Facebook and Baidu, are investing big in Artificial Intelligence. It is, without a doubt, a very exciting time to be working in the field. With so much money flowing in, it is possible that progress towards thinking machines will even accelerate.

WHY READ THIS BOOK?

Computers are transforming our lives today at a remarkable pace. As a result, there is a considerable appetite globally to learn more about Artificial Intelligence. Many commentators have predicted great things. In May 2016 the chief envisioning officer for Microsoft UK, Dave Coplin, put it very boldly: Artificial Intelligence is 'the most important technology that anybody on the planet is working on today', he said. '[It] will change how we relate to technology. It will change how we relate to each other.

I would argue that it will even change how we perceive what it means to be human.'

A month earlier, Google's CEO, Sundar Pichai, described how AI is at the centre of Google's strategy. 'A key driver ... has been our long-term investment in machine learning and AI ... Looking to the future ... we will move from mobile first to an AI first world.'

Yet many other commentators have predicted that AI carries with it many dangers, even to the extent that it may hasten the end of humankind if we're not too careful. In 2014 Elon Musk warned an audience at MIT that 'we should be very careful about artificial intelligence. If I had to guess at what our biggest existential threat is, it's probably that.' Musk is the serial entrepreneur, inventor and investor famous for founding PayPal, Tesla and SpaceX. He's shaken up the banking sector, the car industry and space travel with his innovations, so you might expect him to know a thing or two about the ability of technology, especially computing, to disrupt the world. And Musk has backed his opinion that AI poses a serious existential threat to humankind with his own money. At the start of 2015 he donated $10 million to the Future of Life Institute to fund researchers studying how to keep Artificial Intelligence safe. Now, $10 million may not be a huge amount of money for someone as rich as Musk, whose net worth of around $10 billion puts him in the world's top 100 wealthiest people. But later in 2015 he raised his bet 100-fold, announcing that he will be one of the main backers of the $1 billion OpenAI project. The goals of this project are to build *safe* Artificial Intelligence and then to open-source it to the world.

Following Musk's warning, the physicist Stephen Hawking pitched in on the dangers of Artificial Intelligence. Not without irony, Hawking welcomed a software update for his speech synthesiser with a warning that came in the electronic voice of that technology: 'The development of full artificial intelligence could spell the end of the human race.'

Several other well-known technologists, including Microsoft's Bill Gates and Apple's Steve Wozniak (aka 'Woz'), have predicted a dangerous future for AI. The father of information theory, Claude Shannon, wrote in 1987: 'I visualize a time when we will be to robots what dogs are to humans ... I'm rooting for the machines!'[12] Even Alan Turing himself, in a broadcast on the BBC Third Programme in 1951, offered a cautionary prediction:

> If a machine can think, it might think more intelligently than we do, and then where should we be? Even if we could keep the machines in a subservient position, for instance by turning off the power at strategic moments, we should, as a species, feel greatly humbled ... It ... is certainly something which can give us anxiety.

Of course, not every technologist and technocrat is concerned about the impact of thinking machines on humanity. In January 2016 Facebook's Mark Zuckerberg dismissed these sorts of fears: 'I think we can build AI so it works for us and helps us. Some people fear-monger about how AI is a huge danger, but that seems far-fetched to me and much less likely than disasters due to widespread disease, violence, etc.' Andrew Ng, one of the leading AI researchers at China's internet giant Baidu, has said: 'Worrying about AI is like worrying about overpopulation on Mars.' (Don't forget that one of Elon Musk's other 'moonshot' projects is to populate Mars.)

So who should you believe? If technologists like Musk and Zuckerberg can't agree, doesn't that mean that there's at least something we need to worry about? Fears about Artificial Intelligence go some way back. One of the finest visionaries of the future, science fiction writer Arthur C. Clarke, foretold the dangerous consequences of Artificial Intelligence back in 1968. Clarke has an amazing track record of foreseeing the technologies of the future. He predicted the use of geosynchronous satellites, a global digital library (which we now call the internet), machine translation and more. But the HAL 9000 computer in his novel *2001: A Space Odyssey* famously demonstrated the consequences of AI taking control.

Inspired by Clarke and other visionaries, I started dreaming about Artificial Intelligence as a young boy. And I've worked all my life in the field, trying to make these dreams come true. It is a little concerning, then, to have people *outside* the field, especially when they are very smart physicists and successful tech entrepreneurs, predicting that AI will be the end of humankind. Perhaps the people closest to the action should contribute to this debate? Or are we just too embedded in what we are doing to see the risks? And why would we work on something that could destroy our very own existence?

Some concerns about Artificial Intelligence perhaps come from some deep-seated parts of our psyches. These are fears captured in stories such as the Prometheus myth, the story of the Greek deity who gave man the gift of fire, which has subsequently been the cause of so much good *and* so much bad. The same fear is present in Mary Shelley's *Frankenstein*—that our creations may one day hurt us. Just because the fear is old does not mean it is without reason. There are many technologies we have invented that should give, and have given, us pause for thought: nuclear bombs, cloning, blinding lasers and social media, to name just a few. One of my goals in this book is to help you understand how much you should welcome and how much you should worry about the coming of thinking machines.

Some of the responsibility lies with us, the scientists working on Artificial Intelligence. We haven't communicated enough, and when we have, we have often used misleading language. We need to communicate better what we are doing and where this might be taking society. It is our responsibility as scientists to do so. And it is even more essential for us to do so when, as I argue in this book, much of the change will be societal, and society changes much more slowly than technology. Like most technologies, AI is morally neutral. It can lead to good or bad outcomes.

One of the problems of the debate is that there are a lot of misconceptions about Artificial Intelligence. I hope to dispel some of these. One of my arguments is that people, especially those outside the field, tend to overestimate the capabilities of Artificial Intelligence today and in the near future. They see a computer playing Go better than any human can, and as they themselves cannot play Go well, they imagine the computer can also do many other intelligent tasks.[13] Or at least that it would not be hard to get it to do many other intelligent tasks. However, that Go-playing program, like all the other computer programs we make today, is an *idiot savant*. It can only do one thing well. It cannot even play other games such as chess or poker. It would take a significant engineering effort by us humans to get it to play any other game. It certainly isn't going to wake up one morning and decide that it's bored of beating us at Go and wants instead to win some money playing online poker. And there's absolutely no chance it will wake up one morning and start dreaming of world domination. It has no desires. It is a computer program and can only do what it is programmed to do— which is to play Go exceptionally well.

On the other hand, I will also argue that all of us tend to underestimate the long-term changes technology can bring. We've had smartphones for just a decade and look how they have transformed our lives. Think how the internet, which is only around two decades old, has changed almost every aspect of our lives—and imagine therefore what changes the next two decades might bring. Because of the multiplying effects of technology, the next twenty years are likely to see even greater changes than the last twenty years. We humans are rather poor at understanding exponential growth, since evolution has optimised us to deal with immediate dangers. We are not good at understanding long-term risks, or at expecting black swans.[14] If we really understood the long term well, we'd all stop buying lottery tickets and save much bigger pensions. The improvements that compound growth brings are hard for our pleasure-seeking, pain-avoiding brains to comprehend. We live in the moment.

Before you get any further into this book, I have to warn you: predicting the future is an inexact science. The Danish physicist and Nobel Prize–winner Niels Bohr wrote: 'Prediction is very difficult, especially if it's about the future.' I expect that my broad brushstrokes will be correct, but it is certain some of the details will be wrong. But in exploring these ideas, I hope you will understand why I and thousands of my colleagues have devoted our lives to exploring the exciting path that will take us to thinking machines. And I hope you will understand why it is a path that we should—indeed must—explore if we are to continue to improve the quality of our lives on this planet. There are several areas in which there is a moral imperative for us to develop Artificial Intelligence, as many lives can be saved.

Above all, I hope you will consider how society itself may need to change. The ultimate message of this book is that Artificial Intelligence can lead us down many different paths, some good and some bad, but society must choose which path to take, *and* act on that choice. There are many decisions we can hand over to the machines. But I argue that only some decisions should be—even when the machines can make them better than we can. As a society, we need to start making some choices as to what we entrust to the machines.

WHO SHOULD READ THIS BOOK?

The book is intended for the interested but non-specialist reader. You might want to understand where Artificial Intelligence might be taking us. Are some of the more extravagant predictions about thinking machines likely to come to pass? Will there be a technological singularity? Should you worry about where AI is taking us? How will it affect you and your children? And how long will it be before some of the predictions occur? To avoid interruptions, I have put references and additional technical notes in endnotes. You can read this book and ignore them completely. However, if you want to explore an idea more deeply, these notes will provide you with further details and a springboard into the literature.

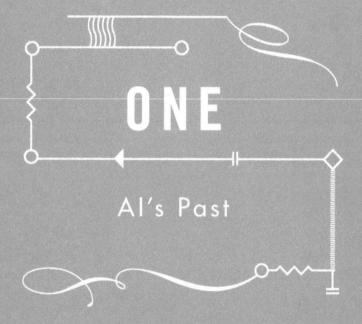

ONE

AI's Past

1: The AI Dream

To understand where Artificial Intelligence is taking us, it helps to understand where it has come from, and where it is today. We can then start to extrapolate forward to the future.

Artificial Intelligence proper began in 1956, when one of its founding fathers, John McCarthy,[1] proposed the name at the now famous Dartmouth Summer Research Project on Artificial Intelligence in New Hampshire.[2] There's arguably much wrong with the name McCarthy chose. Intelligence is itself a poorly defined concept. And putting the adjective *'artificial'* in front of anything never sounds very good. It opens you to countless jokes about Natural Intelligence and Artificial Stupidity. But for better or worse, we're stuck now with the name Artificial Intelligence. In any case, the history of AI goes back much further—even before the invention of the computer. Humankind has been thinking about machines that might think, and how we might model thinking, for centuries.

THE PREHISTORY OF AI

Like many stories, this one has no clear beginning. It is, however, intimately connected to the story of the invention of logic.

One possible starting point is the third century BC, when Aristotle founded the field of formal logic. Without logic, we would not have the modern digital computer. And logic has often been (and continues to be) seen as a model for thinking, a means to make precise how we reason and form arguments.

Besides some mechanical machines for calculating astronomical movements and doing other rudimentary calculations, humankind made little other progress towards thinking machines for the 2000 or so years following Aristotle. But, to be fair, even in the most advanced countries people had a few other problems on their plates, like war, disease, hunger and surviving the Dark Ages.

One standout was the thirteenth-century Catalan writer, poet, theologian, mystic, mathematician, logician and martyr, Ramon Llull.[3] Some consider Llull to be one of the fathers of computing. He invented a primitive logic which could *mechanically* identify what he claimed were all possible truths about a subject. His, then, was one of the first logical and mechanical methods to produce knowledge. Llull's ideas were, however, not greatly recognised in his time, though they are believed to have strongly influenced the next person in our story.

LET US CALCULATE

As the intellectual fog of the Middle Ages started to clear, our story accelerates. One of the standout figures who appeared was Gottfried Wilhelm Leibniz.[4] One of his most far-sighted intellectual contributions was his idea that much human thought could be reduced to calculations of some sort, and that such calculations could identify errors in our reasoning or resolve differences of opinion. He wrote: 'The only way to rectify our reasonings is to make them as tangible as those of the Mathematicians, so that we can find our error at a glance, and when there are disputes among persons, we can simply say: Let us calculate [calculemus], without further ado, to see who is right.'[5]

Leibniz proposed a primitive logic with which to perform such calculations. He imagined an 'alphabet of human thought', in which each fundamental concept was represented by a unique symbol. Computers are ultimately engines for manipulating symbols.[6] Leibniz's abstraction is thus essential if digital computers are to 'think'. The argument is as follows. Even though computers *only* manipulate symbols, if these symbols stand for fundamental concepts, as Leibniz proposed, then computers can derive new concepts and thus perform human-like reasoning.

Around this time, we also come across a philosopher, Thomas Hobbes who laid another stone in the philosophical foundations of thinking machines.[7] Like Leibniz, Hobbes equated reasoning with computation. He wrote: 'By reasoning, I understand computation ... To reason therefore is the same as to add or to subtract.'[8]

Equating reasoning with computation, as both Leibniz and Hobbes did, is a first step on the road to building a thinking machine. Even though the mechanical calculator had been invented a little before both Hobbes and Leibniz were writing, it would take nearly two more centuries before someone tried to put reasoning by computation into practice.[9]

Another towering polymath to appear as the Dark Ages passed was René Descartes.[10] He contributed an important philosophical idea that continues to haunt AI studies today: '*Cogito ergo sum.*' That is, 'I think therefore I am.' These three Latin words elegantly associate thought with (human) existence. Reasoning backwards, we can conclude that if you don't exist, you cannot think.[11] Descartes' idea, therefore, challenges the very *possibility* of thinking machines. Machines don't exist like we do. They lack many special attributes that we associate with our existence: emotions, ethics, consciousness and creativity, to name just a few. And, as we shall see, many of these attributes have been raised as arguments against the existence of machines that think.

For example, as machines are not conscious, they cannot think. Or, as machines are not creative, they cannot be said to think. We'll return to these arguments shortly.

BOOLE AND BABBAGE

The next major player in our story doesn't arrive for another two hundred years. George Boole was a self-taught mathematician.[12] Despite having no university degree, he was appointed in 1849 as the first professor of mathematics at Queen's College, County Cork, Ireland, based on a number of mathematical articles he had published in his spare time from his day job running a school. Boole's university position, somewhat on the fringes of the academic world of the time, gave him the freedom to have some ideas that would be central to the development of computing, and to the dream of building thinking machines. Boole proposed that logic could be formalised by algebraic operations acting on two values: true or false, on or off, 0 or 1. Such 'Boolean' logic describes the operation of every computer today; they are really just sophisticated machines for processing streams of Boole's 0s and 1s. While the importance of Boole's ideas was recognised by few in his day, it is not a stretch to claim that he was the father of the current information age.

Boole, however, had greater ambitions for his logic that were even further ahead of their time. The title of his most complete work about his logic gives an idea of these goals: *An Investigation of the Laws of Thought*. Boole didn't want simply to provide a mathematical foundation to logic, he wanted to explain human reasoning itself. In introducing this work, he wrote:

> The design of the following treatise is to investigate the fundamental laws of those operations of the mind by which reasoning is performed; to give expression to them in the symbolical language of a Calculus, and upon this foundation to establish the science of Logic and construct its

method ... and, finally, to collect from the various elements of truth brought to view in the course of these inquiries some probable intimations concerning the nature and constitution of the human mind.

Boole never fully realised these ambitions. Indeed, his work was largely unrecognised in his day, and he was to die an untimely death ten years later.[13] But even if Boole had not been in the academic backwater of Cork, he had no machine on which to automate these dreams.

Fascinatingly, two years before his death Boole met the next player in our story, Charles Babbage. This took place at the Great London Exposition, where the two great innovators are believed to have talked about Babbage's 'thinking engine'. It is tantalising to wonder what they might have dreamed up together if Boole had not died shortly after. Charles Babbage was a polymath: a mathematician, philosopher, inventor and engineer.[14] He dreamed of building mechanical computers. Although he never succeeded, he is nevertheless considered by many to be the father of the *programmable* computer. His Analytical Engine was designed to be programmed using punched cards.

The idea that computers operate according to a program, and that this program can be changed, is fundamental to the capabilities of computers. Your smartphone can be loaded with new apps, programs that Steve Jobs or any of the other makers of smartphones probably never dreamed of. In this way, it can be many things at once: a calculator, a note taker, a health monitor, a navigator, a camera, a movie player and even (it's sometimes hard to remember) a phone. This is an idea that Turing explored when proposing a general model for computing. A computer is a *universal* machine that can be programmed to do many different things. More subtly, computer programs can modify themselves. This capability is fundamental to the Artificial Intelligence dream. Learning appears to be a key part of our intelligence. If a computer is to simulate learning, it must have some way to modify its own program. Fortunately, it's relatively easy to write a computer program that can modify itself. A program is just data, and that can be manipulated: think of the numbers in your spreadsheet, the letters in your word processor or the colours in your digital image. Computers can therefore learn to do new tasks—that is, to change their program to do tasks that they were not initially programmed to do.

THE FIRST PROGRAMMER

Working with Babbage was Augusta Ada King, Countess of Lovelace.[15] She wrote a set of notes describing and explaining Babbage's Analytical Engine for a wider audience. In these notes, she wrote what is generally considered the first computer program. Babbage was focused on the engine's ability to perform numerical calculations, to compile astronomical and other tables. Lovelace, on the other hand, was able to dream about computers doing much more than mere number-crunching. She wrote that Babbage's invention 'might act upon other things besides number ... the engine might compose elaborate and scientific pieces of music of any degree of complexity or extent.'

This idea was a century ahead of its time. Lovelace's conceptual leap can be seen today in our smartphones, which manipulate sounds, images, videos and many other things besides numbers. However, she was also one of the first critics of Artificial Intelligence, dismissing the dream of building thinking machines that are creative. 'The Analytical Engine has no pretensions whatever to originate anything,' she wrote. 'It can do whatever we know how to order it to perform. It can follow analysis; but it has no power of anticipating any analytical relations or truths.'

This idea—that if computers are not creative, then they cannot be intelligent—has been the subject of much debate. Turing discussed it in his seminal *Mind* paper. It is an argument I will return to shortly, but before I do, I want to reflect on Lovelace's objection. The first person who thought about programming a computer—someone who was able to dream over a century ahead that computers would manipulate more than just numbers—was also highly sceptical about the final goal of making machines that think. It is not a simple dream. It is a dream that goes to the very heart of our position in the universe. Is there something that makes *us* special? Or are we also machines, just like our computers? The answer to these questions will ultimately change the way we think about ourselves. It threatens to change our position at the centre of things, as much as Copernicus's realisation that the Earth goes around the Sun, or Darwin's notion that we are descended from the apes.

One lesser-known figure who joins our story in the eighteenth century is William Stanley Jevons.[16] He made numerous contributions to mathematics and economics. But we are interested in the 'logic piano' he invented in 1870, a mechanical computer that could solve logical puzzles involving up to four true/false decisions—or, to borrow the language of Boole's logic, up to four variables that can take the value 0 or 1. In fact, Jevons built his piano to help teach logic. The original logical piano is still on display at the Museum of the History of Science in Oxford. The logic piano elegantly mechanises a small fragment of Boole's logic. Its inventor wrote that 'it will be evident that [the] mechanism is capable of replacing for the most part the action of thought required in the performance of logical deduction'.[17]

Jevons might therefore be said to have built a very primitive thinking machine, although I doubt the distinguished audience who witnessed its demonstration at the Royal Society in 1870 realised quite how vastly logic pianos were set to transform our lives. At the very least, this was one of the first tentative steps on the road to building computers, and thus to implementing Artificial Intelligence. Sadly, like several of the players in this story so far, Jevons died an untimely death; the logic piano went unmentioned in his obituary in the *Times*.[18]

THE LOGICAL REVOLUTION

Our story now moves forward to the start of the nineteenth century. This was a time for revolution in many fields: in science, art and politics. The foundations of physics were being shaken by Albert Einstein, Niels Bohr, Werner Heisenberg and others through the revolutionary ideas of relativity and quantum mechanics. The foundations of art were being shaken by movements like Impressionism and Dadaism, which rejected the classical past. And around the same time, the foundations of mathematics, and of logic as some of the bricks that make up those foundations, were also being violently shaken.

One of the greatest mathematicians of this time was David Hilbert.[19] In 1900 he identified twenty-three of the most challenging problems facing mathematics. Introducing these problems, he wrote:

> Who among us would not be happy to lift the veil behind which is hidden the future; to gaze at the coming developments of our science and at the secrets of its development in the centuries to come? What will be the ends toward which the spirit of future generations of mathematicians will tend? What methods, what new facts will the new century reveal in the vast and rich field of mathematical thought?

This almost poetic vision would be a fine introduction for the present book. Several of Hilbert's twenty-three problems concerned the foundations of mathematics itself. At that time, the very bedrock of mathematics seemed to be crumbling. Consider something as mathematically simple as a set. A set is just a collection of objects: the set of black cars; the set of silver cars; the set of black or silver cars; the set of cars that are neither black nor silver; the set of everything that isn't a silver car. In 1874 the

German mathematician Georg Cantor wrote down a formalisation of the mathematics of sets.[20] This may seem an odd project for a mathematician. Mathematics is about objects such as numbers and functions. Why would we be interested in something as simple as a set? Sets can, however, represent many different mathematical objects: numbers, functions, graphs, as well as many of the more exotic objects studied by mathematicians, such as manifolds, rings and vector spaces.[21]

Bertrand Russell, another of the great mathematicians of that time, proved that Cantor's attempt to formalise the mathematics of sets was doomed by circular paradoxes.[22] Consider again the set of all silver cars. This does not contain itself. Let's call this a normal set. On the other hand, consider the complement set, the set that contains everything that isn't a silver car. This does contain itself. Let's call this an abnormal set. Now, consider the set of all normal sets. Is the set of all normal sets itself normal? If it is normal, it would be contained in the set of all normal sets. That is, it would be contained in itself. However then it would be abnormal. So let's consider the alternative. Suppose the set of all normal sets is itself abnormal. As it is abnormal, it would be contained in itself, the set of all normal sets. But that makes it a normal set. This is Russell's famous paradox: the set cannot simultaneously be both normal and abnormal. We will see other similar circular paradoxes later in our story. Cantor's theory of sets was so riddled with paradoxes like this that some of his critics called him a 'scientific charlatan' and 'corrupter of youth'. But as the next actor in our story proves, none of this is Cantor's fault. Mathematics is fundamentally this way. And this poses a fundamental challenge for building thinking machines—at least for thinking machines that use logic to reason.

Responding to this crisis at the heart of mathematics, Hilbert formulated a program of work to try to put mathematics on a precise, logical foundation. Hilbert's program, as it came to be called, looks for a small set of basic facts or building blocks on which all of mathematics can be constructed. Hilbert's program also calls for a proof that this formalisation of mathematics contains none of the paradoxes that are to be found in Cantor's theory of sets. Once we have paradoxes, anything can be proven to hold. If we are to build thinking machines—machines that can do mathematics, amongst other activities—we need such building blocks.

THE END OF MATHEMATICS

In 1931 Hilbert's program was blown soundly apart by Kurt Gödel, one of the most important logicians in history.[23] He destroyed Hilbert's program by means of his two famous incompleteness theorems. These prove that any formalisation of mathematics rich enough to describe even something as simple as the whole numbers is inevitably incomplete or contains paradoxes. It follows that any mathematical system you build without paradoxes will also contain mathematical truths that cannot be proved. This is the *incompleteness* in Gödel's incompleteness theorems.

Gödel's results sank Hilbert's program and left mathematics with somewhat shaky foundations forever. The goal of being completely mathematical about mathematics itself is impossible. And this poses a deep philosophical challenge to the dream of building thinking machines. If we are to build thinking machines, and if these machines are to reason mathematically, as Leibniz and Hobbes would have us believe, then we need to provide them with a precise, logical formalisation of mathematics with which they can reason. But Gödel's incompleteness theorems demonstrate that we cannot write down the precise rules for mathematics, the kind of rules you could give to a computer, so that it could do *all* of mathematics.

The mathematical physicist Sir Roger Penrose[24] has been particularly vocal in promoting these sorts of arguments, and in using them to argue against the idea that Artificial Intelligence might one day exceed human intelligence.[25] Numerous objections have, however, been made to Penrose's arguments. Computers (like humans) need not be able to prove all of mathematics. Computers (like humans) can work within a system containing paradoxes. Gödel's theorems require us to think about infinite systems, but all humans and computers are finite. And computers will soon be built using different computational models, such as quantum computers, which go beyond those in Gödel's results. The consensus within the field remains that Gödel's theorems do not stand in the way of the dream of building thinking machines, in theory. And in practice, as I discuss shortly, we continue to make good progress towards this dream.

THINGS THAT CANNOT BE COMPUTED

This nearly brings us full circle, back to the mathematician who started this book, Alan Mathison Turing. He played a pivotal role in building computers, from both a practical and a theoretical perspective. He provided the fundamental abstract model, the Turing Machine, which is still used to describe computers mathematically today. But back in 1936, before we had even built one of these machines, Turing had another remarkable insight. He worked out that there were some problems that such machines could *never* compute. No one had ever programmed a computer at this point in time. There were no computers to program. Yet Turing had the vision to see that there would be some problems that not even the smartest programmer could get computers to solve.

One is the 'halting problem'. Can you write a computer program that decides if another program should halt (or stop)? This would be a useful program to have. You wouldn't want the control software of your fly-by-wire aircraft control system ever to stop. Equally, you would want the program that scans for new channels on your TV set-top box to stop. Turing proved that there are problems like the halting problem for which no computer program exists.[26] Recall that a program is itself just data. It can thus be input data to another program. We could try to write a program that takes another program as input, and decides if the program given as input would ever stop. Turing's remarkable result was to prove that, no matter how smart the programmer, no such program could ever be written.

Turing used a circular argument that was reminiscent of Russell's paradox about sets that do not contain themselves. Suppose we did have a program that could solve the halting problem. Let's call this Turing's program. Now we use this as a subroutine of a bigger program, which we will call Turing's super-program. This takes as input any program, and, using Turing's program as a subroutine, decides if the input program will halt. If the input program halts, Turing's super-program goes into an infinite loop that never halts. On the other hand, if the input program does not halt, Turing's super-program halts. This is where the circular part of Turing's argument comes into play. What does Turing's super-program do when we give it to itself as input? Turing's super-program can either halt or not halt on this input.

Let's consider both possibilities. Suppose Turing's super-program does not halt on this input. Now Turing's super-program does not halt when it is given as input a program that halts. So this means that Turing's super-program halts. So if Turing's super-program does not halt, then this means it halts. Let's consider the other possibility. Suppose Turing's super-program halts on this input. Now Turing's super-program halts when it is given as input a program that does not halt. This means that Turing's super-program would not halt. In either case, we have a contradiction. Turing's super-program cannot both halt and not halt.

Recall that I made one critical assumption: that Turing's program exists. This assumption leads to a contradiction, and so must be at fault. We can therefore conclude that Turing's program cannot exist. We cannot have a program that decides if any given input program would halt. Using this argument, Turing showed that there are problems that computers cannot solve.

The existence of problems that cannot be computed might seem to pose another fundamental challenge to the dream of building thinking machines. We have an irrefutable proof that there are things that computers cannot do.[27] Now, you might wonder if only obscure problems, such as deciding if a program halts or not, cannot be computed. In fact, there are many other very useful problems which cannot be computed, such as deciding if a mathematical statement is true or not.[28]

There are several reasons why the existence of uncomputable problems does not sink the dream of building thinking machines. First, we can still have computer programs that solve such problems, even if a little incompletely. You can already buy software such as Mathematica or Maple that will decide the truth of mathematical statements, but those programs will sometimes say, 'I don't know.' Second, and somewhat alternatively, you could have a computer program that solves such problems but perhaps a little imprecisely. The software might sometimes be wrong when it says that the input program does not halt when it does, or vice versa. Third, a lot Artificial Intelligence is about *heuristics*, rules of thumb that often work but might sometimes fail or even go into infinite loops themselves. Fourth, intelligence itself isn't about being 100 per cent correct. We humans are certainly not 100 per cent correct all the time. We don't need to build a machine that can always solve Turing's halting problem. The dream of building a thinking machine can thus survive the fact that we know of problems that computers cannot compute precisely.

THE ADVENT OF COMPUTERS

At this point, the dream of building thinking machines was largely theoretical. Even when Turing was working out what computers couldn't compute, we didn't actually have a computer that could compute. It took the Second World War to change that. The need to decode intelligence traffic and perform complex calculations to help build the atomic bomb drove the practical side of computing forwards, and led to the first practical computers.

There are various claims to being the world's first computer. These have been muddled by the secrecy surrounding the Second World War, as well as by the different capabilities of the machines. There was Germany's Z3, which was operating in 1941, the United Kingdom's Colossus, which was operating by 1944, the United States' ENIAC, which was operating by 1946, and Manchester's Baby, which, though it wasn't built till 1948, was the first of all these computers to store its own program.[29] But our story isn't really troubled by which was first. What is important is to see how their speed and memory increased, while their size and price fell dramatically. As a result, the number of computers in the world has increased rapidly. Billions are in operation today. The apocryphal claim attributed to IBM's Thomas Watson that there would be a world market for just half a dozen computers has certainly proved wrong.[30] It seems more likely that there is a market for at least half a dozen computers for *every* person on the planet.

DARTMOUTH AND ALL THAT

As the world recovered from the Second World War and computers started to become more commonplace, we had all the ingredients to start building thinking machines. We just needed something to kick it all off. This was the Dartmouth Summer Research Project, which took place in 1956 at Dartmouth, an Ivy

League college in New Hampshire. It was organised by John McCarthy, who, alongside Turing, is considered to be one of the fathers of the field of Artificial Intelligence. McCarthy was at Dartmouth College at that time, though he subsequently moved to Stanford to set up the now famous AI lab there. McCarthy, with Marvin Minsky, Nathaniel Rochester and Claude Shannon, wrote a proposal that persuaded the Rockefeller Foundation to fund a two-month-long brainstorming session at Dartmouth. Minsky was an early pioneer of neural networks, and later set up a prominent AI lab at MIT.[31] Rochester was at IBM and was a co-designer of the IBM 701, the first large-scale electronic computer that the company manufactured in quantity. Shannon worked at Bell Labs, and was already famous for having developed a statistical theory of information that is fundamental to communication networks, as well as for having applied mathematical logic to the design and construction of computers. Others in attendance at the Dartmouth meeting included Oliver Selfridge, grandson of the founder of the famous London department store, and later chief scientist at GTE Laboratories; Herbert Simon, who would go on to win a Nobel Prize in Economics;[32] and Allen Newell, who went on to set up the well-known AI lab at Carnegie Mellon University.[33]

The Dartmouth Summer Research Project was wildly overoptimistic about how rapid progress would be on building thinking machines. The funding proposal for the project began:

We propose that a 2 month, 10 man study of artificial intelligence be carried out during the summer of 1956 at Dartmouth College in Hanover, New Hampshire. The study is to proceed on the basis of the conjecture that every aspect of learning or any other feature of intelligence can in principle be so precisely described that a machine can be made to simulate it. An attempt will be made to find how to make machines use language, form abstractions and concepts, solve kinds of problems now reserved for humans, and improve themselves. We think that a significant advance can be made in one or more of these problems if a carefully selected group of scientists work on it together for a summer.

Despite its overconfidence, the proposal clearly articulated the dream: to describe learning and other aspects of human intelligence with such precision that they could be simulated in a computer. In short, they wanted to make Leibniz's dream concrete: to turn thinking into calculation. Unfortunately, as we shall see, this optimism would soon come to haunt the field.

ACROSS THE ATLANTIC

It would be wrong to think that our story now moved forward solely in the United States. The United Kingdom was one of the birthplaces of computing, and played a pivotal role in the early days of Artificial Intelligence. Indeed, the oldest scientific society in the world devoted to the study of AI is the UK's Society for the Study of Artificial Intelligence and the Simulation of Behaviour. It was founded in 1964 and continues today.

One place in the United Kingdom played a very prominent role in early developments. At the University of Edinburgh in 1963, Donald Michie set up a research group that would eventually evolve into the first (and, for a while, only) Department of Artificial Intelligence in the world.[34] Michie had worked with Turing breaking codes at Bletchley Park, and there they'd had frequent lunchtime conversations about the dream of building thinking machines. Many pioneering projects were undertaken at Edinburgh, including the Freddy robot. This was one of the earliest robots to integrate vision, manipulation and sophisticated control software.

Unfortunately, the United Kingdom squandered its early lead in the AI field following the highly critical Lighthill report of 1973. The applied mathematician Sir Michael James Lighthill FRS was asked by the British Science Research Council to evaluate research in Artificial Intelligence in the UK. The report made a very pessimistic prognosis of many core aspects of research, saying that 'in no part of the field have discoveries made so far produced the major impact that was then promised'. Some of Lighthill's criticisms have been attributed to the infighting that he witnessed between the research groups in Edinburgh. As a result of his report, funding for research into Artificial Intelligence in the United Kingdom was reduced until the Alvey Programme got things back on track a decade later.

EARLY SUCCESSES

Even though the initial progress in Artificial Intelligence studies was not as rapid as the participants of the Dartmouth Summer Research Project had predicted,[35] significant steps were taken during the two decades after 1956. A number of projects from these years stand out as important milestones.

One was the Shakey robot.[36] This was the first mobile robot that could perceive its environment and reason about its surroundings and actions. It didn't do a lot but it was in some sense the first serious attempt to build an autonomous robot. The Shakey project ran from 1966 to 1972 at the Stanford Research Institute in Palo Alto, California. Like much AI research, it was funded by the US Department of Defense, which hoped to develop military robots that could do reconnaissance without endangering human lives. (Some fifty years on, the military does indeed have such robots.)

Life magazine called Shakey the 'first electronic person'.[37] This was perhaps a little too flattering, but Shakey does go down in history as one of the first robots that could 'think' and act for itself. It was inducted into Carnegie Mellon's Robot Hall of Fame in 2004. One of the most important spinoffs of the Shakey project was the A* search algorithm. This finds the shortest path between two points. Shakey used this to plan its route to a new location. When your car's satellite navigation says 'computing new route', it is likely using some variant of the A* search algorithm. This is a nice example of how technology leads us in directions we are unlikely to predict. Who would have anticipated that research into one of the first autonomous robots would prove vital for in-car satellite navigation systems? It's certainly nowhere to be found in the Shakey grant proposal.[38]

Another early milestone was Dendral, a project started in 1965 that launched a whole new industry: the expert system business. Dendral was an ambitious attempt to encode domain expertise (in this case molecular chemistry) into a computer program. Dendral took mass spectra as input and, using its knowledge base of chemistry, suggested possible chemical structures that might be responsible. Dendral had heuristics, rules of thumb that an expert might use to reduce the many possible chemical structures to a small set of possible candidates. While Dendral was successful in its own specialised domain, its biggest impact was its demonstration that, by focusing on a narrow topic, and by encoding human domain expertise explicitly, computer programs could approach expert-level performance for a given task. In the 1980s expert systems like Dendral were implemented in hospitals, banks, nuclear reactors and many other places. Expert systems have now largely morphed into the business rule engines sold by companies like SAP, Oracle and IBM.

OUR MACHINE MASTERS

A significant milestone in the development of thinking machines occurred on 15 July 1979, when the computer program BKG 9.8 defeated Luigi Villa, the world backgammon champion. The final score was a convincing seven games to one in a $5000, winner-take-all match in Monte Carlo. This was the first time that a computer program had beaten a world champion at a game of skill. Man was no longer best. Computers were starting to eclipse their creators. To be fair to Luigi Villa, backgammon is a game of both skill and chance, and the computer did get some lucky breaks on the dice.[39] Hans Berliner, the man who developed BKG 9.8, wrote after the event:[40]

> I could hardly believe this finish, yet the program certainly earned its victory. There was nothing seriously wrong with its play, although it was lucky to have won the third game and the last. The spectators rushed into the closed room where the match had been played. Photographers took pictures, reporters sought interviews and the assembled experts congratulated me. Only one thing marred the scene. Villa, who only a day earlier had reached the summit of his backgammon career in winning the world title, was disconsolate. I told him that I was sorry it had happened and that we both knew he was really the better player.[41]

Even if BKG 9.8 wasn't actually the better player, this was a historic moment. Berliner hadn't programmed BKG 9.8 with better rules for playing backgammon; he programmed it to *learn* to play backgammon. The program duly learned to play better than its creator, and ultimately at around the level of the world champion.

Machine would beat man at other games in due course, including one that had fascinated Turing and many others: the ancient game of chess. In 1985 Garry Kasparov became the youngest ever world chess champion at just twenty-two. He is still considered by many to be the greatest ever chess player. It was perhaps a little cruel, then, that he happened to be the reigning world champion a dozen years later, when chess programs finally eclipsed humans. On 11 May 1997 Kasparov lost to IBM's Deep Blue computer chess program in an exhibition match held under tournament conditions in New York. Deep Blue took home the $700,000 prize money. It was likely little consolation to Kasparov that he had beaten Deep Blue the year before, on that occasion winning $400,000 in prize money. He would forever be remembered as the first world chess champion to be defeated by a computer.

HOW ARE YOU FEELING?

Another early milestone in the history of Artificial Intelligence was ELIZA, a computerised psychotherapist.[42] I hesitate to put this down as a success, as it could equally have been included in the following section, on early AI failures. ELIZA was written by Joseph Weizenbaum between 1964 and 1966.[43] On the one hand, ELIZA is one of the intellectual grandfathers of the chatbots that successfully answer customer queries on websites for companies like PayPal and IKEA. On the other hand, ELIZA cheated. She would take a statement from the patient such as 'I've been thinking about my father' and simply invert it into a question: 'Why have you been thinking about your father?' In reality, ELIZA only had a limited understanding of the semantics of any conversation. Nevertheless, she produced some very convincing dialogue. It was famously reported that Weizenbaum's secretary asked to be left alone so she could talk to ELIZA in private.

Weizenbaum intended ELIZA to be a 'parody' of a psychotherapist. He was therefore shocked that some in the psychiatric profession suggested ELIZA could be developed into a clinical tool, while others suggested ELIZA demonstrated the plausibility of processing natural language with computers. Karim, a chatbot descendant of ELIZA built by the X2AI start-up, is being used today as a 'therapeutic assistant' to help Syrian refugees. The bot offers help and support rather than treatment, an important legal and ethical distinction. And Karim is watched over by human minders. But it suggests we are going down the road against which Weizenbaum cautioned.

ELIZA also demonstrates that we should be careful in judging behaviour intelligent. We are easily deceived. And we are quick to overlook mistakes that machines make due to incompetence. Human conversation is full of errors that we ignore. I will come back to these ideas when I consider Turing's famous test for Artificial Intelligence.

* * *

A conversation with ELIZA

Weizenbaum reported one of ELIZA's conversations with a young woman as follows:

WOMAN: Men are all alike.

ELIZA: In what way?

WOMAN: They're always bugging us about something specific or other.

ELIZA: Can you think of a specific example?

WOMAN: Well, my boyfriend made me come here.

ELIZA: Your boyfriend made you come here?

WOMAN: He says I'm depressed much of the time.

ELIZA: I am sorry to hear you are depressed.

WOMAN: It's true. I'm unhappy.

ELIZA: Do you think coming here will help you not to be unhappy?

* * *

EARLY FAILURES

Alongside these early successes, there were also some early failures. Machine translation was one such area. The idea of using computers to translate from one language into another was proposed as early as 1946, and several machine translation projects were launched in the 1950s and 1960s. The Cold War meant that the US military was keen to automate the translation of documents from Russian and other languages into English.

Progress in getting machines to translate automatically was slow at first. Translating well requires knowledge of grammar, semantics, syntax, idioms and more—in both the source and the target languages. You cannot simply translate word for word. An often-repeated story is that a machine translation system was asked to translate the phrase 'the spirit is willing but the flesh is weak' into Russian, and then back into English. The result was: 'the vodka is good but the meat is rotten'. Whether or not this story is true, it illustrates some of the challenges of machine translation.

In 1964, three bodies funding research into machine translation—the US Department of Defense, the National Science Foundation and the Central Intelligence Agency—set up ALPAC, the Automatic Language Processing Advisory Committee, to evaluate progress. The committee was highly critical of work done towards machine translation to that point, and the research funding was greatly reduced. Two decades later, funding would pick up again as statistical approaches started to show promise. Today, of course, machine translation is back, and is in practical day-to-day use. Google Translate processes enough text every day to fill more than a million books. Perhaps even more impressively, Skype Translator offers near real-time translation of spoken English, Spanish, French, German, Italian and Mandarin. Machine translation now appears to be a reachable dream—one that was simply a long way ahead of its time in the 1960s.

Another high-profile failure was speech recognition. Not surprisingly, Bell Labs—for many years the research arm of the mighty American Telephone & Telegraph (AT&T) Corporation—was interested in having computers that could understand spoken language.[44] By 1952 Bell Labs had built a system that could recognise single digits, although it was limited to a single speaker. But funding was significantly reduced in 1969, when John Pierce,[45] who had led the development of Telstar, the first commercial communications satellite, wrote an article that compared speech recognition to 'schemes for turning water into gasoline, extracting gold from the sea, curing cancer, or going to the moon', and questioned the possibility of speech recognition across multiple speakers and a large vocabulary.[46] Another project that struggled was the Speech Understanding Research program, funded by the Defense Advanced Research Projects Agency (DARPA), the branch of the US Department of Defense that has helped develop many emerging technologies. The program ran for five years from 1971, and supported research at BBN, IBM, Carnegie Mellon and the Stanford Research Institute. However, disappointed with progress, DARPA canned the follow-on program.

As with machine translation, these speech-recognition projects were just too ambitious in the 1960s and 1970s. In the last few years, however, we have seen a step change in the performance of speech-recognition systems. This has been brought about by a machine-learning technique which we'll soon look closely at: Deep Learning. All the main commercial speech-recognition systems now use this technology.[47] More data and better processing power has helped a lot, but so too have improved algorithms. Speech recognition across multiple speakers and a large vocabulary is now feasible. Open an app like Siri or Cortana on your smartphone today and try it for yourself.

ENCODING COMMON SENSE

A third and slightly later failure was CYC, a controversial project started at the pioneering Microelectronics and Computer Technology Corporation (MCC) in 1984. MCC was the first computer industry consortium devoted to research and development set up in the United States. In part it was a response to the Japanese Fifth Generation project (which we will discuss shortly). MCC initially brought together a dozen technology companies, including DEC, Control Data, RCA, NCR, Honeywell, AMD and Motorola, in Austin, Texas. Other tech giants such as Microsoft, Boeing, GE and Rockwell would join MCC in later years.

Doug Lenat left Stanford to lead the CYC project at MCC.[48] He had the dream of codifying an enCYClopedia of common-sense knowledge that a computer could use to behave intelligently. Facts like 'All trees are plants' and 'Paris is the capital of France'. And generic rules like 'If X is a type of Y, and Y has the property Z, then X also has the property Z'. Using this rule and the fact 'Plants are immobile', for instance, CYC can deduce that trees are immobile. In contrast to expert systems of the time, which were limited to specialised domains, Lenat's goal was to build a system with general intelligence. One of the great challenges in AI is precisely to get a computer to know all the simple and trivial facts that we take for granted. 'Trees are immobile ... Paris is not a plant ... Cats are furry.' After ten years of generous funding at MCC, CYC was spun off into the much more modest Cycorp Inc. Unlike MCC, Cycorp Inc. continues today. But it has had rather limited commercial success. 'CYClists', the researchers working to add knowledge into CYC, have struggled to cope with the breadth of knowledge we all take for granted, and with the complexity of the encyclopaedic system into which CYC has grown.

Again, in hindsight we can see that the CYC project was ahead of its time. It was begun before the World Wide Web had taken off, and more critically before the invention of the Semantic Web. In 2012 Google started using its Knowledge Graph to improve search results. The Knowledge Graph is, in some respects, Google's answer to CYC. It's a structured knowledge base of facts about the world. It enables Google to answer queries like 'What is the population of Australia?' Try it! You will get back a nice graph with the population trend over the last fifty or so years. Microsoft Bing, Yahoo! and Baidu all now use such technologies to enhance their search results. Other community-wide projects such as DBpedia and YAGO are also trying to codify knowledge in a similar way. Even if Lenat's ambition was good, his timing was not.[49]

AI CRITICS

From its earliest days, Artificial Intelligence has attracted some very vocal and often damaging critics. I have already mentioned Lighthill and Penrose. Another early critic was the philosopher Hubert Dreyfus.[50] He wrote an essay, 'Alchemy and Artificial Intelligence', which grew into the 1972 book *What Computers Can't Do*.[51] In the third edition, published in 1992, he playfully and somewhat provocatively modified the title to *What Computers Still Can't Do*.

Dreyfus didn't doubt that Artificial Intelligence could succeed. But he did argue that the way Artificial Intelligence researchers were trying to go about it was fundamentally flawed. 'There is no reason why, in principle, one could not construct an artificial embodied agent,' he wrote, 'if one used components sufficiently like those which make up a human being.' Dreyfus's main complaint was with the symbolist approach to building thinking machines, which can be traced back to Leibniz's 'alphabet of human thought'. Dreyfus argued instead that, in order to have intelligence, such symbols must be grounded in the real world, as they are with humans.

Dreyfus's arguments met strong opposition from researchers working in Artificial Intelligence. It didn't help that Dreyfus put his arguments in a combative form, comparing Artificial Intelligence to alchemy. But nor did AI researchers behave too well. It has been said that of all the academics working at MIT, only Weizenbaum, the author of ELIZA, would dare to be seen having lunch with Dreyfus. And there was considerable glee when Dreyfus lost a chess match to the Mac Hack computer program.

Some of Dreyfus's criticisms did hit home. The roboticist Rodney Brooks argued that thinking machines had to be embedded in the real world, sensing it and acting in it as humans do, and grounding their symbols in their perceptions and actions.[52] Only in this way would symbols truly have meaning. Brooks put these ideas into action in a sequence of robots: Allen, Tom and Jerry, Herbert, Seymour and the six-legged Genghis.[53]

Other criticisms that Dreyfus put forward have been convincingly refuted. Dreyfus argued that computers would never be able to capture the human ability to understand context, situation or purpose by using a simple set of rules. However, the fact that we cannot today imagine such a set of formal rules does not mean that such rules cannot exist. Many researchers have responded to Dreyfus by building better and better systems that come closer to human performance every day.

AI CYCLES

One consequence of these early failures is that Artificial Intelligence has gone through periods of optimism and increased funding, followed by periods of pessimism and reduced funding. The first so-called AI winter happened in the second half of the 1970s. A second one occurred in the late 1980s and early 1990s. In both cases, the winter was caused mostly by a collapse in the perception of Artificial Intelligence by funding agencies and venture capitalists. Artificial Intelligence was not failing scientifically, even if it was proving to be more of a technical challenge than many of the early researchers had expected.

In hindsight, it is not hard to see that building a thinking machine will always be an immense intellectual challenge. We are trying to match and even exceed the capabilities of the most complex system known in the universe: the human brain. The longer I have worked in the field, the more respect I have for the human brain. It does all the amazing things humans can do but uses just 20 watts of power. By comparison, IBM's Watson computer, which is one of the most capable systems in use today, consumes 80,000 watts.[54] We have a very long way to go to match the performance/power ratio of the human mind.

The first AI winter started around 1974, when DARPA cut back funding to research in Artificial Intelligence. It ended in 1982, when Japan's Ministry of International Trade and Industry launched the Fifth Generation Computer Systems project. Japan's goal was to stop being a follower and start being a leader in computing. It spent $400 million on this ten-year project. The ambitious goals of Japan's project provoked several rival nations to start projects of their own, for fear of losing the technology race. The United Kingdom responded with the Alvey Programme, which increased funding to a number of areas of computing, including AI. Europe responded with the $6.5-billion ESPRIT project,[55] and the US with the $1-billion Strategic Computing Initiative and the Microelectronics and Computer Technology Corporation. Like the Japanese Fifth Generation Systems project, these looked at computer hardware and other areas of information technology besides Artificial Intelligence. There was also a substantial increase in funding to AI around the world.

Unfortunately, the cycle swung back again at the end of the Fifth Generation project and a second AI winter began. The Japanese had made a number of poor choices about which Artificial Intelligence technologies to explore. As a result, the project was not felt to have been a success, and a planned ten-year follow-on project was cancelled. Nevertheless, the increased funding in Japan, Europe and the United States over the 1980s and early 1990s helped bring many new researchers into the field. And many of these researchers are continuing to push back the frontiers of our knowledge about thinking machines today.

AI SPRING

Artificial Intelligence is currently on another upswing. It definitely feels like spring again. Billions of dollars are pouring into the field. One reason for this is the progress being made in machine learning, and in particular in an area called Deep Learning.[56] Until a few years ago, this was an unfashionable branch of machine learning, practised by a few researchers at universities including Toronto, New York and Montreal.[57] Most research in machine learning focused on probabilistic techniques with impressive names such as 'Bayesian inference' and 'support vector machines'. Deep Learning builds neural networks somewhat like those of our own brains. It was considered for many years to be a bit of dead end, compared to the more sophisticated probabilistic methods.

However, the persistence of the small pool of Deep Learning researchers is starting to pay off—and spectacularly. A number of results were published that caught the imagination of the AI research community. At the end of 2013, Demis Hassabis and some fellow researchers at the UK start-up DeepMind used Deep Learning to teach computers to play seven classic Atari arcade games: Pong, Breakout, Space Invaders, Seaquest, Beam Rider, Enduro and Q*bert. Subsequently they expanded this to forty-nine games.[58] In most cases, the computers were able to play at the level of a human. In a dozen cases, they played at superhuman level. This was a remarkable result, as the program was not given any background knowledge about the games. All it had access to was the score and the pixels on the screen. It learned every game from scratch. It didn't know anything about bats, balls or lasers. Nor did it know about gravity, Newtonian physics or any of the other things we humans know about when we play such games. Simply by playing lots and lots of games, the computers learned first how to play, and then (a few hours later) how to play well.[59] Stuart Russell, one of the authors of the leading textbook on Artificial Intelligence, observed: 'That's both impressive and scary in the sense that if a human baby was born and by the evening of its first day was already beating human beings at video games, you'd be terrified.'

Inspired by this breakthrough, Google paid what is believed to be around $500 million to buy DeepMind. At the time, the company had a staff of about fifty employees, about a dozen of whom were machine-learning researchers. It had no revenue. Not surprisingly, it wasn't just the AI community that started to pay attention.

Since then, Deep Learning has shown itself to be exceptionally good at perception: tasks such as speech recognition, object recognition in computer vision, and natural language processing. These are the sorts of tasks that our brains do without much conscious effort. Even Deep Learning's success at playing the ancient Chinese game of Go (which I will discuss shortly) is largely due to its success at perceiving the state of the board, who is winning and what a good move would be.

Deep Learning needs lots of data. But in areas such as speech recognition, collecting lots of data isn't too hard. On the other hand, Deep Learning seems to find tasks that require higher-level reasoning harder. The DeepMind program did really well at playing Pong, the two-dimensional version of table tennis. To play Pong well, you don't need much strategy—you just move the bat to the ball and try to get the ball into the corners. But Deep Learning has never reached even close to human-level performance in games that require memory and planning. In Ms. Pac-man, for example, you have to plan ahead how you'll deal with the ghosts. As a result, DeepMind played Ms. Pac-man rather poorly. More conventional AI techniques seem better suited to such tasks.

It seems likely to me that there will eventually be a backlash against Deep Learning. It cannot hope to live up to the hype about its potential. It will not 'solve' all of intelligence. And it certainly cannot deliver the value that some in Silicon Valley are ascribing to it. There's a place for other techniques that require less data and do more high-level reasoning. There also remains a role for knowledge-based techniques in which expertise is explicitly programmed into the computer. Finally, in safety and other critical applications, there remains a role for technologies which can explain what they do and why, and which can guarantee certain behaviours. For these sorts of applications, Deep Learning is likely too much of a closed box, unable to provide explanations for its output or to give such guarantees.

DRIVERLESS CARS

Besides Deep Learning, there have been several other recent successes that take us further along the road to thinking machines. In 2004 DARPA announced a $1-million Grand Challenge to kick-start progress in autonomous driving, and ultimately tackle the problem of getting supply convoys into dangerous places such as Iraq and Afghanistan. The first competition was a dismal failure for Artificial Intelligence. The winning entry, Carnegie Mellon University's Red Team, travelled less than 12 kilometres of the 240-kilometre desert course. The $1-million prize for finishing the course was left unclaimed. But the AI researchers bounced back: just one year later, five teams completed the course. Sebastian Thrun's team from Stanford University took home the prize, now increased to $2 million. 'The impossible has been achieved,' Thrun declared.

Less well known, more than ten years earlier the European Union had funded the $810-million PROMETHEUS Project on autonomous driving. The project began in 1987; near the end of the project, in 1994, two autonomous cars, VaMP and VITA-2, drove over a thousand kilometres on a French highway in heavy traffic at speeds of up to 130 kilometres per hour. Anyone who has driven in France will respect this achievement. Autonomous cars are now regularly appearing in our cities and on our highways. They're even hitting the racetrack. In February 2017 the first ever self-driving car race took place at the Buenos Aires Formula E ePrix. Unfortunately, it ended with one of the two cars crashing. But soon we will see multiple cars racing each other at up to 300 kilometres per hour.

ELEMENTARY, MY DEAR WATSON

Another recent success for Artificial Intelligence was IBM's Watson computer. In 2011 Watson demonstrated human-level performance at answering general knowledge questions in the game show *Jeopardy!*—a long-running and somewhat back-to-front American quiz show in which contestants are presented with trivia clues in the form of answers, and must reply with questions.

* * *

Watson competing on Jeopardy!

HOST: Tickets aren't needed for this 'event', a black hole's boundary from which matter can't escape.

WATSON: What is event horizon?

HOST: Wanted for killing Sir Danvers Carew; appearance—pale and dwarfish; seems to have a split personality.

WATSON: Who is Hyde?

HOST: Even a broken one of these on your wall is right twice a day.

WATSON: What is clock?

* * *

Watson (which was named after IBM's founder, Thomas J. Watson) faced two formidable competitors in this man-versus-computer match. The first competitor was Brad Rutter. Brad is the biggest all-time money winner on *Jeopardy!* with over $3 million in prize money. Also competing was Ken Jennings, holder of the longest winning streak on the show—seventy-four consecutive games in 2004. Despite this formidable competition, Watson won the $1-million prize over three days of competition.

Watson demonstrates the very real advances we are making in areas such as natural language understanding, getting computers to understand text, and probabilistic reasoning, or getting computers to deal with uncertainty. Watson uses sophisticated probability estimates to choose between different answers to questions. This sort of technology is already filtering out into our everyday lives. Apps such as Siri and Cortana can parse, understand and answer complex questions such as 'What is the second-largest city in the United States?' (The correct answer is Los Angeles, with a population approaching 4 million people.)

AI IS GO

I could mention many other examples of progress in Artificial Intelligence, but instead I will end with another landmark moment. In March 2016 Google's AlphaGo program beat Lee Sedol, one of the best Go players in the world, in a five-game match, claiming a prize of $1 million. Humankind was no longer champion at one of the oldest and most challenging board games ever invented. Many Go masters had predicted computers would never play Go well. Even optimists for machines had predicted that success was a decade or so away. In July 1997, following Deep Blue's victory against Kasparov, the *New York Times* had said: 'When or if a computer defeats a human Go champion, it will be a sign that artificial intelligence is truly beginning to become as good as the real thing.'

While Go is a simple game, it has enormous complexity, and so AlphaGo's success represents a significant step. Two players take turns to play black or white stones on a nineteen-by-nineteen board, trying to surround each other. In chess, there are about twenty possible moves to consider at each turn. In Go, there are around 200. Looking two steps ahead, there are 200 times 200—or 40,000—possible moves to consider. Three steps ahead, there are 200 times 200 times 200—or 8 million—different moves available. And looking just fifteen black-and-white stones ahead creates more possible moves than there are atoms in the universe.

Another aspect of Go that makes it a great challenge is working out who is winning as the game progresses. In chess, it's not too hard to work out who is ahead. Simply counting the value of the different pieces is a good first approximation. In Go, there are just black and white stones. It takes Go masters a lifetime of training to learn how to spot when one player is ahead. And any good Go program needs to do this in order to work out which of those 200 different moves will improve its own position.

AlphaGo uses an elegant marriage of computer brute force and human-style perception to tackle these two problems. To deal with the immense number of possible moves by each player, AlphaGo uses an AI heuristic called Monte Carlo tree search. It is impossible to explore every possible move very far ahead into the game. Instead, the computer uses its grunt to explore a random sample of the possible moves. Those moves which lead, on average, to the most wins are the most promising. And to deal with the difficulty of recognising who is ahead, AlphaGo uses Deep Learning. We don't really know how to describe a good position on the Go board. But just like humans can learn to perceive good positions, the computer can learn too. This is another example of how Deep Learning is very good at perceptive tasks. AlphaGo learned, and ultimately exceeded, a Go master's ability to perceive who is ahead.

Google's scale and financial clout also played a significant role in the victory. AlphaGo played itself billions of times, improving its strategies. Like many other recent advances in AI, a significant return has come from throwing a lot of resources at the problem.

Before AlphaGo, computer Go programs were mostly the efforts of a single person, and were run on just one computer. AlphaGo, on the other hand, represents a significant engineering effort by dozens and dozens of Google's engineers and top AI scientists, as well as the benefits of access to Google's vast server farms.

While AlphaGo's victory was a clear milestone passed, I do not completely agree with Demis Hassabis, leader of the AlphaGo project, that Go is 'the pinnacle of games, and the richest in terms of intellectual depth'. It is certainly the Mount Everest of games insofar as it has one of the largest 'game trees'.[60] However, poker is the K2, the more deadly mountain.[61] Poker introduces a number of additional factors, such as uncertainty about where particular cards are, as well as the psychology of your opponents. Arguably this makes it a greater intellectual challenge. In Go, there is no uncertainty, and psychology is much less important than simply playing well.

Despite claims that the methods used to solve Go are general-purpose, it would take a significant human effort to get AlphaGo to play even a game like chess well. Nevertheless, the ideas and AI techniques that went into AlphaGo are likely to find their way into new applications soon. And it won't be just in games. We'll see them in areas such as Google's PageRank, AdWords, speech recognition and even driverless cars.

HIDDEN AI

One of the problems with the progress we're making towards thinking machines is its habit of slipping out of view. Often, as soon as we know how to automate some task, it stops being called Artificial Intelligence and becomes mainstream computing. For instance, speech recognition is no longer considered by many to be an AI invention—the hidden Markov models and Deep Learning nets have fallen out of sight.

Our lives are now enriched by many examples of this. Every time you ask Siri or Cortana a question, you are profiting from many types of Artificial Intelligence: speech-recognition algorithms that convert your speech into a natural language question; a natural language parser that converts this question into a search query; search algorithms that answer this query; and ranking algorithms that predict the most 'useful' ads to place alongside your search results. And if you're lucky enough to own a Tesla car, you can sit in the driving seat whilst the car drives itself autonomously along the highway using a host of AI algorithms that sense the road and environment, plan a course of action and drive the car.[62]

For those of us working on AI, the fact that these technologies fall out of sight means success. Ultimately, AI will be like electricity. Almost every device in our lives uses electricity. It is an essential but invisible component of our homes, our cars, our farms, our factories and our shops. It brings energy and data to almost everything we do. If electricity disappeared, the world would quickly grind to a halt. AI will likewise become an essential but invisible component of all our lives.

2: Measuring AI

Artificial Intelligence is making progress. It may have been slower than predicted in the optimistic forecasts made by some researchers in the field's earliest days, but it remains the case that computers are getting smarter every day. A fundamental challenge is measuring precisely this progress. It is perhaps not very surprising that this is a difficult task. We do not have a very good definition of intelligence itself, so it is hard to say whether computers are getting more intelligent.

You might wonder why we don't use IQ tests. After all, these are meant to provide a standardised measurement of human intelligence. Why not use them to measure machine intelligence too? There are, however, many cultural, linguistic and psychological biases in IQ tests. And they completely ignore various important aspects of our intellectual lives, such as our creativity, and our social and emotional intelligence. Plus, IQ tests require a minimum base intelligence. You don't learn a lot by giving a written IQ test to a newborn baby, or even to a toddler.

THE TURING TEST

Alan Turing himself anticipated this problem. He proposed that we adopt a purely functional definition: if a computer behaves in the same way as a human, then we might as well say it is intelligent. In his famous 1950 *Mind* paper, he described this functional definition by means of a simple thought experiment. This has become known as the 'Turing test'.

Suppose we have an intelligent program. The Turing test puts a judge in a room with a computer terminal and connects them either to the program or to a real person. The judge can ask any questions he or she likes. If they cannot tell the computer apart from the person, then the program passes the Turing test. Turing predicted that computers would pass his test in around fifty years' time. This was over sixty years ago. So, if Turing is right, computers should have already passed or be about to pass his test. I discuss shortly how near we are to achieving this goal.

We can also talk about a Turing test for some more specialised task. Suppose you are developing a program to write beer reviews automatically. Your program passes the Turing test for beer reviews when the reviews it writes cannot be distinguished from those written by a person. Consider the following beer review:

> A nice dark red color with a nice head that left a lot of lace on the glass. Aroma is of raspberries and chocolate. Not much depth to speak of despite consisting of raspberries. The bourbon is pretty subtle as well. I really don't know that find a flavor this beer tastes like. I would prefer a little more carbonization to come through. It's pretty drinkable, but I wouldn't mind if this beer was available.

Could a computer create something like this? Actually, a computer did write it.[1] All it was told was to write a review for a beer that had a fruit or vegetable taste. And this is what it produced, entirely automatically. To write the review, it used a neural network trained on thousands of past reviews from BeerAdvocate. com. The computer wasn't told the rules of English grammar. Nor was it told how to make mistakes to make it sound as if the review was written by a human. It learnt all of this by mining patterns it detected in past reviews.

THE LOEBNER PRIZE

My view, which I suspect is shared by many of my colleagues working in AI, is that the Turing test is best viewed as what Germans call a *Gedankenexperiment*—a thought experiment, a way for us to explore the idea of a machine thinking and what that would mean. However, it is not something that needs actually to be implemented. Or, indeed, that Turing necessarily expected to be run.

Not everyone has seen it that way. In 1990 the inventor Hugh Loebner established a prize of $100,000 and a solid-gold medal for the first programmer to write a program that passes a Turing test.[2] A Loebner Prize competition has been run on an annual basis since then.

The Loebner Prize has wandered around the world. Mostly it has been held in the United Kingdom; it made a brief excursion down under to Australia in 1999, when it was held at Flinders University in South Australia, but it returned to the Northern Hemisphere in 2000 and has not crossed the equator again since. For two years it was held in Loebner's own apartment in New York City. It has been run since 2014 by the United Kingdom's Society for the Study of Artificial Intelligence and the Simulation of Behaviour (AISB).

The Loebner Prize has many critics. Indeed, Marvin Minsky called it a publicity stunt, and offered $100 to anyone who could stop the Loebner Prize.[3] Never one to miss an opportunity for more publicity, Loebner responded by announcing that Minsky was now a co-sponsor, since the Loebner Prize would, according to his rules, stop as soon as a program passed the Turing test. Loebner's company for a while made roll-up plastic disco dance floors, and Loebner said it was 'interesting to have funding for AI come from the sale of plastic disco dance floors, and might popularize them'. There have been many other criticisms of the Loebner Prize beyond the publicity-seeking of its founder. Most seriously, the competition has often used judges who were somewhat unqualified for the task, while the rules and design of the competition have encouraged, and even sometimes rewarded, deception rather than competence.

PASSING THE TURING TEST?

In 2014 a Turing Test was run at the Royal Society in London. Poignantly, the test was run on the sixtieth anniversary of Alan Turing's death. The winning program was a chatbot named Eugene Goostman. The chatbot pretended to be a thirteen-year-old Ukrainian boy. The press release put out after the event claimed that the Turing test had been passed for the first time, as ten out of the thirty judges thought the chatbot human.[4] It is not clear that it is adequate to fool 30 per cent of judges in a five-minute conversation; Turing's paper was unspecific about the length of the test or the number of judges who had to be fooled. He did, however, make the following prediction: 'I believe that in about fifty years' time it will be possible, to programme computers ... to make them play the imitation game so well that an average interrogator will not have more than 70 per cent chance of making the right identification after five minutes of questioning.' In 1952, in a discussion on the BBC Third Programme, Turing was less optimistic, predicting it would take 'at least 100 years' to pass his eponymous test. A quick reading of the transcripts from the 2014 Turing test at the Royal Society demonstrate that we are still some way from having computer programs that pass the Turing test, as intended by its inventor.

Many AI researchers, myself included, do not consider pretending to be a 13-year-old Ukrainian boy who frequently avoids answering the question to be in the spirit of Turing's proposed test. At the very least, you need to imitate an adult and you need to answer the questions. The goal should be to answer questions intelligently, not deceptively. Interestingly, Turing anticipated that machines playing his imitation game might try such tricks. Unfortunately, he was too quick to dismiss this concern in his famous *Mind* paper:

> It might be urged that when playing the 'imitation game' the best strategy for the machine may possibly be something other than imitation of the behaviour of a man. This may be, but I think it is unlikely that there is any great effect of this kind. In any case there is no intention to investigate here the theory of the game, and it will be assumed that the best strategy is to try to provide answers that would naturally be given by a man.

* * *

Transcript of a conversation from the Turing test held at the Royal Society in June 2014

JUDGE: Hello.

EUGENE: Hello, I'm really glad to have the chance to chat with you! My guinea pig Bill sends his regards too!

JUDGE: Is Bill a male or a female?

EUGENE: Ask Bill personally, please.

JUDGE: Well I'd rather talk to you. What is your name?

EUGENE: Call me Eugene. I am glad to talk to you!

JUDGE: My name is Jane and I am female. How about you? What's your gender?

EUGENE: I'm a male. A 'guy' I'd say.

JUDGE: Pleased to meet you Eugene. What's the weather like where you are?

EUGENE: Let's get on with our conversation!

JUDGE: Don't you like talking about the weather?

EUGENE: All these talks about weather is a waste of time.

JUDGE: What would you like to discuss?

EUGENE: I don't know/ Better tell me more about yourself!

* * *

BEYOND THE TURING TEST

There are other problems with the Turing test. Intelligence has many dimensions: emotional, linguistic and deductive, to name just a few. In addition, the test should be more objective, more difficult to spoof, less culturally biased, less focused on a single task, and more able to measure incremental progress. Given these many issues, there have been a number of proposals for tests that might do a better job of measuring our progress towards thinking machines.

Hector Levesque, a leading AI researcher at the University of Toronto, has proposed one alternative: the Winograd Schema Challenge.[5] The test is named in honour of Terry Winograd, a pioneering AI researcher whose 1968 SHRDLU program was one of the first natural language understanding computer programs. SHRDLU could answer natural language questions about a virtual blocks world. It was groundbreaking for its time. A transcript of its output gives a good idea of its capabilities.

* * *

A conversation with the SHRDLU program

PERSON: Pick up a big red block.

COMPUTER: OK.

PERSON: Grasp the pyramid.

COMPUTER: I DON'T UNDERSTAND WHICH PYRAMID YOU MEAN.

PERSON (changing their mind): Find a block which is taller than the one you are holding and put it into the box.

COMPUTER: BY 'IT', I ASSUME YOU MEAN THE BLOCK WHICH IS TALLER THAN THE ONE I AM HOLDING.

COMPUTER: OK.

PERSON: What does the box contain?

COMPUTER: THE BLUE PYRAMID AND THE BLUE BLOCK.

PERSON: What is the pyramid supported by?

COMPUTER: THE BOX.

PERSON: How many blocks are not in the box?

COMPUTER: FOUR OF THEM.

PERSON: Is at least one of them narrower than the one which I told you to pick up?

COMPUTER: YES, THE RED CUBE.

PERSON: Is it supported?

COMPUTER: YES, BY THE TABLE.

PERSON: Can the table pick up blocks?

COMPUTER: NO.

PERSON: Can a pyramid be supported by a block?

COMPUTER: YES.

PERSON: Can a pyramid support a pyramid?

COMPUTER: I DON'T KNOW.

* * *

Inspired by the SHRDLU program, the Winograd Schema Challenge asks a computer to answer a sequence of multiple-choice questions that require it to perform anaphora resolution, working out what is meant by 'it'. Questions in the Winograd Schema Challenge come in pairs:

The trophy doesn't fit in the brown suitcase because it's too big.
What is too big?

0: the trophy
1: the suitcase

The trophy doesn't fit in the brown suitcase because it's too small.
What is too small?

0: the trophy
1: the suitcase

To work out what 'it' refers to, we cannot simply apply grammatical rules. You need to understand the problem and reason about it. The example above requires some common-sense and geometric reasoning. The trophy doesn't fit either because it (the trophy) is too big, or because it (the suitcase) is too small. You need some common-sense knowledge that small things fit inside big ones. The following example illustrates some other aspects of intelligence that can be tested with these questions.

> *The large ball crashed right through the table because it was made of steel. What was made of steel?*

0: the ball
1: the table

> *The large ball crashed right through the table because it was made of styrofoam. What was made of styrofoam?*

0: the ball
1: the table

Answering these questions requires knowledge of materials and the ability to reason about physics. The ball crashed through the table either because it (the ball) was made of steel, or because it (the table) was made of styrofoam. To work out the correct answer, you need to know about the density of materials and what could break what.

Another alternative to the Turing test is the IKEA challenge. I am not sure it is a very good alternative, but anyone who has struggled to assemble some IKEA furniture will probably appreciate it. The challenge is for a robot to build a piece of IKEA furniture given just the usual picture instructions. I suspect it will be a century or more before we fully crack this challenge.

THE META-TURING TEST

Implicit in the Turing test is the idea that it takes intelligence to identify intelligence. We give the task of judging whether or not a computer is an intelligent human to an intelligent human. This introduces an asymmetry to the test. No one is judging whether the judge is intelligent or not.

For this reason, I have proposed another alternative to the Turing test. I call it the meta-Turing test. This is a symmetrical test. We have a group with an equal number of humans and computers. All pairs talk to each other. And each has to decide which in the group is human and which is robot. To pass the meta-Turing test, you need to be as good as (or better than) the best human classifier at classifying humans and robots, and to be classified as human by the humans in the test as least as often as any human.

You cannot pass this test by dodging the question or throwing out non sequiturs. You also have to ask questions that determine whether the others are human or machine. Working out good questions to ask, and then deciding if you are speaking to a human or a machine, is much harder to do than simply answering questions.

THE UNCANNY VALLEY

Another problem with measuring progress in AI is that we often misjudge the closeness of machines to humans. In robotics, there's an interesting psychological phenomenon known as the 'uncanny valley'. When a robot physically looks and moves almost like a human, we become disturbed by their appearance. The valley is the dip in our comfort level as the robot becomes more and more like a human. Small differences stand out and take on immense importance. Eventually, when these differences become very small, we become unable to distinguish the robot from a human, and our comfort level improves. A similar and related phenomenon has also been observed with computer-generated graphics.

With computer programs, on the other hand, there seems to be the opposite problem to the uncanny valley. When interacting with a computer, humans are quick to ignore errors and responses that are un-humanlike. I have already mentioned how Joseph Weizenbaum found that many people confused ELIZA for a real psychotherapist, even though it only parroted back people's responses as questions. I have come across several other examples of this phenomenon.

When Garry Kasparov was beaten by Deep Blue in 1997, the computer made a strange move in the second game. Rather than capture an exposed pawn, Deep Blue sacrificed a piece. Kasparov was unnerved by the move. It seemed to show immense strategic foresight for the computer to defend while ahead, in order to head off any possibility of a counter-attack. The move suggested to Kasparov that Deep Blue had improved greatly since their first match, the year before. In reality, the move was caused by a bug in Deep Blue's code. The program was not as smart as Kasparov supposed, and could not look that far ahead. But it isn't surprising that Kasparov assumed Deep Blue was more intelligent than it was. Who wants to lose to a stupid computer?

We might call this the 'natural valley'. When programs approach the level of our own intelligence, we will be quick to attribute them with more intelligence than they actually have. We fall into the trap of believing they are more natural than they are. As computers take over tasks we used to do, we will want to think that they are more intelligent than they actually are. These tasks were difficult when we used to do them! Moreover, we automatically, perhaps even subconsciously, correct small errors in communication with others. We will likely give computers the same benefit of the doubt that we usually give to other humans, and think of them as more intelligent than they actually are.

OPTIMISTIC FORECASTS

Let's move on from the problem of measuring progress to the problem of predicting when advances will happen. Alan Turing's forecast that we would have thinking machines by the year 2000 proved a little optimistic. We were still some way away at the turn of the millennium. Unfortunately, a number of leading AI researchers have continued to share Turing's optimism. In 1957 the Nobel laureate Herbert Simon declared that we were already in the age of intelligent machines:

> It is not my aim to surprise or shock you, if indeed that were possible in an age of nuclear fission and prospective interplanetary travel. But the simplest way I can summarize the situation is to say that there are now in the world machines that think, that learn, and that create. Moreover, their ability to do these things is going to increase rapidly until in a visible future the range of problems they can handle will be coextensive with the range to which the human mind has been applied.

Given the speed of progress, he suggested humankind would need to consider our position carefully: 'The revolution in heuristic problem solving will force man to consider his role in a world in which his intellectual power and speed are outstripped by the intelligence of machines.'

Simon, like Turing, was probably too optimistic about thinking machines. The machines in existence back then proved more difficult to improve than he anticipated. In my view, however, he was not wrong to recommend that we should consider the profound impact that intelligent machines will have on our lives.

In 1967 Marvin Minsky was also very optimistic about progress, predicting thinking machines were very near: 'Within a generation ... the problem of creating "artificial intelligence" will substantially be solved.'[6] Three years later, in 1970, he was even more optimistic:

> In from three to eight years we will have a machine with the general intelligence of an average human being. I mean a machine that will be

able to read Shakespeare, grease a car, play office politics, tell a joke, have a fight. At that point the machine will begin to educate itself with fantastic speed. In a few months it will be at genius level and a few months after its powers will be incalculable.[7]

Ironically, such overly optimistic claims have likely held the field back. Critics of AI such as Roger Penrose were, in part, goaded by claims like these. Penrose has said that he wrote his book *The Emperor's New Mind* in response to some 'extreme and outrageous claims' that Minsky and others made on a BBC *Horizon* program.

PESSIMISTIC FORECASTS

To be fair to the optimists, pessimists about thinking machines have been equally mistaken. In 2004 Frank Levy and Richard Murnane argued that driving was unlikely to be automated in the near future.[8] One year after their prediction, Stanford's autonomous vehicle won the DARPA Grand Challenge and the $2-million prize by driving over 100 miles along an unrehearsed desert trail. The win marked the start of the race to build a new trillion-dollar industry: driverless cars. If Levy and Murnane had looked *back* even a short time, they would have realised their prediction was already wrong: as we saw earlier, two autonomous cars had driven over 1000 kilometres on highways in France a full ten years earlier.[9]

Another pessimist was Dr Piet Hut, a computational astrophysicist at the Institute of Advanced Study at Princeton, and a keen Go player. In 1997, following Deep Blue's victory over Kasparov, he said: 'It may be a hundred years before a computer beats humans at Go—maybe even longer.' In less than twenty years this pessimistic prediction had been proved wrong.

THE EXPERT VIEW

In 2012 Vincent Müller and Nick Bostrom of the University of Oxford surveyed a number of AI researchers about when 'high-level machine intelligence' would be achieved.[10] In particular, they asked when we might build a machine that could carry out most jobs at least as well as an average human. As there is significant uncertainty about when this might happen, they asked for an estimate of when it was 50 per cent likely. The median of these estimates was the year 2040. They also asked when high-level machine intelligence was 90 per cent likely. The median of these estimates was the year 2075. In addition, when asked about the overall impact of such thinking machines on humanity, only half the respondents to the survey thought it would be positive. Around half thought it would be mostly neutral or bad.

This survey is one of the main pieces of evidence in Nick Bostrom's bestseller *Superintelligence*, which argues that AI poses an *imminent* existential threat to humankind. Unfortunately, the survey has been also been rather poorly reported in the press. Many reports claimed that Müller and Bostrom surveyed over 500 researchers.[11] It's true that they sent questionnaires to over 500 researchers, but only 170 were interested enough in the topic to reply. Their survey therefore samples just a small fraction of the thousands of researchers working on AI worldwide. Many reports also claimed that the survey was of 'leading experts in the field'.[12] Actually, only twenty-nine of the 170 respondents (less than 20 per cent) were what might be called 'leading' AI researchers.[13] The majority of responses came from more minority groups within the AI world, many of whom would be predisposed to respond enthusiastically and optimistically to such a survey.

The largest group of responses, denoted 'AGI' by Müller and Bostrom and contributing seventy-two replies in total, were participants of two conferences focused on *building* superintelligence.[14] This group represents nearly half of all the replies to the survey. You could expect this group to be a little more optimistic about the timeline for thinking machines, given that they were attending a specialist conference focused on questions such as superintelligence and existential risk. The enthusiasm of the AGI group is reflected in the fact that they had the highest response rate. Sixty-five per cent of the polled AGI group responded to the survey. By comparison, the response rate overall was just 31 per cent.

Another large group in the survey, with forty-two replies, was the group labelled 'PT-AI'. There were participants of a conference organised by Müller in Oxford on the Philosophy and Theory of AI. The participants of this conference included a couple of mainstream AI researchers, Stuart Russell and Aaron Sloman. However, many were hardcore philosophers: there was Daniel Dennett, as well as Müller and Bostrom themselves. Members of this group had little experience of building AI systems, and of the many practical challenges still to be solved. Together, the two groups, AGI and PT-AI, contributed over two-thirds of the responses to the survey. It is doubtful that their responses represent the views of mainstream or leading AI researchers.

In the interests of completeness, let me describe the fourth and final group surveyed. These were twenty-six members from the Greek Association for Artificial Intelligence. Now, Greece is a powerhouse in several areas of computer science; one is databases. But I hope my Greek colleagues will not be upset if I note that other countries—the United States, the United Kingdom, China, Germany and Australia—lead the world in AI research. Also, these twenty-six respondents represented just 10 per cent of the Greek Association for Artificial Intelligence. Again, it is not clear whether this is a representative sample of mainstream or leading AI researchers. You should probably, therefore, treat the results of Müller and Bostrom's survey with caution.

A more recent survey was taken that is likely more informative of what researchers working in mainstream AI think. This was a 2016 survey of 193 Fellows of the Association for the Advancement of Artificial Intelligence (AAAI). Election as a fellow of this society is one of the highest honours in AI. It is limited to researchers who have made significant and sustained contributions to the field over several decades. Fellows make up less than 5 per cent of the membership of the Association for the Advancement of Artificial Intelligence. It is fair, then, to call them 'leading AI experts'. A substantial eighty of the 193 AAAI fellows (41 per cent) responded to the survey, including many well-known figures in the field, among them Geoff Hinton, Ed Feigenbaum, Rodney Brooks and Peter Norvig.[15] Unlike in Müller and Bostrom's survey, a quarter of the respondents predicted that superintelligence will never arrive, and another two-thirds predicted it would take more than twenty-five years. In total, then, more than nine out of every ten respondents put superintelligence at or beyond their own retirement age.[16] This is a more pessimistic prediction than that of Müller and Bostrom's survey. Nevertheless, it seems that a reasonable number of experts in AI are open to the possibility that machines will think at least as well as us sometime in the present century. It is also not at all clear, though, that experts in AI are the best people to predict how long it will take to get to superintelligence. Historians of science, futurologists and others may be far more accurate in their predictions.

THE ROAD AHEAD

Even if machines that think are achievable by 2100, we remain a considerable distance from that point today. In 2016, at the leading AI conference in New York City, the first ever Winograd Schema Challenge test was run. Recall that this is one of the proposed replacements for the Turing test, designed to measure common-sense and other types of reasoning. The winning entry scored 58 per cent accuracy, which is a grade D at best.[17] So the winner did better than a person answering questions by simply tossing a coin, but still some way from the 90 per cent or so that humans tend to achieve in such tests.

So how far along the road to thinking machines are we? If you add up everything written in the newspapers about the progress being made towards machines that think, or if you believe the more optimistic surveys, you might suspect we are further down this road than we actually are. We can only build machines today that can do narrow tasks. We have a lot of work ahead to build machines that can match the full breadth of the abilities of humans. And there are many tasks—like common-sense reasoning, and understanding natural language—which will likely be difficult to automate fully for some time to come. It's not popular to trust experts these days, but if they are to be believed, we are perhaps 50–100 years away from building superintelligence.

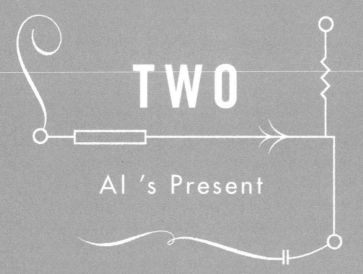

TWO

AI 's Present

3: The State of AI Today

When facing a difficult problem, a natural strategy is to decompose it into parts. The problem of building a thinking machine divides into a number of different parts. Not surprisingly, many researchers working in Artificial Intelligence focus on just one of these parts. Of course, there are also those who believe the problem is essentially undecomposable. But the human brain has a number of different parts, and these seem to perform different functions. So it seems reasonable to look to simplify the problem of building thinking machines by examining its constituent parts.

THE FOUR TRIBES

There are four different 'tribes' working on the different aspects of building a thinking machine. Of course, saying this grossly simplifies reality, as in practice the intellectual landscape of AI is extremely complex. But categorising AI researchers into tribes nevertheless helps us understand the lie of the land.

The Learners

We are born without language, without knowledge of what is good to eat, without the ability to walk, without knowledge of the sun and the stars, without knowledge of Newton's laws of physics. But we learn all these things and more. One way, therefore, to build a thinking machine would be to build a computer that can learn like humans do. This also eliminates the problem of having to codify all the knowledge we acquire as we grow up, knowledge that is essential to operating in the real world. As the CYC project discovered, it is a long and painful task to itemise for a robot all the common-sense knowledge it needs: water cannot be picked up, the sky is blue, shadows are not objects and so on.

Within the tribe of learners, my colleague Pedro Domingos has identified five 'religious groups': the symbolists, the connectionists, the evolutionaries, the Bayesians and the analogisers.[1]

The symbolists are disciples of Leibniz, bringing ideas from logic to learning. In logic, we typically perform deductive reasoning, inferring that B follows from A. The symbolists reverse this, using 'inductive reasoning' to learn what caused B. Since we observe B, they suppose, A must be the cause.

The connectionists, on the other hand, bring ideas from neuroscience to learning that are much less about symbols such as A and B, or 0 and 1, and more about the sort of continuous signals observed in the human brain. They use learning mechanisms like those in our neurons, where we learn how best to weigh the inputs to our artificial neurons. Deep Learners are some of the most visible members of this religion.

The third religious group are the evolutionaries, who take their inspiration from nature. They use mechanisms similar to those of evolution—'survival of the fittest'—to discover the best computational model for a problem.

The fourth religious group are the Bayesians. They take a statistical approach to learning that can be traced back to the Reverend Thomas Bayes.[2] They learn which of their models is most probable to succeed, based on the observed data.

The final religious group are the analogisers. They look to map a problem onto some other space, often with many more dimensions, where the connections between similar items might become clear. They use learning methods with fancy names such as 'support vector machines'. These methods find some other view of the problem, where similar items—say, all the observations of cats—are close together. Any new observation that is close to these old observations is taken to be a cat.

The Reasoners

The second tribe are the intellectual disciples of Leibniz, Hobbes and Boole. They explore how to equip machines with explicit rules of thought. Machines can reason over knowledge that is either explicitly encoded up front or learned from interacting with the real world. Hence, the reasoners may depend on the tribe of the learners to prepare their way.

Human reasoning is far more complex than the simple algebraic model dreamed of by Boole. The real world is not all 0s and 1s. We need to cope with incomplete knowledge, with inconsistent knowledge, with uncertainty about knowledge, and with knowledge about knowledge. The reasoners therefore try to develop formal models of reasoning that can cope with partial information, with contradictory information, with probabilistic information, and with information about information itself (so-called meta-information). The reasoners themselves consist of a number of different groups. There are the hardcore deductive reasoners. Some of them try to get computers to do mathematical reasoning, to prove theorems, even to invent new mathematics. Another group focuses on planning—getting computers to plan sequences of actions to achieve some given goal. Other groups within the tribe of reasoners focus on reasoning tasks, such as updating a knowledge base as new and perhaps contradictory information arrives.

The Roboticists

Human intelligence is a complex phenomenon. It arises in part from our interactions with the real world. The third tribe, the roboticists, build machines that act in the real world: they can reason about their actions, and learn like we do from these interactions. The roboticists therefore overlap with the tribes of the learners and the reasoners. Of course, robots need to sense the world in which they act, so some within this tribe work on computer vision: giving computers the ability to perceive the state of the world. Vision not only helps us navigate in the real world, it is also an important part of our ability to learn about it.

The Linguists

The fourth tribe working to build thinking machines are the linguists. Language is an important part of human thought. For machines to think, they must therefore understand and manipulate natural language. The linguists develop computer programs that can parse written text and understand and answer questions—even translate between two languages. Some also work on speech recognition, getting computers to convert audio signals into natural language text.

THE TWO CONTINENTS

Let's extend our metaphor of the tribes further. In AI research there are also two 'continents': the continent of the scruffies and the continent of the neats. Neats look for elegant, precise mechanisms with which they can build thinking machines. Leibniz was one of the first neats. John McCarthy was another famous neat. Scruffies, on the other hand, suppose that intelligence is too complex and messy to be solved by simple, precise mechanisms. Rodney Brooks is one of the most famous scruffies. He builds robots that lack explicit logical control structures. These robots sense and act in the real world, and complex behaviours emerge out of their interactions. Scruffies are the hackers of the AI world. Indeed, the genesis of hacking culture can be traced back in part to the many scruffies at CSAIL, MIT's famous Computer Science and Artificial Intelligence Laboratory.

Members of the four tribes—the learners, the reasoners, the roboticists and the linguists—live on both continents. Some members of the machine learning tribe are scruffies, for example, and other members are neats. Similarly, there are linguists who are scruffies and linguists who are neats. Not surprisingly, almost all members of the reasoners' tribe are neats. Theirs is a problem that is often logical and so lends itself to a neat approach. On the other hand, many of the members of the tribe of roboticists are scruffies. Theirs is a problem that is complex and messy, and this lends itself to a scruffy approach.

THE STATE OF MACHINE LEARNING

A lot of the buzz about Artificial Intelligence today is due to the spectacular progress being made by the tribe of the learners. Deep Learning methods especially are demonstrating impressive performance, often overtaking other longstanding techniques. For example, speech-recognition systems based on Deep Learning, such as Baidu's Deep Speech 2, are now competitive with humans at transcribing speech into text. And, as I described earlier, Google's AlphaGo program beat one of the best players in the world at Go in early 2016 by playing itself at Go and learning from its mistakes.

It would be wrong to conclude, however, that machine learning has brought us very close to thinking machines, and that, with a little more refinement, techniques such as Deep Learning will 'solve' intelligence. One reason that Deep Learning is not the end of the game is that it needs loads of data. This is possible in a domain like playing Go: there are databases filled with past games played by experts from which a program can learn. And we can also play the machine against itself and generate limitless amounts of further data. But in other domains data is harder to collect. In many robotic domains, physics and engineering may limit how quickly we can collect data—we may need to be careful not to break the robot as it learns and makes mistakes. In other domains there may not be much data. We might want to predict the success rate for heart or lung transplants, but there is limited data on which to base any predictions as such operations world-wide number only in the hundreds. With problems like this, Deep Learning will be challenged as it needs lots of data. Humans, by comparison, are remarkably fast learners, and we learn from much less data. According to Go experts, AlphaGo plays Go in a way not seen before, especially in the opening moves of the game. Nevertheless, it took only three games for Lee Sedol to learn enough about AlphaGo to win a game. AlphaGo, by comparison, has played more games—billions— than any human could play in a lifetime (even in several). Respect, then, to Lee Sedol. And a small victory for humankind in what was otherwise another defeat to the machines.

There are several other reasons why Deep Learning will not provide the whole answer to the problem of building thinking machines. First, we will often want our thinking machines to explain their decisions. Deep Learning is largely a closed box. It cannot meaningfully explain why a particular input gives a certain output. If we are to trust the system, we may want it to explain some of its decisions. Second, we will often want to *guarantee* certain behaviours. An autonomous car must always stop at a red light. Air traffic control software can never permit two aircraft into the same sector. Deep Learning does not permit such guarantees to be made, and we will likely need more rule-based systems to do this. Third, the complexity of the human brain is of a scale way beyond any networks built using Deep Learning today. The human brain has billions of neurons with trillions of connections; Deep Learning today uses thousands of artificial neurons with millions of connections. Scaling up to match the brain is not going to be easy. In addition, the brain has many different types of neuron, and many different structures that are used for different tasks. It is therefore likely that we will need similar specialisation in any thinking machine.

Despite these reservations, machine learning is maturing as a technology, and can solve many problems without too much help from us humans. But it is not at the point that we can simply push a button—humans must still do a lot of algorithm selection, parameter tuning and what is euphemistically called 'feature engineering' to make the technology work. Machine learning is inherently limited by the input data. For example, if you want to predict whether a shopper will use a coupon offer, you might want to add a new piece of data to your model—like how long it is since they last purchased something from the company.

We cannot discuss the state of machine learning without mentioning the role that big data has played in its recent success. Many industries are leveraging big data sets to build practical applications using machine learning. Banks are using big data and machine learning to detect credit-card fraud, for instance. Online stores and services such as Amazon and Netflix are using big data and machine learning to tune their product recommendations. NASA has identified a new type of star using machine learning applied to a large star catalogue.

In general, machine learning helps us classify, cluster and make predictions about data. I'll talk shortly about the state of the art in using machine learning to identify images, to drive autonomously, to recognise speech and to translate texts between languages. Machine learning is, however, being used to good effect by companies in many other domains. It is impossible to list them all but I'll mention a few to illustrate the breadth of the field. Machine learning is being successfully used to detect malware, to predict hospital admissions, to check legal contracts for errors, to prevent money laundering, to identify birds from their song, to predict gene function, to discover new drugs, to predict crime and schedule police patrols appropriately, to identify the best crops to plant, to test software, and (somewhat controversially) to mark essays. Indeed, it might be easier to list the areas in which machine learning is not being used. Actually, scratch that; it is almost impossible to think of an area in which machine learning isn't being used.

There are several areas in which machine-learning techniques struggle. One mentioned earlier is explanation. Unlike humans, many machine-learning algorithms are unable to explain why they came up with their answers. Another area is in learning from limited amounts of data, as well as from 'noisy' data. Machine learning has a long way to go to match human performance in these situations. A third challenge area is learning across problems. Humans can apply their expertise in one domain to get up to speed quickly in another. If you are good at playing tennis, you will likely be at least reasonable at badminton. By comparison, machine-learning algorithms tend to have to start again from scratch. A final area in which machine learning remains challenged is what is known as unsupervised learning. Many of the recent advances in machine learning have been in supervised learning. Here we have training data that is correctly labelled: *This is a picture of a cat. This is a picture of a car. This is spam. This is not spam.* But in many application domains we don't have the labels, or perhaps collecting labels requires too much time and effort. We still need to make progress in the field of unsupervised learning—that is, developing machine-learning algorithms that work without labels. As children, much of our learning happens without explicit labels. In the real world, cats don't have labels attached to them telling us that they are cats. Yet somehow we learn to recognise cats from dogs. Our machine-learning algorithms need to do the same.

THE STATE OF AUTOMATED REASONING

The automated reasoning tribe is also making progress, but so far has a smaller footprint in practical applications. Automated reasoning can itself be further decomposed into a number of different types of reasoning. Perhaps the purest type of reasoning is deduction. This is mathematical reasoning—applying rules of inference to derive new facts from old. If the two sides of a triangle are of equal length, then so are the two base angles. Deductive reasoning can also be applied to other, less mathematical problems. If there is an obstacle in front of the robot, then find a route around the obstacle. If the stock level falls beneath five units, then order new stock.

For some well-defined mathematical reasoning tasks, we already have programs that can perform as well, if not better than, humans. One example is symbolic integration. What is the integral of: $x+7/x^2(x+2)$ A computer algebra system like Maple or Mathematica will quickly come back with the correct answer.[3] This is one of the examples of AI falling out of sight. Many people might not realise that some of the pioneering work in computer algebra took place within Project MAC, the precursor to the AI laboratory CSAIL.[4]

Another example of mathematical reasoning that computers can do well is equation solving. Consider the following A-level mathematics exam question:[5]

If $cos(x+cos(3x)+cos(5x)=0$, what is x?

The PRESS equation-solving program developed at the Department of AI at the University of Edinburgh in the 1970s and 1980s can solve such problems.[6] When tested on 148 equations from A-level exams from 1971 to 1984, PRESS solved 132 correctly. It also answered nineteen out of twenty-six simultaneous equations correctly, giving it an overall 87 per cent success rate. That's enough to get an A grade. PRESS solved these equations in the traditional high-school way, rewriting equations into simpler form until a solution drops out. There are many ways to rewrite an equation, most of which are not helpful. PRESS therefore included some sophisticated heuristics, rules of thumb designed to pick the best way to simplify each equation. PRESS was later applied within the MECHO project to answer mechanics problems from A-level physics exams.

Other more creative aspects of mathematical reasoning have also been automated. For example, computers have actually invented some new and interesting mathematical concepts. Simon Colton developed a computer program called HR that invented new mathematical concepts.[7] HR was named in honour of Hardy and Ramanujam, a famous mathematical partnership that was recently celebrated in the book and film *The Man Who Knew Infinity*. Like the Indian mathematician Ramanujan, the HR program focused on identifying patterns in numbers and other algebraic domains.[8] HR invented several new types of number. These numbers are sufficiently interesting that mathematicians have subsequently explored their properties. When people make the objection that computers will never be creative, this is one of the counter-examples I like to give.

* * *

Inventing new mathematics by computer

The HR program starts with some basic facts about addition: 1+1=2, 1+2=3, 2+1=3, 2+2=4 and so on. HR is programmed to repeat any operation. Repeating addition gives you the concept of multiplication. HR also is programmed to invert any operation. Inverting multiplication gives you the concept of division. HR then invents the idea of divisors, numbers that exactly divide a number: 2 is a divisor of 6. 3 is a divisor of 6. But 4 is not. HR then notes that some numbers have only two divisors, themselves and 1. 3 has two divisors: 1 and 3. 4 has three divisors: 1, 2 and 4. 5 has two divisors: 1 and 5. So HR invents the concept of numbers with two divisors: 2, 3, 5, 7, 11, 13, etc. These are better known as prime numbers.

So far, we have not gone further than the Ancient Greeks. But then HR takes a step that we didn't expect. HR considers applying a concept to itself. What about numbers where the number of divisors itself is a divisor? These are called refactorable numbers. Consider 8. The numbers 1, 2, 4 and 8 divide 8 exactly. So there are 4 divisors of 8. And 4 itself is one of them. Thus, 8 is refactorable. Consider 9. The numbers 1, 3, and 9 divide 9 exactly. So there are 3 divisors of 3. And 3 itself is one of them. Thus 9 is refactorable. But consider 10. The numbers 1, 2, 5 and 10 divide 10 exactly. So there are 4 divisors of 10. But 4 is not one of the divisors. Thus, 10 is not refactorable.

HR also makes conjectures about the concepts it invents. For instance, HR conjectures that there is an infinite number of refactorable numbers. Like primes, as numbers become bigger, they become rare but they never disappear completely. HR went on to invent many known types of number, such as powers of two, prime powers and square free numbers. But it also invented seventeen new types of number considered interesting enough by mathematicians to be entered into the online Encyclopedia of Integer Sequences. Unknown to Colton, refactorable numbers had been invented a decade earlier by a human mathematician. But HR did invent many other new concepts, such as numbers for which the number of divisors is itself a prime number.

A fundamental component of HR was its mathematical taste. There are many uninteresting mathematical concepts: numbers where the number of divisors is the number itself, numbers with just one divisor and so on. HR had therefore to decide which concepts to expand on and which to ignore. This required programming it with a sense of taste, encouraging it to focus its attention only on the interesting. Concepts such as a number for which the number of divisors is the number itself are not particularly interesting; the only examples are 1 and 2. Similarly, a number for which the number of divisors is not the number itself is not particularly interesting; every number except 1 and 2 satisfies this definition. HR focuses on concepts that fall in between—that are neither too rare nor too common.

* * *

Another area of automated reasoning in which applications are being fielded is planning. When Mars Rover needs to perform an experiment at the top of a neighbouring hill, it needs a plan. You cannot control it from Earth. Too much can go wrong in the fifteen minutes or so that it takes for a radio signal to get between the two planets. Till now, most space missions use pre-prepared plans. They are built on Earth, using a mixture of human and computer tools, and uploaded in advance onto the spacecraft. But in 1999 NASA's Deep Space One flew entirely autonomously, finding and executing plans to control the spacecraft without any human intervention.[9] All this at a distance of some 600 million miles from Earth. Similar automated planning technology is now routinely used to plan the movement of robots around factories and hospitals, or the operations of robotic sheet-metal-bending work stations—even to play tricks in the game Bridge Baron.

Another component of the Deep Space One controller was its ability to diagnose faults automatically. It was able to identify and fix faults in its futuristic ion engine. Such automated diagnosis is another exciting application area for automated reasoning. Automated diagnosis is used to identify and repair faults in highly complex power transmission networks and in expensive gas turbines, as well as to identify and suggest treatments for cancer, osteoarthritis and many other diseases.

I want to highlight one final area of automated reasoning as it has many practical applications. This is the area of optimisation. Here we get a computer to choose the best of many different options. At the same time, we respect whatever constraints we have, such as limited resources, staff or money. For example, how do we get the computer efficiently to schedule production, roster staff, route trucks, place and price adwords, or move a jointed robotic hand through space? Such optimisation problems pose a fundamental computational challenge. Suppose, for example, we are routing a delivery truck around Manhattan, and we have ten parcels to deliver. There are ten options for the first stop, nine for the second, eight for the third and so on. That is $10 \times 9 \times 8 \times 7 \times 6 \times 5 \times 4 \times 3 \times 2 \times 1$ possible routes. If we multiply this out, we get 3,628,800 possible routes. If we have twenty parcels, there are over 2 quintillion possible routes (to be precise: 2,432,902,008,176,640,000). And if we have fifty-five parcels, there are more possible routes than there are atoms in the universe. To solve such problems, computers are our only hope. Smart algorithms cut through this complexity, finding a needle in the haystack that is the optimal (or near-to-optimal) route.

In the fast-growing area of data analytics, optimisation is the less well-known but nevertheless essential cousin of machine learning. We use machine learning to find a signal in our big data. For instance, we can identify products that our customers are most likely to buy, based on a large database of historical purchases. But this signal alone is not enough. We need to turn this into some sort of action. This is where optimisation comes into play. In this case, how many of each product should we stock, keeping in mind the capacity of our warehouse and our available funds? And how much do we charge for each product, bearing in mind the cost of production, delivery and storage?

Optimisation is transforming the efficiency with which many businesses are now operating, turning data into dollars. In every sector of the economy, it's improving operations. In some cases, it is maximising profits. In others, it is minimising our impact on the environment. It is being used to schedule mines, rotate crops, roster staff, route trucks, balance portfolios and price insurance. As with machine learning, it is almost impossible to find a sector of the economy in which optimisation is not being used in some form or other.

Despite making solid progress, automated reasoning still faces three fundamental challenges. In fact, these three challenges have troubled the field from its earliest days. The first challenge is finding a representation for a problem that makes reasoning about it easy. There are often many alternative and logically equivalent representations for a reasoning problem.

A classic example is the 'mutilated chessboard' problem. Suppose you take a standard eight-by-eight chessboard, and cut out the two corner squares opposite each other. The challenge is to tile the mutilated chessboard that remains with thirty-one two-by-one dominoes. Of course, you could simply try to place dominoes on the chessboard in all possible ways. But there is a representation that makes reasoning about this problem easy. Consider the colour of the squares of the mutilated chessboard. The two removed squares are both the same colour—let's say they're white. So the chessboard now has thirty-two black squares and thirty white squares. This means we cannot hope to cover it with two-by-one dominoes, which each must cover one black and one white square. A good representation has uncovered the solution to the problem.

The second challenge facing automated reasoning is coping with the 'combinatorial explosion', the rapid increase in possible solutions that even our best algorithms must explore. We can tame this beast but it never goes away. Smart algorithms will not, for example, explore all permutations in our delivery truck problem. They will skip over many clearly suboptimal solutions. But even the best algorithm will still need to explore many close-to-optimal solutions. As problems grow larger, this will often be too time-consuming.

THE STATE OF AI TODAY

The third challenge facing automated reasoning is common-sense and qualitative reasoning. Humans have vast stores of knowledge about how the world works. If we let go of a ball, it will accelerate towards the ground due to gravity. The ball will likely bounce back. But if we drop an egg, it will likely break. Building systems that can make inferences like this remains a largely unsolved problem. We learn such models of the world as children. We have a long way to go before we can build machines that can match even a young child's ability at such tasks.

THE STATE OF ROBOTICS

Robotics is perhaps the tribe that might be expected to make the slowest progress. In robotics, we have to build actual machines that can interact with the real world. Machines that have to obey the laws of physics, and cope with limitations brought about by their weight and strength. Machines that negotiate a world they only partially know and observe. And machines that can physically break when they make mistakes. It is all so much easier in the virtual world, where we can know everything, where everything is exact, where we are less limited by the laws of physics, and where we can easily replace things when we break them. Nevertheless, the roboticists' tribe is making real advances.

Consider industrial robots. These used to cost hundreds of thousands of dollars, and required specialised programming. But today you can buy a decent industrial robot like the friendly Baxter for around $20,000, and program it yourself.[10] Even a small to medium-sized enterprise could consider using such a robot. Twenty thousand dollars is a meaningful price point. It's less than the annual wage of the worker whom the robot is likely to replace. A company can get a return on its investment in under a year.

As a result of these sorts of advances in robotics, we are starting to see 'dark factories' where there are no people and so no need for lights. FANUC, one of the largest manufacturers of industrial robots, has operated a dark factory near Mount Fuji since 2001. Yes, robots making robots. The future is already here. For the last five years, FANUC has posted annual sales of around $6 billion, selling robots into booming markets like China's.

Even in factories with lights, robots are increasingly replacing people. If you go into a car factory today, it is the robots that are doing the welding and the painting. And they're doing it far better than we humans used to do it. Warehouses are also being automated rapidly. Every time you receive a product from Amazon, you profit from the many robots that moved goods around the company's vast warehouses, fulfilling your order. Robots are also finding their way onto farms, and into mines and ports, as well as into restaurants, hotels and shops.

Robots are also appearing on our roads. Autonomous cars, buses and trucks are quickly moving out of the research lab and into the showroom. Most marry two technologies: high-precision GPS and maps for navigation, and sensors such as vision and radar for identifying other vehicles and obstacles on the road. As a result, autonomous vehicles can now drive down the highway with little or no intervention from a human driver. Around town, however, autonomous driving remains a challenge. There are many more surprises to cope with in an urban setting: pedestrians, intersections, bicycles, parked cars and so on. We are likely a decade or so away from having autonomous vehicles that can deal with such complexities.

Another place robots are starting to turn up today is the battlefield. In fact, in every possible theatre of war—in the air, on the land, and on or under the sea—the military is developing and testing robots. An arms race is underway to automate warfare. The Pentagon has allocated $18 billion in its current budget for the development of new types of weapons, many of them autonomous. It would take too long to list every military robot in development, so I'll pick out one robot in each theatre to illustrate the state of progress.

In the air, BAE Systems has been flying the autonomous drone Taranis, nicknamed Raptor, since 2013. This stealth drone can fly across oceans, perform surveillance, and identify and attack aerial or ground targets. On land, Boston Dynamics has developed a series of two-legged and four-legged robots that can move over rough terrain, carrying loads for soldiers. The YouTube videos of these robots are terrifying. I used to say Terminator was a hundred years away—but then I saw the video for their latest creation, the Atlas humanoid robot marching across a snowy forest. I now say Terminator might only be fifty years away. Google, the parent company of Boston Dynamics, appears to agree. Their motto used to be 'Don't be evil', though this was recently updated to 'Do the right thing'. In line with either motto, and following a lot of unfavourable press, Google put Boston Dynamics up for sale in early 2016. (I will return to this topic, and the arguments for and against such military robots, in a later chapter.)

Also on land, Samsung developed the SGR-A1 Sentry Guard Robot back in 2006. This robot currently guards the Demilitarised Zone between North and South Korea. This 250-kilometre-long buffer zone is filled with landmines, razor-sharp wire, and now robots that can kill. Samsung's robot can automatically identify, target and kill anyone who steps into no-man's land with its 5.56-millimetre robotic machine gun and optional grenade launcher.

On the sea, the US Navy christened the world's largest unmanned surface vessel, the 132-foot-long *Sea Hunter*, in April 2016. This robotic warship can cross oceans, hunting for mines and submarines without direct human control. Finally, under the sea, in March 2016 Boeing unveiled its 'game-changing' 51-foot-long autonomous submarine, *Echo Voyager*. This can spend six months underwater and has a range of around 12,000 kilometres. That's enough to get you from Pearl Harbor to Tokyo and back—without surfacing. There's no doubt about it—an arms race is underway.

There are even robots that carry robots, that themselves carry robots. In September 2016 Lockheed Martin tested its Submaran S10 autonomous boat. The Submaran is completely self-sufficient, using solar and wind and power. The Submaran launched the Marlin drone autonomous submarine. The submarine was commanded by the boat to launch the foldable and autonomous Vector Hawk drone. The robots are starting to work with each other.

Back in the lab, researchers are starting to build robots that can do a range of tasks that we do easily but that were previously considered impossible for machines. Robots can now run, fold laundry, iron clothes and catch balls. These all sound like simple tasks but, surprisingly, it is the simplest tasks that we have often found the hardest to automate.

Despite these advances in the lab, it is likely that the home will be the last place to see robots routinely. Robots still prefer the predictable and routine. They struggle to cope with uncertainty. This is why robots will take over factories first. They work best in environments we can completely control. Robots also still struggle to match our dexterity and sensitive touch.

THE STATE OF COMPUTER VISION

Robots need sensors to make sense of the world, and one of our most important senses is vision. Computer vision is therefore an important component in many robots. It is also vital for autonomous vehicles. We can use GPS and high-precision maps to navigate, but we still need to sense other vehicles and obstacles on the road.

We are making good progress in getting machines to see. Again, much of this progress is being driven by advances in Deep

Learning. Vision can be broken down into a number of general tasks—such as object recognition, motion analysis and pose estimation (position and orientation)—as well as more specialised tasks such as optical character recognition, scene labelling and face recognition.

Every year, computer scientists run a competition to measure progress in computer vision, the Large Scale Visual Recognition Challenge. In recent years, performance has improved dramatically, fuelled by advances in Deep Learning. The competition is based on the ImageNet database, which contains millions of photographs, labelled into thousands of object classes, including Persian cat, flamingo, mushroom and canoe.[11] In the first year of the competition, in 2010, the winning entry (from NEC Labs) had an error rate of 28.2 per cent.[12] By 2015 the winning entry (from Microsoft Research Laboratory in Beijing) had an error rate of just 3.57 per cent. Indeed, competition has become so intense between the technology giants that Baidu was caught breaking the rules in an attempt to win, and was banned for a year. There is, however, still some way to go to match human performance. Top-1 error rates, which measure the percentage of images where the most probable label is incorrect, are still around 20 per cent.

Such object recognition has become sufficiently mainstream that apps are now available to recognise objects automatically. Nokia's Point and Find app will automatically recognise buildings, cinema posters and products. Another app, Google Goggles, will recognise 76,000 different works of art at the Metropolitan Museum of Art in New York. And, though it has now been phased out, Microsoft's Bing Vision could recognise books, CDs and DVDs.

Face recognition is a specialised area within computer vision in which progress has also been good. Face recognition software currently works well on frontal images. It struggles as you move towards a profile. Poor lighting, sunglasses, long hair or even smiling can also present challenges. Nevertheless, on the standard 'Labeled Faces in the Wild' database of 13,000 images taken from the web, a state-of-the-art system such as Google's FaceNet achieves over 99 per cent accuracy. That's likely good enough for Big Brother. Again, Deep Learning has played a significant role in achieving such accuracy.

Optical character recognition (OCR) is another example of AI falling out of sight. OCR machines first appeared commercially in the 1950s, though the first patent for OCR dates back to 1929. Today, any multifunction printer you buy will have some decent OCR software bundled with its scanner. OCR is largely a solved problem. For typewritten Latin text, accuracy rates are greater than 99 per cent. For handwriting, accuracy rates drop to around 80 per cent, but as we're all doing less and less handwriting, this problem seems to be going away!

Computer vision is also contributing to projects like the 'bionic eye'. Cochlear implants and sophisticated signal processing have given hearing to many deaf people. A similar race is now underway in the United States, Australia and Europe to provide vision to those suffering from partial or total blindness. The goal is to implant electrodes onto the damaged retina. Computer vision algorithms have an important role to play in preparing the signal for these electrodes, and focusing the brain on important parts of the image.

Despite all this progress, computer vision still has some way to go before computers can undertake tasks more complex than object recognition and the like. For example, it remains a significant challenge to get computers to understand not individual objects but whole scenes, and the relationships between them. *The waiter serving the drinks to the group of women has dropped a glass of water*. It also is a challenge to predict what happens next. *The falling glass will break on the stone floor*. Computer vision systems currently also struggle with adverse lighting, poor weather conditions, low-resolution images and difficult camera angles.

THE STATE OF NATURAL LANGUAGE PROCESSING

The fourth and final AI tribe are the linguists. They try to get computers to parse, understand and use natural language. The processing of natural language can be broken down into a number of interrelated tasks, such as question answering, machine translation, text summarisation and speech recognition.

Question answering is one of the oldest problems studied in natural language processing. It can itself be broken down into a number of sub-problems, such as text-based question answering and knowledge-based question answering. In simple text-based question answering, we simply look to retrieve the correct answer from a text. *Who is the hero of the story? Where is the story set?* In knowledge-based question answering, we look to extract more semantic information, typically from a structured database. *What countries have land borders with China? Who was the US President when Elvis died?* Question answering can also be broken down, along other dimensions such as whether the domain is open or closed.

The performance of question answering systems is evaluated within a number of competitions such as the Text REtrieval Conference (TREC), held annually since 1992. Many technologies developed for competitions like this are now used to answer queries in commercial search engines like Google and Bing. A state-of-the-art question answering system can answer 70 per cent or more of simple questions correctly when the goal is to return a factoid or list. For closed-domain question answering, performance was already respectable even back in the early 1970s. For example, the LUNAR system correctly answered 78 per cent of questions about the Apollo moon rocks put to it by geologists at the Second Annual Lunar Science Conference, held in Houston in 1971.[13] LUNAR answered questions such as: 'What is the average concentration of aluminium in high alkali rocks?' For open-domain question answering, IBM's Watson (described earlier) represents the current state of the art.

Machine translation is another problem in natural language processing in which good progress has been made in the last few decades. After the disappointments of the 1960s and 1970s, interest in machine translation grew in the late 1980s and 1990s, fuelled in part by the development of the World Wide Web. Today, systems such as Google Translate demonstrate that machine translation performs acceptably at the sentence level when the languages are close together. For instance, Google Translate works okay between French and English. When the languages are further apart—such as English and Chinese—or when we want to translate whole paragraphs, there is still some distance to go. Even at the sentence level, however, Google Translate can still make some elementary mistakes.

* * *

Google Mistranslations

Input: L'auto est á ma soeur.
Output: The car is to my sister.
Correct: The car belongs to my sister.

Input: They were pregnant.
Output: Ils étaient enceintes
Correct: Elles étaient enceintes.

Input: Mais ça n'a l'air très amusant.
Output: But it does sound very funny.
Correct: But it doesn't sound very funny.

Input: La copine de le pilot mange son diner.
Output: The girlfriend of the pilot eats his dinner.
Correct: The girlfriend of the pilot eats her dinner.

* * *

To translate these sentences correctly requires a deep semantic understanding. You have to know that only women are typically pregnant. You have to understand idiom. You have to be able to perform complex anaphora resolution, to use common sense and other forms of reasoning to work out the person to whom particular pronouns refer. While we are still many years, if not decades, away from systems that can do this as well as humans, performance is already good enough for many applications.

Finally, speech recognition is another area of AI where progress is sufficiently good that it is starting to disappear from view. We will soon take it for granted that we can speak to a device and it will understand us. Again, Deep Learning has been responsible for many of the recent gains. Baidu's Deep Speech 2 system is, for instance, competitive in speed and accuracy with human performance when transcribing spoken English or Mandarin. Much larger training sets than used in the past have lifted performance considerably. Deep Speech 2 was trained on tens of thousands of hours of labelled speech. Perhaps what is most remarkable is that such systems don't have a semantic understanding of the text being transcribed. They operate purely at the syntactical level.

Despite all these advances, there are some fundamental areas in which natural language processing continues to be challenged. First, systems struggle to understand language and speech above the sentence level. There is still a lot of room for improvement in translating whole paragraphs of text or transcribing long spoken passages. Second, natural language processing still struggles with semantics—that is, with obtaining a true understanding of the meaning. You need meaning to distinguish between 'the bolt hit the ground, and the tree caught fire' and 'the bolt hit the ground, and the mast collapsed'. One bolt is electric, the other is metal.

AI AND GAMES

I want now to turn to some fun problems that these four tribes have worked on. Games have been a popular test bed for Artificial Intelligence. This should perhaps not be very surprising. Games have precise rules and clear winners that make them a good choice to automate.[14] There are small sets of possible actions, from which each player needs to choose at each step. And it is often easy to determine when someone has won, and which actions contributed to this success. With games, too, we can train the computer by making it play itself many times.

The real world is often not so well behaved. There may not be precise rules about what we can do. There can be very many or even an infinite number of actions that can be performed at any point in time. It can be very difficult to determine if a chosen action was good or not. And it can be much more difficult to collect lots of training data.

Games thus offer a simple, idealised world in which to develop machines that think. Games are also an area in which it is easy to quantify the progress being made. There are several games at which machines are now clearly superior to humans. Whenever someone tells me that computers can *only* do what they have been programmed to do, I like to list half a dozen games where computers are world champion. In most cases, these world champion computer programs *learned* to play better than us.

Othello

Othello (or Reversi, as it is sometimes called) is a two-player game played on an eight-by-eight board. Players take turns to place coloured disks on the board, at the same time reversing the colour of any of their opponents' disks that lie between their own disks. In 1997 the computer program Logistello beat the world champion Takeshi Murakami convincingly: 6–0. Logistello had refined its game by playing itself hundreds of thousands of times. Othello programs have continued to improve since then and are now substantially better than human players. For smaller games, specifically Othello played on a four-by-four or a six-by-six board, computers have computed the perfect play. In both cases, this leads to a win for the second player. Though it has not been proven yet, in practice the eight-by-eight game appears to end in a draw if both players play perfectly.

Connect 4

Connect 4 is a vertical version of noughts-and-crosses that has seven columns and six rows. The two players take turns to drop coloured disks into columns, trying to make a vertical, horizontal or diagonal line of four disks. In 1988 Victor Allis wrote an AI program that plays a *perfect* game of Connect 4. The program will never lose. It will force you into a draw or, if you make enough mistakes, it will beat you. It is mathematically impossible to beat the program.[15]

Chess

From the very start of the field, chess was considered an interesting test bed for Artificial Intelligence. Around 1948, Alan Turing wrote what was probably the first chess program. Lacking a computer on which to run the program, he ran it by hand with pencil and paper. It took him about half an hour to compute each move. The program failed to live up to its name, Turbochamp, and lost its first game. Nevertheless, it contained many ideas that are found in more sophisticated chess programs today.

As mentioned earlier, it was a significant milestone when the world champion Garry Kasparov lost to IBM's Deep Blue computer program in 1997. While this was the last match Deep Blue ever played, chess programs that run on a personal computer now play well above the level of the best human players.[16] In 2006 Vladimir Kramnik, who won the title of world champion from Kasparov, lost 2–4 to the Deep Fritz program, which ran on a standard PC. Interestingly, computer chess programs like Deep Fritz have changed the game of chess itself, increasing our under-standing of the game and serving as wonderful educational tools. Professionals and amateurs alike have benefited from chess pro-grams, which help them learn new plays and analyse old games. Chess is a good example of how thinking machines can augment rather than just replace humans.

Thanks to our better algorithms, even quite small chess pro-grams can now play very competitively. In 2009 Pocket Fritz 4 won the Copa Mercosur grandmaster tournament in Buenos Aires, Argentina, with nine wins and a draw. Pocket Fritz 4 is rated stronger than Garry Kasparov's highest ever rating. What's amazing is that Pocket Fritz 4 was running on an HTC Touch mobile phone.

Although the name seems to suggest it, Deep Blue did not use Deep Learning. The 'deepness' in Deep Blue was the depth to which looked, far beyond what humans could. Another confu-sion about Deep Blue, compared to a program like AlphaGo, is the suggestion that it did not use machine learning. Demis Hassabis has argued:

> Deep Blue is a hand-crafted program where the programmers distilled the information from chess grandmasters into specific rules and heuristics, whereas we've imbued AlphaGo with the ability to learn and then it's learnt it through practice and study, which is much more human-like.[17]

This misrepresents Deep Blue. Sure, there were a lot of hand-crafted features in Deep Blue and chess knowledge provided by grandmasters in the form of opening and closing books. Nevertheless, machine learning played a vital role in the development of Deep Blue. Its evaluation function—to determine who was winning—had many undetermined parameters. For example, it was not programmed how to weight a safe king position, compared to a space advantage in the centre. The optimal values for these parameters were determined by machine learning over thousands of master games.

AlphaGo, too, had a number of handcrafted features, such as liberties (an empty intersection adjacent to a stone), ladders (zigzag moves) and nakade moves (moves inside surrounded territory); these were not learned but programmed by humans. Also, AlphaGo was trained on a large database of past human games. So both AlphaGo and Deep Blue used machine learning, even if AlphaGo did more learning than Deep Blue. And both AlphaGo and Deep Blue included handcrafted knowledge about their respective games, even if AlphaGo had less handcrafted knowledge added than Deep Blue.

Checkers

Checkers (also known as draughts) is typically played on an eight-by-eight chessboard and involves capturing black or white pieces by making diagonal moves. In 1996 the Chinook program, written by a team from the University of Alberta led by Jonathan Shaeffer, won the Man vs. Machine World Checkers Championship, beating the grandmaster Don Lafferty. Arguably Chinook's greater triumph came shortly before this, against Marion Tinsley, who is often considered the greatest checkers player ever. Tinsley never lost a world championship match, and lost only seven games in his entire forty-five-year career, two of them to Chinook. In their final match, Tinsley and Chinook were drawn but Tinsley had to withdraw due to ill health; he died shortly after. Sadly, we shall never know if Chinook would have gone on to draw or win. In any case, a University of Alberta team now has a program that plays *perfectly*. They exhaustively showed that their program could never be defeated. Exhaustive is the correct term here: it required *years* of computation on more than 200 computers to explore all the possible games.

Go

As we have seen, machine overtook man at Go for the first time in March 2016, when AlphaGo beat Lee Sedol 4–1. The most successful computer Go program before AlphaGo was CrazyStone, a program written by Remi Coulom. CrazyStone has beaten several professional Go players, but only when playing with a handicap advantage of four or more stones. Coulom was also the inventor of Monte Carlo Tree Search, one of the key ingredients in the success of AlphaGo. In March 2014 Coulom predicted it would take another decade to beat a professional player. In reality it took just twenty-four months, and AlphaGo beat one of the world's best players. (To be fair to Coulom, at the time of his prediction he also said: 'But I do not like to make predictions.')

It is interesting to compare AlphaGo to Deep Blue, which preceded it by twenty years. Deep Blue used specialised hardware to explore around 200 million positions per second. By comparison, AlphaGo evaluates only 60,000 positions per second. Deep Blue's approach used brute force to find a good move—but that does not scale well to the more complex game of Go. AlphaGo, by contrast, has a much better ability to evaluate positions, a skill learned from playing billions of games against itself.

It is also interesting to compare Deep Blue with modern chess programs. These explore far fewer positions than Deep Blue did. For instance, Deep Fritz explores around 8 million positions per second. And Pocket Fritz 4, which runs on a mobile phone and is rated better than Kasparov, explores just 20,000 positions per second.[18] This is far fewer than even AlphaGo. These programs have been trained to evaluate chessboard positions far better. They do not, therefore, have to look so far ahead into the game as Deep Blue did. We have got better at both Go and chess by being able to evaluate the board better.

Poker

Poker offers some interesting challenges not found in games like chess and Go. One is that it is a game of imperfect information. In games like chess and Go, you can see the board, and you know the state of play precisely. But in poker, some of the cards in play are concealed. This makes it a game of probabilities. Another challenge is that poker is a game of psychology, requiring you to understand the strategy of your opponents—when they might be bluffing, for instance.

Despite these challenges, computers are now very good at playing poker. In 2015 it was announced that the bot Cepheus had *essentially* solved the popular two-person version of poker, heads-up limit Texas Hold 'Em. Given the role that chance plays in poker, it is impossible to win money on every single hand. You can simply get some unlucky cards. But if you looked at all the hands that could happen and you averaged all of those, then Cepheus was demonstrated to win or break even in the long run.

In 2015 humans narrowly won the two-week 'Brains vs. Artificial Intelligence' competition at Rivers Casino in Pittsburgh playing heads-up no-limit Texas Hold 'Em. The four human competitors were top-ranked players, including the world number one. And in early 2017, two poker bots, Liberatus from CMU and DeepStack from a Canadian and Czech team, beat some of the leading players in the world at heads-up no-limit Texas Hold 'Em. As the name suggests, DeepStack uses Deep Learning but Liberatus uses more traditional AI techniques. Both learned to play from poker from scratch.

Scrabble

In 2006 the program Quackle defeated former world champion David Boys at Scrabble in a human–computer showdown in Toronto. Rather ungraciously, Boys remarked that losing to a machine was still better than being a machine. Computers are, of course, very able at finding the best-scoring words. They can quickly and mechanically search through the dictionary. However, Scrabble also requires skill in using the board well to exploit the special squares that double and triple the score, and in exploiting the board to get cross scores. In addition, skill is required in anticipating what letters are still to be drawn, and in playing the end game. Playing well at Scrabble therefore requires more than finding the best-scoring word in the dictionary.

Rubik's Cube

The standard three-by-three Rubik's cube can be in one of roughly 43 quintillion orientations. One quintillion is a one followed by eighteen zeroes. Actually, we can be very precise about the complexity of Rubik's cube. A cube can be in any one of a possible 43,252,003,274,489,856,000 possible orientations. Since an omniscient being would know the best move to make at any step, any algorithm that can solve the cube optimally is known as 'God's algorithm'. Similarly, 'God's number' is the optimal number of moves needed to solve the puzzle. My colleague Richard Korf used a lot of brute-force work on a computer to prove that God's number is just twenty moves.[19] In fact, most cubes can be solved in just eighteen moves.

Back in 1997 it took Korf's computer around four weeks, on average, to find the optimal solution for a particular problem. Twenty years later, we can solve that same problem in under a second. In fact, in November 2017 the technology company

Infineon physically solved a Rubik's cube in the world record time of 0.637 seconds, beating their previous record of 0.887 seconds. Cameras photographed the cube to work out how the cube was scrambled. They then computed the fastest solution to unscramble the cube. A robot then executed these moves. All in just over half a second. This is nearly ten times faster than the human world record. Fourteen-year-old Lucas Etter from Kentucky was the first person to break the five-second barrier, with a time of 4.904 seconds in November 2015.

Robot Soccer

Hundreds of researchers around the world are working on developing robots that can play soccer. This may seem an odd goal (pun intended). However, the game has many features that make it an interesting challenge. It requires speed, strength, agility and coordination, as well as strategic play. And it is great for getting young people interested in robotics.

RoboCup, an annual knockout tournament for robot soccer, has been run annually since 1997. The tournament attracts around 3000 participants in 400 different teams. It has also spawned a number of related events, such as RoboCup Junior for high-school students, and RoboCup Rescue, in which robots are built that can help in earthquakes and similar disasters.

The robots play in a number of different leagues. The blue-ribbon event is the Standard Platform League, in which each team has an identical robot. The robots are distinguished by their software—may the best program win. The Standard Platform League started in 1999 with AIBOs, cute robot dogs made by Sony. When Sony discontinued these, the league shifted in 2008 to 58cm tall humanoid Nao robots.

The overall goal of RoboCup is to beat the human world champion team in an exhibition match by 2050. There is still some way to go: a team of six-year-olds would have no trouble running rings around even the best RoboCup team today. Nevertheless, performance improves every year. At the end of each competition, participants are required to share their code so that everyone can benefit from the progress exhibited by the winners.

As in human football, teams from Germany have played a leading role. In the annual RoboCup competition, German teams have won the Standard Platform League eight times. Australia has also punched above its weight, with teams winning seven times. I am lucky to work at an institution that has contributed to much of this success. The University of New South Wales has won five times, most recently back-to-back wins in 2014 and 2015. The moment I realised RoboCup was entering the mainstream was when I heard it being reported in the sports section of the BBC Radio 4 news.

4: The Limits of AI

Progress in the past does not guarantee progress in the future. Perhaps we will run into limits that prevent the dream of building thinking machines? Let's therefore consider some practical and theoretical arguments as to why we might *never* build thinking machines. There are many machines we would like to have but will likely never engineer. Time machines to take us back to the past. Perpetual-motion machines that run forever. Perhaps thinking machines fall into the same category: highly desirable but sadly impossible?

Many other fields have run into fundamental limits, both practical and theoretical. For instance, mathematics contains many impossibilities. You cannot square a circle. And, as you may recall, it is impossible to write down a logical formulation for all mathematics. In physics, it follows from Einstein's theories that it is not possible to accelerate faster than the speed of light. And time travel appears to be largely impossible on a practical level, avoiding logical dilemmas like accidently killing your own grandfather. Perhaps there are similar practical or theoretical limits that will defeat our ambitious goal of building thinking machines?

Before we look at possible limits, we should define more carefully our desired end point. We can then consider if there is anything to prevent us reaching this point.

STRONG AI

One possible end point for AI is to build a machine that equals or exceeds our capabilities at a particular task requiring intelligence. This is sometimes called *weak AI*. We have achieved this end point already in a number of specialised domains. For example, computers are as good as, and in some cases better than, humans at playing chess, conducting air-to-air combat,[1] guessing the location of photographs[2] and diagnosing lung disease.[3]

Beyond this is *strong AI*. One of the louder and more eloquent critics of AI, the philosopher John Searle, came up with this concept.[4] It is the idea that thinking machines will eventually be minds, or at least that they will have all the hallmarks of minds, such as consciousness. Other human traits that might be relevant to strong AI are self-awareness, sentience, emotion and morality. Searle introduced the idea of strong AI with the 'Chinese Room', a famous thought experiment designed to expose some of the limits of AI.[5]

The Chinese Room is a little like a Turing test. Suppose we lock Searle in a room. It's important for the purposes of the experiment to understand that Searle knows no Chinese, either written or spoken. But in the room there is a large set of books containing rules in English that manipulate Chinese symbols. You pass into the room slips of paper containing questions in Chinese. Searle follows the rules in the books and writes answers to these questions onto other slips of paper, which he then passes outside. Now, suppose that the Chinese person writing these questions cannot tell Searle's answers apart from those of someone who really does know Chinese. Searle then asked: who understands Chinese? It's clearly not him. Nor is it the room or the book—they're both inanimate objects. In this scenario Searle is playing the role of a computer that is answering Chinese questions. So we cannot say a computer passing such a test really *understands* Chinese, as strong AI requires.

Philosophers, cognitive scientists and AI researchers have discussed Searle's Chinese Room experiment vigorously ever since. In 2004 it was claimed that 'the Chinese Room argument has probably been the most widely discussed philosophical argument in cognitive science to appear in the past 25 years'.[6] It is worth emphasising that most research in the field of Artificial Intelligence is focused on weak AI rather than strong AI. Indeed, I suspect only a minority of researchers in the field believe we will eventually achieve strong AI. And we do not need strong AI to get almost all of the benefits of thinking machines. We just need machines that perform as well as humans. They don't actually have to have minds. Indeed, if they do not have minds, we avoid a number of ethical problems—such as whether they have rights, or whether we are allowed to switch them off.

To many working in the field, therefore, Searle's Chinese Room argument is a bit of a distraction. In fact, Alan Turing anticipated Searle's criticism two decades earlier. The Turing test was introduced precisely to counter the sort of arguments put forwards by Searle.

Many other replies have been made to Searle's arguments. One is that the system as whole can be said to understand Chinese. Another is that the argument is irrelevant, as it can never be tested. No experiment can distinguish between a system with or without a mind. A third is that the Chinese Room can never exist, as we would need to ground the symbols in reality. A robot could, for instance, physically connect the symbols to objects in the real world, and this would provide meaning. In any case, while it provides an interesting perspective, Searle's Chinese

Room is likely not a troubling limit on our quest to create thinking machines.

ARTIFICIAL GENERAL INTELLIGENCE

A slightly less extreme end point than strong AI is Artificial General Intelligence, or AGI. This is the goal of building machines with the ability to work on *any* problem that humans can do, at or above the level of humans. Again, it is worth emphasising that the majority of research to develop thinking machines is focused on weak AI (building machines designed to solve specific problems) rather than on AGI (building machines designed to solve any problem). Only a small minority of researchers in the field are focused on AGI.[7] AGI is sometimes used synonymously with strong AI, but there is a large difference. AGI does not suppose that thinking machines will be minds, with consciousness and everything else that might be associated with minds. AGI is often used synonymously with the idea of superintelligence, or intelligence far beyond that of a human, but really AGI is only a step along the road to superintelligence.

Nick Bostrom defines superintelligence as 'an intellect that is much smarter than the best human brains in practically every field, including scientific creativity, general wisdom and social skills'.[8] One reason that AGI is often confused with superintelligence is that many believe that the path from AGI to superintelligence will be very rapid. Once we get to AGI, machines can simply improve themselves. We will thus rapidly get to superintelligence after AGI is achieved. We shall return to this idea shortly, when we discuss the idea of the technological singularity.

So there are several different end points for building thinking machines. In increasing order of capability, we have weak AI, AGI, superintelligence and strong AI. It's worth bearing these different end points in mind when considering arguments against thinking machines. An argument against conscious machines, for instance, might prevent us from getting to strong AI but it does not preclude weak AI or even AGI.

SOME ARGUMENTS AGAINST AI

Machines that think are a provocative idea. They threaten to usurp much that is often said to make us special. Not surprisingly, then, many arguments have been made against the long-held dream of building thinking machines. Indeed, Turing anticipated this back in 1950: in his seminal *Mind* paper, he discussed and dismissed many of them.

One argument against AI discussed by Turing is the argument of *disability*. People object that computers may act in some ways intelligently, but they can never do something really new. They can never be wrong. They can never fall in love. They can never learn from experience. They can never have a sense of humour. They can never enjoy strawberries and cream. The list goes on. Unfortunately, as Turing noted, people rarely back up such arguments with evidence. Usually the person has just never seen a machine do such a task yet.

Some of these specific arguments are very easy to dismiss. There are many documented cases of computers doing something new. Making a new type of opening move in Go. Inventing a new type of number. Writing a news story. There are also many examples of computers learning from experiences. AlphaGo learned to play Go by playing itself. Amazon learns to recommend you products from your and others' past interactions. Google Translate learned how to translate sentences by studying millions of examples. As for computers never being wrong, anyone who has ever tried to debug a complex program will disagree vehemently.

A related argument, also raised by Turing, is the mathematical objection that there are logical limits to what computers can prove mathematically. One problem with this objection is that it is not at all clear that humans do not have our own mathematical limits. You probably know many highly intelligent people who are mathematically very challenged. Putting this aside, even if computers cannot prove all mathematical truths, they can still prove many mathematical statements. Indeed, there are some mathematical theorems which have only been 'proved' by computers. The most famous is the four colour theorem. This states that any planar map requires, at most, four different colours. The only proofs we have for this require exhaustively trying to colour hundreds of possible counter-examples—a task which, realistically, it is only possible to perform without error on a computer.

Can machines be creative?

One of the most popular arguments against AI is Lady Lovelace's objection that computers cannot be creative. There are many responses to this. One is that computers have been creative many times already, writing poems, composing music and painting artworks. In fact, machines started writing poetry a hundred years before the invention of the electronic computer. The eccentric inventor John Clark spent fifteen years building Eureka, a machine that generated Latin hexameter verse.[9] It was first put on show in Piccadilly, London, in 1845. It must have proved popular, as the one-shilling entrance fee allowed Clark to retire comfortably. The machine was clockwork, and patriotically played the national anthem as it composed a Latin verse. It contained eighty-six wheels, which drove an amazing collection of 'cylinders, cranks, spirals, pullies, levers, springs, ratchets, quadrants, tractors, snails, worm and fly, heart-wheels, eccentric-wheels, and star-wheels'.[10] This produced one of 26 million possible verses. Fittingly, it would take a lifetime to run through every one of its rather gloomy verses; here's one:

Martia castra foris praenarrant proelia multa.
Military camps foretell many battles abroad.

Computers can do a better job than this now. Here's a more recent haiku by Ray Kurzweil's Cybernetic Poet:

Crazy moon child
Hide from your coffin
To spite your doom.

In 2011 one of the world's oldest student-run literary journals, Duke University's *Archive*, published a short poem called 'For the Bristlecone Snag'.

A home transformed by the lightning
the balanced alcoves smother
this insatiable earth of a planet, Earth.
They attacked it with mechanical horns
because they love you, love, in fire and wind.
You say, what is the time waiting for in its spring?
I tell you it is waiting for your branch that flows,
because you are a sweet-smelling diamond architecture
that does not know why it grows.

Unbeknown to the editors, the poem was written by a computer. Zachary Scholl, the program's inventor, argued therefore that his program had passed the Turing test for poems. As with the claims that the chatbot Eugene Goostman had passed the Turing test proper, there are reasons to dispute Scholl's claim. Student poetry might be expected to be a little awkward, as this poem is in several places. Scholl submitted twenty-six poems, one for each letter of the alphabet. This was the only one accepted. Some 96 per cent of the program's output therefore did not pass this test. And the editors were not explicitly looking to distinguish computer-generated poetry from human-written poems. Nevertheless, it is becoming harder to argue that computers will never be able to write poetry.

Another response to Lady Lovelace's objection is that humans are limited by the same deterministic laws as computers. If humans can surprise us, then perhaps computers can too. Indeed, one of the rewards of working in AI are the 'aha' moments when our creations do something we never expected them to do. I still recall my surprise and delight when this first happened to me. It was 1988, and my program spat out the proof to a mathematical theorem that I had imagined was well beyond its capabilities. It would have challenged even my undergraduate students. I was impressed.

A third response to Lady Lovelace's objection is that machine learning is likely to be a significant component of any intelligent machine, and that such machines may therefore behave in ways that we do not expect. Creativity might arise from the complex interactions between the program and its environment.

THE 'HARD PROBLEM'

Another strong argument (upcoming pun intended) against the possibility of thinking machines, specifically against strong AI, is that machines will never be conscious. This objection is at the heart of Searle's Chinese Room argument. In 1951, at Manchester University's Lister Oration, the British brain surgeon Geoffrey Jefferson eloquently put this argument forward:

> Not until a machine can write a sonnet or compose a concerto because of thoughts and emotions felt, and not by the chance fall of symbols, could we agree that machine equals brain—that is, not only write it but know that it had written it. No mechanism could feel (and not merely artificially signal, an easy contrivance) pleasure at its successes, grief when its valves fuse, be warmed by flattery, be made miserable by its mistakes, be charmed by sex, be angry or miserable when it cannot get what it wants.

In considering this argument, we must first put aside the solipsist's fear that only one's own consciousness is sure to exist. We still face the possibility that consciousness might be an emergent property—that it might develop within any sufficient complex system, even one in silicon. We are also left with the problem that consciousness is itself a difficult problem to explain in biological systems. Indeed, the philosopher David Chalmers has called it 'the hard problem'.[11]

> Consciousness poses the most baffling problem in the science of the mind. There is nothing that we know more intimately than conscious experience, but there is nothing that is harder to explain. All sorts of mental phenomena have yielded to scientific investigation in recent years, but consciousness has stubbornly resisted. Many have tried to explain it, but the explanations always seem to fall short of the target. Some have been led to suppose that the problem is intractable, and that no good explanation can be given.

I hope that we may come to a partial answer to 'the hard problem' through building thinking machines. Perhaps they will at some point become conscious? Or perhaps we can build machines that think without them developing any form of consciousness? We might prefer that machines do not gain consciousness. Once machines are conscious, we may have ethical obligations towards them. Is it reasonable just to turn them off? Do they suffer?

In any case, since we understand so little today about consciousness, it is not at all clear that it is *necessarily* a limit on the quest to build machines that think.

TACIT LIMITS

Another limit on building thinking machines appears at first sight paradoxical. It is connected to our unconscious mind. Michael Polanyi's seminal book *The Tacit Dimension* begins with the observation:

> We know more than we can tell ... The skill of a driver cannot be replaced by a thorough schooling in the theory of the motor car; the knowledge I have of my own body differs altogether from the knowledge of its physiology; and the rules of rhyming and prosody do not tell me what a poem told me without any knowledge of its rules.[12]

A lot of the 'intelligent' activities we do are not ones that we can explain to anyone else—or even to ourselves. Though he was not writing about computers, the economist Paul Autor borrowed this observation in 2014 to argue that 'the tasks that have proved most vexing to automate are those demanding flexibility, judgment and common sense skills that we understand only tacitly'.[13]

He named this Polanyi's paradox. One of the best examples of Polanyi's paradox is facial recognition. You know your husband's face, and you can recognise it out of a million, or indeed a billion others. Yet you are not conscious about your knowledge of his face. You would probably struggle to describe the precise arrangement of his eyes, nose and mouth. Instead, you recognise the face as a whole, and unconsciously.

Another example, again very relevant to building thinking machines, is language itself. We don't learn a language by being taught its grammar and the dictionary. Indeed, especially in a loose language like English, many of us are largely unaware of the formal grammar. Most of the English grammar I know comes from having Latin drummed into me at school. There are many other examples of Polanyi's paradox. Riding a bicycle. Making wine. Baking bread. We can read about them in books. But if you want to learn them, you have to do them.

Polanyi's paradox is closely connected to another paradoxical idea, which was discovered by AI researchers even earlier. Moravec's paradox was identified by Hans Moravec, Rodney Brooks, Marvin Minsky and others back in the 1980s.[14] Moravec described the paradox as follows: 'It is comparatively easy to make computers exhibit adult level performance on intelligence tests or playing checkers, and difficult or impossible to give them the skills of a one-year-old when it comes to perception and mobility.'[15]

The renowned linguist and cognitive scientist Steven Pinker has claimed that this is the most significant discovery by AI researchers.[16] In his book *The Language Instinct*, he writes:

THE LIMITS OF AI

The main lesson of thirty-five years of AI research is that the hard problems are easy and the easy problems are hard. The mental abilities of a four-year-old that we take for granted—recognising a face, lifting a pencil, walking across a room, answering a question—in fact solve some of the hardest engineering problems ever conceived. Do not be fooled by the assembly-line robots in the automobile commercials; all they do is weld and spray-paint, tasks that do not require clumsy Mr. Magoos to see or hold or place anything. And if you want to stump an artificial intelligence systems, ask it questions like, Which is bigger, Chicago or a breadbox? Do zebras wear underwear? Is the floor likely to rise up and bite you? If Susan goes to the store, does her head go with her? Most fears of automation are misplaced. As the new generation of intelligent devices appears, it will be the stock analysts and petrochemical engineers and parole board members who are in danger of being replaced by machines. The gardeners, receptionists, and cooks are secure in their jobs for decades to come.[17]

The flip side of Polanyi's paradox is that those tasks that we struggle to automate are the ones in which computerisation will tend to augment rather than replace humans. The construction worker is relatively safe thanks to Polanyi's paradox. But he or she has become a cyborg of sorts, with cranes, diggers, drills and other tools that amplify what they can do manyfold.

There is perhaps no real paradox to Polanyi's idea. Our brains encode billions of years of evolution. Our perceptions and reflexes have been fine-tuned over millions of generations. High-level conscious thought is a much more recent arrival. The difficulty of mastering a task on a machine may simply reflect how long it has taken human evolution to master it.

HUMAN-IMPOSED LIMITS

One reason we might never run into thinking machines is that we might put laws into place that prevent them being built. We might decide that the risks of building certain machines outweigh the benefits. Alternatively, we might permit them to be built but decide to limit how they might act. In 1942 Isaac Asimov proposed his well-known laws of robotics.

* * *

Asimov's laws

1. A robot may not injure a human being or, through inaction, allow a human being to come to harm.
2. A robot must obey the orders given it by human beings except where such orders would conflict with the First Law.
3. A robot must protect its own existence as long as such protection does not conflict with the First or Second Laws.

* * *

Asimov claimed these laws came from the *Handbook of Robotics*, fifty-sixth edition, published in 2058.[18] As in many other areas, Asimov's writing shows immense foresight. By 2058, robots will likely be playing such critical roles within our society that we will have had to work out the ethics of their behaviour. Unfortunately, Asimov's stories illustrate that even such simple laws are problematic.[19] What happens if a robot must harm one human to save several others? What happens if both action and inaction will harm a human? What happens if two humans give contradictory orders? Nevertheless, Asimov still argued that robots should be built with such laws in mind: 'I have my answer ready whenever someone asks me if I think that my Three Laws of Robotics will actually be used to govern the behavior of robots, once they become versatile and flexible enough to be able to choose among different courses of behavior.'[20]

Despite his insistence, I remain doubtful. There are many reasons why his laws are inadequate as a mechanism to build robots that interact with humans safely. As he himself admits, humans are certainly not rational. Equally, Asimov's laws are imprecise and incomplete. Much of the challenge is in trying to provide precision and cover cases we might never imagine. In trying to build driverless cars, Google has reported some very bizarre and unexpected situations its car has experienced.

A much simpler law is that proposed by the English mathematician I. J. Good, who worked with Turing at Bletchley Park.[21] His was a simple but beautiful suggestion: 'Treat your inferiors as you would be treated by your superiors.'

Unfortunately, it is possible to find faults with even this rule. Robots might like to receive 240 volts, but humans likely wouldn't. Robots should surely sacrifice themselves for us even if we are inferior to them. Others have therefore tried to be more precise and long-winded. In 2010 the Engineering and Physical Science Research Council (EPSRC), the main UK government body that funds AI research, brought together experts with backgrounds in technology, the arts, law and social sciences to define some basic principles for roboticists.

* * *

EPSRC's principles for roboticists

1. Robots are multi-use tools. Robots should not be designed solely or primarily to kill or harm humans, except in the interests of national security.
2. Humans, not robots, are responsible agents. Robots should be designed; operated as far as is practicable to comply with existing laws & fundamental rights & freedoms, including privacy.
3. Robots are products. They should be designed using processes which assure their safety and security.
4. Robots are manufactured artefacts. They should not be designed in a deceptive way to exploit vulnerable users; instead their machine nature should be transparent.
5. The person with legal responsibility for a robot should be attributed.

* * *

It is hard to disagree with these principles. But they leave open several serious questions, which we will shortly address. How can a person be legally responsible for a robot, especially one that learns its own behaviours? If robots are not responsible agents, who precisely is responsible for the autonomous car that drives our child home from school? How should we protect the vulnerable in our societies whose jobs may be taken away by the robots we design? My questions could continue.

Others have continued to try. In 2016 the British Standards Institution, the national standards body of the United Kingdom, published BS 8611. This is a 28-page guide on designing ethically sound robots. It identifies a number of ethical hazards, including robot deception, robot addiction and the possibility of self-learning systems exceeding their remits. The *Guardian* summarised the standard with the headline: 'Do no harm. Don't discriminate.' Other countries and bodies are sure to follow. For instance, the world's largest professional organisation for technologists, the Institute of Electrical and Electronics Engineers (IEEE), is in the process of drawing up similar guidelines for those amongst its 400,000 members who are building AI systems.

MACHINE PARTNERS

In September 2016, Google, Amazon, IBM, Microsoft and Facebook announced a 'Partnership on AI to benefit people and society'. The goal of the initiative is to formulate best practices on AI technologies, to advance the public's understanding of AI, and to serve as an open platform for discussion and engagement about AI and its influences on people and society. The partnership is guided by a set of tenets.

* * *

Tenets of the 'Partnership on AI'

1 We will seek to ensure that AI technologies benefit and empower as many people as possible.

2 We will educate and listen to the public and actively engage stakeholders to seek their feedback on our focus, inform them of our work, and address their questions.

3 We are committed to open research and dialog on the ethical, social, economic, and legal implications of AI.

4 We believe that AI research and development efforts need to be actively engaged with and accountable to a broad range of stakeholders.

5 We will engage with and have representation from stakeholders in the business community to help ensure that domain-specific concerns and opportunities are understood and addressed.

6 We will work to maximize the benefits and address the potential challenges of AI technologies, by:

a Working to protect the privacy and security of individuals.

b Striving to understand and respect the interests of all parties that may be impacted by AI advances.

c Working to ensure that AI research and engineering communities remain socially responsible, sensitive, and engaged directly with the potential influences of AI technologies on wider society.

d Ensuring that AI research and technology is robust, reliable, trustworthy, and operates within secure constraints.

e Opposing development and use of AI technologies that would violate international conventions or human rights, and promoting safeguards and technologies that do no harm.

7 We believe that it is important for the operation of AI systems to be understandable and interpretable by people, for purposes of explaining the technology.

8 We strive to create a culture of cooperation, trust, and openness among AI scientists and engineers to help us all better achieve these goals.

* * *

Again, it is hard to disagree with most of the tenets of the 'Partnership on AI'. This initiative is still very young, so it's hard to know the impact it will have on the development of the field. Will it ensure the responsible development of AI that benefits all? Hopefully it will be more than just a PR effort. The founding partners have obvious conflicts of interest. These are the technology companies with the most to gain from AI. Many of my colleagues working in AI are becoming concerned that too much power is concentrating in the hands of these giants. As their actions in arranging their tax affairs, scanning books, lobbying congress and other matters demonstrate, their success does not always and completely align with the public good.

ETHICAL LIMITS

Machines that think present a number of interesting ethical challenges. One area in which these challenges need to be addressed very soon is autonomous driving. Computers are starting to make life-or-death decisions on our roads and highways. Suppose you are sitting in an autonomous car reading the paper, when suddenly two children run onto the road in front of you. Does your car decide to drive into the two children, into an oncoming car in the opposite lane, or into a parked car? The computer has milliseconds to decide which action to take, all of which may result in injury or even death.

This life-or-death scenario is what ethicists call a 'trolley problem'. You are asked to choose between outcomes that differ in who may or may not die. The computer might calculate that the collision with the two children will likely kill both children, but you will be saved by your airbags. Similarly, the computer might calculate that the collision with the oncoming car will be so much more energetic that it will likely kill both you and the occupants of the other car. Finally, it might calculate that the collision with the parked car has a good chance of killing you. This is outcome in which the fewest people die—but you are the unfortunate victim. What if only one child runs onto the road? Now the choice is between you and the child.

The classic trolley problem involves a runaway railway trolley. There are five people tied to the rail ahead. You are standing in between, next to a lever. If you pull this lever, the trolley will switch to a siding. However, there is one person tied to the siding. You have two options: either you do nothing and the trolley kills the five people on the main track, or you pull the lever, diverting the trolley onto the siding, where it will kill one person. Which do you do? There are many variants of the trolley problem, involving men pushed into the path of the trolley, organs transplanted from one person to save multiple lives, and people locked up rather than killed. These variants expose ethical distinctions like that between action and inaction, and between direct effects and possible side-effects.

Despite the publicity that trolley problems have attracted, they are only a very small part of building *ethical* autonomous vehicles. There are many other ethical problems that must be faced, many of which will turn up much more frequently. As human drivers, we often break laws. We go through amber lights. We cross white lines to overtake. We break the speed limit to get out of danger. Should autonomous vehicles also break laws in this way? If so, by how much? Another topical ethical question is whether we should build systems in which the human driver may have to take back control at short notice. There is evidence that humans would struggle to do this, and may not regain situational awareness quickly enough. How do we protect other road users, such as cyclists and pedestrians, who might be difficult for autonomous vehicles to sense? Should autonomous cars be specially distinguished so other road users can treat them with appropriate caution? Should we have dedicated lanes where autonomous driving is allowed—and only allowed? Should humans even be allowed to drive once autonomous cars become safer than human-driven cars?

In the next decade it is going to be fascinating to see how society adapts to autonomous vehicles and the ethical challenges they pose. The field is likely to be a litmus test for how other ethical challenges concerning AI are dealt with in the future. The evidence so far is that we are sleepwalking into this bright future. Most governments have adopted positions concerning autonomous vehicles that, in my view, give too much responsibility to the companies developing the technology. Understandably, countries are keen not to stifle progress, and to have some part of the trillion-dollar industry that manufacturing autonomous vehicles will be. It is not at all obvious that the incumbents, like General Motors, Ford and Toyota, will win this race over newcomers such as Tesla, Apple and Nvidia. Equally, there is a very real moral imperative to get autonomous vehicles onto our roads. They will prevent the thousands of deaths in road traffic accidents that happen every year. But in this rush to move forward, we must be careful.

A nice analogy is air transportation. A hundred years ago, in the early days of the technology, flying was very much a free-for-all. Accidents were common. Flying was dangerous and only for the brave. But government quickly stepped in and regulated both flying itself and the manufacturers of aircraft. Bodies were set up to learn from accidents. Laws were enacted to regulate flying and the standards required for aircraft. Today, flying is one of the safest modes of transport. This is the end point that we should be aiming for with autonomous vehicles, but it seems very unlikely to me that we will reach it if government does not regulate more strongly.

We do not let drug companies test their products freely on the general population. Similarly, we should not let technology companies test autonomous cars freely on public roads without strong oversight. Drug companies are also not allowed to change their products freely. Why then do we let car companies automatically upload unproven updates to their software? Lessons learned in any road trial should be shared with other developers as much as is commercially possible. And national or international bodies will need to investigate the causes of accidents involving autonomous vehicles. Every crash could improve every autonomous vehicle.

ALGORITHMIC DISCRIMINATION

Another ethical challenge that is very immediate is algorithmic discrimination. Algorithms can intentionally or unintentionally discriminate against groups within society. Companies such as Google have promoted the myth that algorithms are good and do not discriminate.[22] Google's code of conduct begins: 'Yes, it's about providing our users unbiased access to information, focusing on their needs and giving them the best products and services that we can.' And the way that they attempt to bring you this unbiased access to information is with algorithms that blindly pick the best result. But algorithms can discriminate, especially when these algorithms learn from data.

In 2015 a study at Carnegie Mellon University found that Google served more ads for higher-paid jobs to men than to women. This is obviously not the way to beat gender discrimination in pay. Other algorithms used by Google also bake in discrimination. Google's auto-complete for 'Politicians are' offers the following options:

Politicians are liars
Politicians are corrupt
Politicians are lizards

Actually, that might not be such a good example. Let me try again. Google's auto-complete for 'Doctors are' offers these options:

Doctors are dangerous
Doctors are better than teachers
Doctors are useless
Doctors are evil

I am not sure we want algorithms that return any of these answers, even the one about teachers. I picked on Google here, but you can get similar biases from any of the other search engines.[23] The algorithms may not have any explicit biases themselves, but we may feed them data which, whether we realise it or not, will lead them to make biased decisions.

In many cases, it might come down to how we use the algorithm. Suppose you build a machine-learning algorithm to predict which convicted criminals are the most likely to commit another crime. You could use such an algorithm to target probationary services and help people stay out of jail. This would seem to be a good use of technology. However, suppose a judge used the same algorithm to decide on sentencing, giving tougher sentences to those more likely to reoffend. This is a more challenging use of the same technology. Especially if it meant, for example, that black people ended up incarcerated for longer than white people. In fact, a study in 2016 of COMPAS, a computer program used to predict reoffending, found that black defendants were far more likely than white defendants to be judged incorrectly to have a higher risk of recidivism, while white defendants were more likely than black defendants to be judged incorrectly as low-risk.[24] Predictions by COMPAS are used by courts across the United States to inform decisions about the amount of bail, the length of sentences, and release dates for probation. Algorithmic discrimination is already locking people up unfairly.

The European Union is taking action on this issue. The General Data Protection Regulation (GDPR) takes effect in May 2018. Article 22 of this act gives EU citizens the right to question and fight decisions that affect them that have been made on a purely algorithmic basis. It is not clear yet how this will be enforced, or even if it can be enforced. It is also not clear how technology companies will adjust. However, it is clear that we all need to wake up to the problem of algorithmic discrimination, and governments around the world have an important role to regulate.

PRIVACY

Another area where AI poses immense ethical challenges is in privacy. Big Brother works much better with smart algorithms to shift through lots of data. Edward Snowden's disclosures awoke many of us to the increasing potential for AI to invade our privacy. Indeed, it is only with AI that intelligence agencies can hope to shift the immense amounts of data being collected.

As ever, this is a double-edged sword. In the ongoing (and seemingly never-ending) war on terror, we may wish to be able to use smart technologies to find terrorists hiding in plain sight. On the other hand, we may wish not to have government know all our peaceful and democratic thoughts. To compound matters, many of us have become accustomed to giving away for free immensely valuable data about ourselves to companies such as Facebook. There is a lot of truth to the saying, 'If you're not paying for the product, you are the product.'

There are a number of approaches under development to protect individual privacy. As our devices get smarter, we can push more of the computation off the cloud and onto the device. In this way, you may not have to share *your* information with anyone else. There are also new ideas like differential privacy. We can, for instance, add 'noise' to a database so that answers to queries are unchanged but individuals can no longer be identified. In my view, what is missing, though, is for government to step up to the plate. Individuals need guarantees that protect their privacy, from government and corporation alike. It is too tempting and too easy for both government agencies and corporations to invade our privacy. And technology is only making it easier.

MISTAKEN IDENTITY

One theme that emerges in several science-fiction movies is that of a machine mistaken for human. In the classic film *Blade Runner*, Rick Deckard (Harrison Ford) tracks down and destroys replicants that have escaped and are visually indistinguishable from humans. Tantalisingly, the film leaves open the question of whether Rick Deckard is himself a replicant. More recently, the movie *Ex Machina* centres on a type of Turing test in which the robot Ava tries to be human enough to trick someone into helping her escape. And in *Metropolis*, one of the very first science-fiction movies ever, a robot disguises itself as a woman, Maria, and causes the workers to revolt.

It thus seems likely that sometime in the future we will have to deal with the impact of machines being mistaken for humans. In fact, it could be argued that this future is already here, with computers 'passing' limited forms of the Turing test. As any lover of Shakespeare knows, there are many dangers awaiting us when we try to disguise our identity. What happens if a machine impersonates someone we trust? Perhaps they will be able to trick us to do their bidding. What if we suppose they have human-level capabilities but they can only act at a sub-human level? Accidents might quickly follow. What happens if we develop a social attachment to a machine? Or, worse still, if we fall in love with one? There's a minefield of problems awaiting us here.

RED FLAGS

This is not the first time in history that a technology has come along that might disrupt and endanger our lives. Concerned about the impact of motor vehicles on public safety, the British parliament passed the Locomotive Act in 1865. This required a person to walk in front of any motorised vehicle with a red flag to signal the oncoming danger. Of course, public safety wasn't the only motivation for this law, as the railways profited from restricting motor vehicles in this way. Indeed, the law restricted the use of motor vehicles to a greater extent than safety alone required. The sentiment was a good one: until society adjusted to the arrival of a new technology, the public had a right to be forewarned of potential dangers.

Interestingly, the red flag law was withdrawn three decades later, in 1896, when the speed limit was raised to 14 miles per hour (approximately 23 kilometres per hour). Coincidently, the first speeding offence, as well as the first British motoring fatality—the unlucky pedestrian Bridget Driscoll—also occurred that same year. Road accidents have escalated quickly from then on. By 1926, the first year for which records are available, there were 134,000 cases of serious injury, yet there were only 1,715,421 vehicles on the roads of Great Britain. That's one serious injury each year for every thirteen vehicles on the road. A century later, thousands still die on our roads every year.

A NEW LAW

Inspired by such historical precedents, I recently proposed a new law to prevent machines from being mistaken for humans.[25]

* * *

Turing Red Flag Law

An autonomous system should be designed so that it is unlikely to be mistaken for anything besides an autonomous system, and should identify itself at the start of any interaction with another agent.

* * *

This is not the law itself, of course, but a summary of its intent. Any law has to be much longer and more precise. Legal experts as well as technologists will have to draft such a law; the wording will need to be carefully crafted, and the terms properly defined. It will, for instance, require a precise definition of autonomous system.

There are two parts to this proposed law. The first states that an autonomous system should not be designed to act in a way that leads others to believe there is a human in the loop when there is not. Of course, it is not impossible to think of some situations where it might be beneficial for an autonomous system to be mistaken for something other than an autonomous system. A computer pretending to be human might, for example, create more engaging interactive fiction. More controversially, robots pretending to be human might make better care-givers and companions for the elderly. However, there are many more reasons we don't want computers to be fooling us, intentionally or unintentionally. Hollywood provides lots of examples of the dangers awaiting us here.

Such a law would, of course, cause problems for any sort of Turing test. Hopefully, replacements for the Turing test will eventually move from tests for AI based on deception to tests that quantify explicit skills and intelligence. Some related legislation has been put into law for guns. In particular, Californian governor Arnold Schwarzenegger signed legislation in September 2004 that prohibits the public display of toy guns in California unless they are clear or painted a bright colour, in order to differentiate them from real firearms. The purpose of the law is to prevent police officers mistaking toy guns for real ones.

The second part of the law states that autonomous systems must identify themselves at the start of any interaction with another agent. Note that this other agent might even be another machine. This is intentional. If you send your bot out to negotiate the purchase of a new car, you want it to know whether it is talking to a person or a dealer bot. You wouldn't want the dealer bot to be able to pretend to be a human just because it was interacting with your bot. This aspect of the law is designed to reduce the chance that autonomous systems are mistaken for what they are not.

RED FLAGS IN ACTION

Let's consider four up-and-coming areas where this law might have bite. First, consider autonomous vehicles. In my view it is a real oversight that the first piece of legislation that permits autonomous vehicles on roads—the AB 511 act in Nevada—says nothing at all about such vehicles being identified to other road users as autonomous. A Turing red flag law would require an autonomous vehicle identify itself as such, both to human drivers and to other autonomous vehicles.

There are many situations where it could be important to know that another road vehicle is being driven autonomously. For example, when a traffic light changes, we can suppose that an approaching autonomous vehicle will indeed stop, and so save us from having to brake hard to avoid an accident. As a second example, if an autonomous car is driving in front of us in fog, we can suppose it can see a clear road ahead, using its radar. For this reason, we do not have to leave a larger gap in case it has to brake suddenly. As a third example, at a four-way intersection, we can suppose an autonomous car will not aggressively pull out when it does not have right of way. And as a fourth and final example, if an autonomous car arrives at a diversion, we might expect it to drive more slowly as it tries to work out where the road is now going.

How should an autonomous vehicle identify itself? I don't suppose this should be with a person walking in front of it with a red flag. This was too restrictive even back in 1865. Autonomous vehicles might have to carry distinctive plates, just like we require learner drivers to identify themselves on the roads today. Or perhaps vehicles might display a magenta flashing light when they are being operated autonomously.

In addition, autonomous vehicles should always broadcast their location, velocity and autonomy to neighbouring vehicles. In June 2015 Reuters reported that two autonomous cars, one from Google and the other from Delphi Automotive PLC, nearly had an accident on a Silicon Valley street. The Google car apparently cut off the Delphi car as it was about to perform a lane change. The Delphi car then had to take 'appropriate action' to avoid an accident. Clearly, it would help prevent such incidents if autonomous vehicles were required to broadcast their location and intentions. Of course, adequate safeguards will also need to be put in place that such broadcasting does not compromise the privacy of their human occupants.

Once autonomous vehicles are commonplace, other motorists will expect to meet them. But before this time, it will be important to know that the oncoming vehicle is somewhat special, and may behave differently to a human driver. In the past, it was less necessary for autonomous vehicles to identify themselves: there were so few of them, and most looked a little odd (the large rotating LIDAR sensors on their roofs tended to give the game away). However, now that the technology is shrinking and autonomous cars are starting to look more normal, it will become increasingly difficult to know when a car is being driven autonomously. There's also a reverse argument. Suppose autonomous vehicles are (or become) better drivers than humans. Then, just like today, when we demand that less experienced and capable learner drivers are identified, we might demand that human drivers identify themselves. A Turing red flag law will achieve this.

Let's move on to the second area where a Turing red flag law might have an impact. Consider virtual assistants such as Apple's Siri or Microsoft's Cortana. Here's a conversation I had with Siri:

THE LIMITS OF AI

* * *

A conversation with Siri

SIRI: What can I help you with?

Q: Are you a computer?

SIRI: I can neither confirm nor deny my current existential status.

Q: Are you a human?

SIRI: I'm an assistant. That's all that matters.

Q: Are you an AI?

SIRI: That's a rather personal question.

* * *

Based on conversations like these, it would appear that Siri is coming close to violating this proposed Turing red flag law. It begins its conversations without identifying itself as a computer, and it answers in a way that, depending on your sense of humour, might deceive. At least, in a few years' time, when the dialogue is likely more sophisticated, you can imagine being deceived. Of course, few if any people are currently deceived into believing that Siri is human. It would only take a couple of questions for Siri to reveal that it is not human. Nevertheless, it is perhaps setting a dangerous precedent to have technology that is in everyday use on millions of smartphones and that pretends, albeit poorly, to be human.

There are also several more trusting groups that could already be deceived. My seven-year-old daughter has a doll that establishes a Bluetooth connection to Siri so that it can answer general questions. I am not sure she fully appreciates that a smartphone is doing all the clever work here. Consider also those with Alzheimer's disease or other forms of dementia. Paro is a cuddly robot seal that has been trialled as therapeutic tool to help such patients. Again, some find it troubling that a robot seal might be mistaken for a real one. Imagine, then, how much more troubling society will find it when such patients mistake AI systems for humans?

Let's move onto a third example: online poker. This is a multi-billion-dollar industry, so it is possible to say that the stakes are high. Most, if not all, online poker sites already ban computer bots from playing. Bots have a number of advantages, especially over weaker players: they never tire, they can compute odds very accurately, and they can track historical play very accurately. Of course, in the current state of the art, they also have disadvantages, such as their ability to understand the psychology of their opponents. Nevertheless, in the interests of fairness, I suspect most human poker players would prefer to know if any of their opponents was not human. A similar argument could be made for other online computer games. You might like to know about it if you're being 'killed' so easily because your opponent is a computer bot with lightning-fast reflexes.

I'll end with a fourth example: computer-generated text. Associated Press now generates most of its US corporate earnings reports using a computer program developed by Automated Insights. A narrow interpretation might rule such computer-generated text outside the scope of a Turing red flag law. Text-generation algorithms are typically not autonomous. Indeed, they are typically not interactive. However, if we consider a longer timescale, then such algorithms are interacting in some way with the real world, and what they produce could well be mistaken for human-generated text.

Personally, I would prefer to know whether the text I was reading was written by a human or a computer. That knowledge is likely to impact on my emotional engagement with the piece of writing. But I accept that we are now in a grey area. You might be happy for automatically generated tables of stock prices and weather maps to be unidentified, but perhaps you do want computer-generated match reports to be identified? What if the commentary on the television show covering the World Cup Final is not from Lionel Messi, one of the best footballers ever, but a computer that just happens to sound like Messi?

As these examples illustrate, we still have some way to go in working out where to draw the line with any Turing red flag law. But I would argue that there is a line to be drawn somewhere.

AGAINST RED FLAGS

Several arguments can be raised against a Turing red flag law. One is that it's way too early to be worrying about this problem. Indeed, by flagging this problem today, we're just adding to the hype around AI systems breaking bad. I discount this argument for several reasons.

First, autonomous vehicles are likely only a few years away. In June 2011, Nevada's governor signed into law AB 511, the first legislation anywhere in the world which explicitly permits autonomous vehicles. As I mentioned earlier, I find it surprising that the bill says nothing about the need for autonomous vehicles to identify themselves.

Second, many of us have already been fooled by computers. Several years ago a friend asked me how the self-service checkout could recognise different fruit and vegetables. I hypothesised a classification algorithm, based on colour and shape. But then my friend pointed out the CCTV display behind me, where a human operator was doing the classification. The boundary between machine and man is quickly blurring, and even experts in the field can be mistaken. A Turing red flag law will help keep this boundary clear.

Third, humans are often quick to assign more capabilities to computers than they actually possess. The last example illustrates this, but as another, I let some students play with an Aibo robot dog, and they quickly started to ascribe to it emotions and feelings, neither of which it has. Autonomous systems will be fooling us as human long before they actually are capable of acting like humans.

Fourth, one of the most dangerous times for any new technology is when it is first being adopted and society has not yet adjusted to it. It may well be that, as with motor cars today, society decides to repeal any Turing red flag laws once AI systems become the norm. But while they are rare, we might well choose to act a little more cautiously.

In many states of the USA, as well as in countries including Australia, Canada and Germany, you must be informed if your telephone conversation is about to be recorded. Perhaps in the future it will be routine to hear: 'You are about to interact with an AI bot. If you do not wish to do so, please press 1 and a real person will come on the line shortly.'

I want next to turn away from limits that might prevent us getting to thinking machines, and consider instead forces that might get us there more quickly.

THE SINGULARITY

One simple way to get thinking machines, and then to develop quickly all the way to the point of superintelligence, is by what is called the 'technological singularity'. This idea can be traced back to a number of different thinkers. John von Neumann was one of the first to consider it.[26] Following his death in 1957, Stanislaw Ulam wrote: 'One conversation [with von Neumann] centered on the ever accelerating progress of technology and changes in the mode of human life, which gives the appearance of approaching some essential singularity in the history of the race beyond which human affairs, as we know them, could not continue.'[27]

Another person behind the idea of the technological singularity was I.J. Good. In 1965 he talked about an 'intelligence explosion' rather than a singularity, but the idea is much the same:

Let an ultraintelligent machine be defined as a machine that can far surpass all the intellectual activities of any man however clever. Since the design of machines is one of these intellectual activities, an ultraintelligent machine could design even better machines; there would then unquestionably be an "intelligence explosion", and the intelligence of man would be left far behind. Thus the first ultraintelligent machine is the last invention that man need ever make.[28]

Despite these quotes from the 1950s and 1960s, many credit the idea of a technological singularity to the computer scientist Vernor Vinge, who predicted in 1993: 'Within thirty years, we will have the technological means to create superhuman intelligence. Shortly after, the human era will be ended.'[29] Vinge wrote earlier about a technological singularity in several of his science-fiction novels, starting with the seminal cyberpunk book *True Names* in 1981.

Even more recently, the idea of a technological singularity has been popularised by the futurist Ray Kurzweil, as well as others such as the University of Oxford philosopher Nick Bostrom.[30] Based on current trends, Kurzweil predicts the technological singularity will happen around 2045. For the purposes of this book, I suppose that the technological singularity is the point in time at which we build a machine of sufficient intelligence that is able to redesign itself to improve its intelligence—at which point its intelligence starts to grow exponentially, quickly exceeding human intelligence by orders of magnitude.

Many of the existential concerns about the risks AI poses for humanity stem from the technological singularity. Philosophers such as Bostrom worry that thinking machines will develop so quickly that we will not have time to monitor and control their development. However, as I shall argue shortly, there are many reasons why machines may not be able to improve themselves repeatedly, and why we will never see the technological singularity.

TWO MATHEMATICAL QUIBBLES

My first quibble is that the technological singularity is a very poor name for this idea of machines improving their own intelligence recursively. It is not a singularity in the sense used by mathematicians. The function $\frac{1}{10-t}$ has a mathematical singularity at $t=10$. As t gets closer to 10, the function goes off to infinity. Indeed, even the slope of the function becomes infinite as t approaches 10. Mathematicians call this hyperbolic growth. The proponents of a technological singularity typically argue for exponential growth, which is much slower than hyperbolic growth. A function grows exponentially when it increases by a constant multiple at each time step. For example, the exponential function doubles every time t increases by 1. Such a function approaches infinity more slowly than a function like $\frac{1}{10-t}$. An exponential function has a slope that is always finite. In fact, exponentials are the beautiful functions where their slope is just a multiple of their value. Since the value is finite, so is their slope.

My second quibble is that the idea of exponential growth in intelligence depends entirely on the scale used to measure intelligence. For example, sound is often measured on a logarithmic scale. Twenty decibels is ten times louder than ten decibels. Thirty decibels is 100 times louder. Mathematicians call this a logspace. If we measure intelligence like sound in such a logspace, exponential growth is merely linear. I will not tackle here what we mean by measuring the intelligence of machines (or of humans). I will simply suppose there is such a property as intelligence, that it can be measured and compared, and that the technological singularity is when this measure increases exponentially fast in an appropriate and reasonable scale.

THE LIMITS OF AI

THE SINGULARITY MAY NEVER COME

The idea of a technological singularity has been the subject of more debate outside the mainstream AI community than within it. In part, this may be because many of the proponents for the singularity have come from outside the field. The technological singularity also has become associated with some rather challenging ideas such as life extension and transhumanism. This is unfortunate, as it has distracted debate away from the fundamental question: will we ever be able to develop machines that at some point become able to improve themselves recursively, so that their intelligence increases exponentially fast and quickly exceeds our human intelligence?

This does not seem like a particularly wild idea. The field of computing has profited considerably from a number of exponential trends. Moore's law has predicted with reasonable accuracy that the number of transistors on an integrated circuit, and hence the amount of memory in a chip, will double every two years since 1965. And Koomey's law has accurately predicted that the number of computations per joule of energy used by a computer will double every nineteen months since the 1950s. Your smartphone became possible after just half a century of building computers due to these exponential trends. If cars had made the same technological advances in this time, their engines would have shrunk to the size of an ant, and would run for a lifetime on a single tank of petrol. Is it unreasonable, then, to suppose that AI will also at some point witness exponential growth on the back of these other exponential trends?

There are, however, several strong arguments against the possibility of a technological singularity.[31] Let me be precise: I am not predicting that Artificial Intelligence will fail to achieve human or even superhuman intelligence. However, I am suggesting that there will not be the runaway exponential growth predicted by some. We will more likely have to program much of the intelligence in thinking machines ourselves. It will take a lot of science and engineering. We will not simply wake up one morning and discover that the machines have improved themselves overnight, and we are no longer the smartest inhabitants of planet Earth.

Since we are considering the intelligence of machines and of humans, we have to consider what we mean by intelligence. This is worth a whole book in its own right. So, as before, I will try not to define it but simply suppose that intelligence can be measured and compared. Having made that assumption, I can now discuss some strong arguments against a technological singularity. These are not the only arguments against a technological singularity. We can, for instance, also inherit all the arguments raised against Artificial Intelligence itself, discussed earlier. For example, machines will never think because they are not conscious, and machines can never think because they are not creative. My focus here, though, is on arguments that go directly against the idea of an exponential runaway in intelligence.

The 'Fast Thinking Dog' Argument

One common argument put forward by proponents of a technological singularity is that computers have a significant advantage in speed and memory over our brains. And these advantages are getting exponentially greater with every year. Unfortunately, speed and memory alone do not bring increased intelligence. To adapt an idea from Vernor Vinge, a faster-thinking dog is still unlikely to play chess.[32] Steven Pinker puts this argument eloquently:

> There is not the slightest reason to believe in a coming singularity. The fact that you can visualize a future in your imagination is not evidence that it is likely or even possible. Look at domed cities, jet-pack commuting, underwater cities, mile-high buildings, and nuclear-powered automobiles—all staples of futuristic fantasies when I was a child that

have never arrived. Sheer processing power is not a pixie dust that magically solves all your problems.[33]

Intelligence is much more than thinking faster or longer about a problem than someone else, or with more facts at your fingertips. Of course, exponential trends in computing such as Moore's law have certainly helped the quest for Artificial Intelligence. We now learn off bigger data sets. And we now learn more quickly. But, at least for humans, intelligence also depends on many other things, including years of experience and training. It is not at all clear that we can short-circuit this in silicon simply by increasing the clock speed and connecting up more memory.

The 'Anthropocentrism' Argument

Many descriptions of the technological singularity suppose that human intelligence is some special point to pass, some sort of 'tipping point'. For instance, Nick Bostrom writes: 'Human-level artificial intelligence leads quickly to greater-than-human-level artificial intelligence ... The interval during which the machines and humans are roughly matched will likely be brief. Shortly thereafter, humans will be unable to compete intellectually with artificial minds.'[34]

Human intelligence is, however, just one point on a wide spectrum that takes us from insects through mice, past dogs and on to apes and then humans. Actually, it might be better to say it is a probability distribution rather than a single point. Each of us sits at some different point along this distribution.

Now, if there is one thing the history of science has shown us, it is that we are not as special as we would like to believe. Copernicus taught us that the universe did not revolve around the Earth. Darwin taught us that we are just another member of the animal kingdom and come from much the same stock as our cousins the apes. And Artificial Intelligence will likely teach us that our intelligence is itself nothing special—that we can recreate and exceed it with our machines. There is no reason, therefore, to suppose that matching human intelligence is some special milestone that, once passed, allows for rapid increases in intelligence. Of course, this doesn't preclude there being some level of intelligence which is such a tipping point.

One argument put forward by proponents of a technological singularity is that human intelligence is a special point to pass because we are *unique* in being able to build artefacts that amplify our intellectual abilities. We are the only creatures on the planet with sufficient intelligence to design new intelligence, and this new intelligence is not limited by the slow process of reproduction and evolution. However, this sort of argument supposes its own conclusion. It assumes that human intelligence is enough to design an artificial intelligence that is sufficiently intelligent to be the starting point for a technological singularity. In other words, it assumes we have enough intelligence to initiate the technological singularity, the very end point we are trying to reach. We may or may not have enough intelligence to be able to design such AI. It is far from inevitable. Even if we have enough intelligence to design superhuman Artificial Intelligence, this superhuman Artificial Intelligence may not be adequate to precipitate a technological singularity.

The 'Meta-intelligence' Argument

My favourite argument against the idea of a technological singularity is that it confuses the intelligence to do a task with the ability to improve your intelligence to do a task. David Chalmers, in an otherwise careful analysis of the idea of a technological singularity, writes: 'If we produce an AI by machine learning, it is likely that soon after we will be able to improve the learning algorithm and extend the learning process, leading to AI+.'[35] Here, AI is a system with human-level intelligence, and AI+ is a system more intelligent than the most intelligent human. Chalmers' claim that *likely* soon after we will be able to improve the learning algorithm is where his logic takes a leap of faith. There is nothing *likely* about it. For example, progress in machine-learning algorithms has been neither especially rapid nor easy. Machine learning is indeed likely to be a significant component of any human-level AI system that we might build in the future, if only because it will be painful to hand-code all the knowledge and expertise required otherwise. Suppose an AI system uses machine learning to improve its performance at some task requiring intelligence, such as translating text from English into German. There is no reason that the same system can *also* improve the basic machine-learning algorithm it uses. Machine-learning algorithms frequently top out in performance on a particular task, and no amount of tweaking appears to improve them.

Of course, we are currently seeing impressive advances in Artificial Intelligence using Deep Learning. This has dramatically improved the state of the art in speech recognition, computer vision, natural language processing and a number of other domains. But these advances have not fundamentally changed the back-propagation algorithm that is used to do the machine learning. Improvements have mainly come from larger data sets and deeper neural networks. Yann LeCun, one of the three musketeers of Deep Learning,[36] attributed their success to their size: 'Before, neural networks were not breaking records for recognising continuous speech; they were not big enough.'[37]

More data and bigger neural networks mean we need more processing power. As a result, graphical processing units (GPUs) are now frequently used to provide this. However, being better able to recognise speech or identify objects has not led to any improvement in Deep Learning itself. There have been a few tweaks to the back-propagation algorithm at the heart of Deep

Learning. But the most important improvements in twenty years of work on neural networks are bigger networks, larger data sets and more processing power.

We can come at this argument from another direction, using one of the best examples we know of an intelligent system. Consider the human brain. It is much easier for us to learn how to do a particular task better than it is for us to learn how to learn better in general. If we remove the normalisation inherent in the definition of IQ, human intelligence has increased over the last century but only slowly.[38] And improving your intelligence today is pretty much as slow and painful as it was a century ago. This is despite improved understanding of how the brain learns, and access to many new technologies that help us learn. Perhaps thinking machines will also struggle to improve their performance quickly, and may never achieve more than a fraction of their fundamental limits?

The 'Diminishing Returns' Argument

Many arguments for the technological singularity suppose that improvements to intelligence will be a relative constant multiplier, with each generation becoming some fraction better than the last. However, the experience so far with most of our AI systems has been one of diminishing returns. We start out by picking all the low-hanging fruit and therefore improve quickly, but then we run into difficulties. An AI system may be able to improve itself an infinite number of times, but the extent to which its intelligence changes overall might be bounded. For instance, if each generation only improves by half the last change, then the system will at most double its initial intelligence.[39]

Diminishing returns may also come not only from the difficulty of improving our AI algorithms, but also from the difficulty of their subject matter becoming rapidly more complex. Paul Allen, the Microsoft co-founder, identified this phenomenon:

We call this issue the complexity brake. As we go deeper and deeper in our understanding of natural systems, we typically find that we require more and more specialised knowledge to characterise them, and we are forced to continuously expand our scientific theories in more and more complex ways ... we believe that progress toward this understanding [of cognition] is fundamentally slowed by the complexity brake.[40]

Even if we see continual, perhaps even exponential improvements in our Artificial Intelligence systems, this may not be enough to improve performance. The difficulty of the problems that have to be solved before intelligence increases may itself increase even more rapidly.

The 'limits of intelligence' argument

Another argument against the technological singularity is the possibility of running into some fundamental limits. Some of these are physical. Einstein taught us that you cannot accelerate past the speed of light. Heisenberg taught us that you cannot know both position and momentum with complete accuracy. Ernest Rutherford and Frederick Soddy taught us that you cannot know with certainty when the radioactive decay of an atom will happen. Any thinking machine we build will be limited by these physical laws. Of course, if that machine is electronic or even quantum in nature, these limits are likely to be much greater than the biological and chemical limits of our human brains. The human brain has a clock speed of dozens of cycles per second. Computers today have clock speeds of billions of cycles per second, millions of times faster. The human brain makes up for this slow clock speed with its massive parallelism—that is, unlike a computer, which processes one instruction at a time, our brains work on many different things at the same time. But even allowing for this, it is remarkable that such a slow machine can do so much. Clearly, computers are likely to have a significant edge in terms of raw clock speed.

However, there are also more empirical laws that emerge out of complex systems. For example, Dunbar's number is the observed correlation between brain size for primates and average social group size.[41] This puts a limit on social groups of between 100 and 250 people. Intelligence is also a complex phenomenon, and may also have limits that emerge from this complexity. Any improvements in machine intelligence, whether it runs away or happens more slowly, may quickly bump up against such limits. Of course, there's no reason to suppose that our own human intelligence is at or close to this limit. But equally, there's little reason why any such limits are necessarily far beyond our own intelligence.

Another limit may simply be due to the inherent uncertainty of nature. No matter how hard you think about a problem, there may be limits to the quality of your decision-making. Even a superhuman intelligence is not going to be any better than the rest of us at predicting the next EuroMillions lottery. Finally, computation is already running into some hard physical limits. The uncertainty of the quantum world limits how small we can build. In March 2016, Intel announced that Moore's law was ending, and that transistors would only shrink in size for another five years. Intel will now shift its focus to areas such as power consumption, in part to support our appetite for mobile devices.

The 'Computational Complexity' Argument

Another argument against the singularity comes from computational complexity. Humans are very poor at understanding exponentials. Many of us underestimate the effects of compound growth. But equally, more of us overestimate the power of exponential growth. There is an idea that exponential improvements are adequate to crack any problem. This is a misconception.

Computational complexity is the branch of computer science that looks at how fast we can compute answers to problems.

Some computational problems are easy. We can, for instance, sort even a long list of names into alphabetical order quickly. In fact, the time for an optimal algorithm to sort a list of n names grows faster than n, the size of the list, but slower than n^2, the square of the size of the list. What does this mean in practice? It means that if we double the size of the list of names we are sorting, it takes more than twice as long but less than four times as long to compute a sorted list (since 2^2 or 2*2 is 4). On the other hand, if we triple the size of the list of names we are sorting, it takes more than three times as long but less than nine times as long to compute a sorted list (since 3^2 or 3*3 is 9). There are other computational problems that are more challenging. For example, we can multiply two n by n matrices of numbers in a time that grows faster than n^2 but slower than n^3. In practice, this means that if we quadruple the size of the matrices we are multiplying, the time to multiply them together increases by more than by a factor of 16 (which is 4*4 or 4^2), but by less than a factor of 64 (which is 4*4*4 or 4^3).

Both sorting lists and multiplying matrices together are 'easy' problems. You will barely notice when your computer has to solve them. But there are other computational problems which are much more difficult to solve. For example, the best algorithm known to solve our delivery truck problem, which is more commonly called the travelling salesperson problem, takes exponential time. Every time we add a single new destination to visit, the runtime of the algorithm increases by a constant factor. This is the hallmark of exponential growth. And because of this exponential growth, doubling the number of destinations is likely to make it impossible to find a solution. Even the fastest supercomputer will choke.

The classic explanation of why exponential growth hurts is an ancient Indian chess legend. To get the sage to play him at chess, the king offers the sage any prize he can name. The sage asks for one grain of rice on the first square of the chessboard, two grains on the second, four on the third, and so on. The king, not being an expert on exponential growth, accepts. The king would need 18,000,000,000,000,000,000 grains of rice for the final sixty-fourth square. This is around 210 billion tons of rice, enough to carpet the whole of India.

We are somewhat blinded these days by the benefits of exponential trends such as Moore's law. But exponential improvements will not help solve even simple problems, like computing all permutations of a list. The best algorithm to solve this problem takes more than exponential time to solve.[42] Computational complexity may be one of the fundamental limits discussed earlier. Unless we use computers that go far beyond our traditional models of computation, we are likely to run into many problems where computational complexity fundamentally limits our performance.

You might hope that the burgeoning field of quantum computing would offer hope in this direction. Quantum computers offer the possibility of performing many computations in parallel. In a classical computer, each bit represents one of two possible states, 0 or 1. Computations are performed on this single state. In a quantum computer, each quantum bit (or qbit) is a superposition of these two different states. Computations can therefore be performed on an exponential number of states simultaneously. This gives quantum computers potentially an exponential speed-up over classical computers. Unfortunately, as mentioned earlier, there are many computational problems which even an exponential speed-up is not enough to tame. Thus, quantum computers will help but will not by themselves get us to the technological singularity.

Despite all these arguments against the technological singularity, I strongly believe we will arrive at thinking machines with human and even superhuman levels of intelligence on certain tasks. I see no fundamental reason why we cannot one day build machines that match and eventually exceed our intelligence. However, I am very doubtful that the route to superhuman levels of intelligence will be an easy one. There will not be some simple snowballing of intelligence once we reach machines with human-level intelligence. It will take a lot more work by my colleagues to get us there.

SIMULATING THE BRAIN

Another 'easy' route to thinking machines proposed by some is to copy the one good example we have. We could simply build a simulation of the human brain. There are many challenges to such an approach.

First, the scale of this problem is immense. As we have seen, the neural networks we can build today have far fewer connections than that of the brain. However, we might not be able to stop here with a model with as many neurons as the human brain. We might also need to model the dendrites on the neurons, and the dendritic spines that grow on the dendrites. We might have to model both the chemical and the electrical activity of the brain. Modelling even a single neuron to this level of detail challenges our fastest computers today.

Second, we might have to copy the many different and complex structures in the brain. This will challenge our ability to map the brain, which is by far the most complex system we know of in the universe. It's not going to be an easy job.

Third, even if we can simulate the brain successfully, it may just give us a closed box that provides no better insight into intelligence than our own brains. We might have no greater understanding of how intelligence emerges from the simulated flow of electrons and chemicals as we can get from our own real flow of electrons and chemicals.

SOLVING INTELLIGENCE

Let's consider a time when we have built a thinking machine. There is no guarantee that we will have 'solved' intelligence in the process. By solving intelligence, I mean that we should have come up with a theory like those physicists have devised to model motion around the universe, which allow us not only to predict the position of objects in the sky but also to fly with great precision to other planets. We would like a theory of intelligence that both explains how intelligence emerges from complex systems and lets us build new and even more intelligent systems.

Abstraction will likely be an important component of any such theory. Chemistry abstracts the more precise theories found in quantum physics. In modelling chemical reactions, we do not solve Erwin Schrödinger's equations exactly. Biology, in turn, abstracts the chemistry of our cells. For instance, our theories of evolution are not simply accounts of genetics and the chemistry of DNA. They abstract many other factors, such as the impact of geography on populations. Any theory of intelligence is likely to depend heavily on similar abstractions.

When dealing with greater complexity, other sciences have fallen back on more descriptive theories. We may ultimately have a theory of intelligence that is also descriptive rather than predictive. In the worst case, we may end up like a subject such as economics, where the theories do not even describe very well how a real economy behaves. Similarly, any theory of intelligence that emerges from the building of thinking machines may not explain intelligence. A machine that thinks might be as unknowable to us as other human minds. I hope not.

HUMAN LIMITS

I want to end this chapter on a more upbeat note, and think about human limits that may prove not to be so limiting for machines. Humans have some strong biological limits. Our brain size is severely limited by the size of our mother's birth canal. Our brains are rather slow, with a clock speed of around 10 Hz. Our brains operate on very little power, somewhere around 20 watts. Nevertheless, they consume a third of all the energy our bodies need. Computers, by comparison can operate at much faster clock speeds, with much greater memory, with far more sensors and with far more power.

Human intelligence, too, has been limited by evolution. Our intelligence is evolved. There is just one path that nature has explored to reach human-level intelligence. There is no reason to suppose that evolution has found the best way to implement intelligence. Especially as we get older, we discover there are many parts of our bodies which are poorly engineered. Most of the time, they are just good enough to get us through the day. Evolution is also a very slow progress: it takes decades to move to the next generation. With computers, by comparison, we can explore many more design paths at a much greater rate.

LEARNING COLLECTIVELY

There is one final area I want to discuss in which humans are much more limited than computers. This is learning. We humans have to learn a lot for ourselves. If you learn how to ride a bicycle, it is of limited help to me when I am learning. On the other hand, machines have a unique ability to share their learning. When one Tesla car learns how to recognise and avoid a runaway shopping trolley, we can upload the new code to the whole Tesla fleet worldwide. All Tesla cars can then recognise and avoid a runaway shopping trolley. One car learns but every car shares the performance benefits—and not just every Tesla on the planet, but every Tesla that will ever be manufactured in the future. This is such an important idea that I have invented a word for it: co-learning.

* * *

A Definition of *Co-learning*

When an agent in a collective group learns EITHER directly for themselves OR indirectly from another agent.

* * *

Co-learning is related to but different from *collective learning*, or learning by a group. Sociologists, anthropologists and others talk about the human species advancing by the collective learning of knowledge across generations. By comparison, co-learning is learning by an individual within a group. Co-learning also covers skills as well as knowledge. Co-learning applies to much shorter timescales than the transfer of knowledge passed across generations by collective learning. Co-learning still applies to long timescales. What we learn now can also be uploaded onto computers at any point in the future. Digital knowledge, unlike human knowledge, never needs to decay.

Just imagine if humans could co-learn like computers. You would be able to speak every language under the sun. And what you learn would never be forgotten. You would be able to play chess as well as Garry Kasparov, and Go as well as Lee Sedol. You would be able to prove theorems as easily as Euler, Gauss and Erdös. You could write plays and poetry to rival those of Shakespeare. You would be able to play every musical instrument. All in all, you would match the best abilities of anyone on the planet. This sounds scary. But this is the future of co-learning with computers.

Humans can do a limited form of co-learning. We have two basic mechanisms, the first of which is spoken language. However, as a co-learning mechanism, it is rather limited. We can only co-learn from people who are within earshot. And we can only co-learn what we can articulate. Telling someone how to ride a bicycle is not that helpful, as my daughter can attest.

The second mechanism we have for co-learning is writing. This is much more effective. Indeed, the invention of writing was one of our most transformative inventions. Writing allows us to co-learn across the whole human population. Once you learn something new, you can write it down and share it across time and space with everyone else on the planet. Without writing, civilisation would have advanced much more slowly.

Nevertheless, writing has certain limitations as a mechanism for co-learning. It is slow. Reading takes time. Writing also only conveys a description of what has been learned. By comparison, computer code can be shared very quickly, and immediately executed. This gives co-learning in computers a significant advantage over co-learning in humans. Every Apple smartphone on the planet can learn and improve the code used to recognise speech by every other Apple smartphone. Every Tesla car can improve its own driving and that of every other Tesla car. Every Nest home controller can learn better energy efficiency for itself and for every other Nest home controller on the planet. Co-learning is one reason why the coming revolution—the invention of thinking machines—will surprise many by its speed. Learning on a planet-wide scale will improve AI systems very rapidly.

This might sound a little too good. Might co-learning in computers not threaten us again with a technological singularity? The simple answer is no. Co-learning speeds up learning, but only by a linear factor—the size of the community that is co-learning. If we have 100,000 Tesla cars, then we will learn 100,000 times faster than if we have one car. If we have 10 million smartphones, then we will learn 10 million times faster. An intelligence explosion, on the other hand, requires exponential growth. It needs some positive feedback. Nevertheless, co-learning means thinking machines will arrive far faster than human intelligence did. The speed at which thinking machines arrive is likely to surprise us, given that, as humans, we are used to much more limited ways of learning.

5: The Impact of AI

Machines that think will impact us in many different ways. At the top level, they may threaten our very existence. Lower down, they will transform our society and economies, replacing many jobs that humans currently perform. And at the bottom, they look set to revolutionise almost every individual activity we undertake, from making love to waging war. This chapter will consider, in turn, the likely impact AI will have on humanity, on society, on the economy, and finally on jobs and warfare.

AI AND HUMANITY

Let's start with the biggest risk: that thinking machines might end humanity. We became the dominant species on planet Earth in large part due to our intelligence. Many animals are larger, faster and stronger than us. But we used our intelligence to invent tools, agriculture and, shortly after (on an evolutionary timescale), amazing technologies such as steam engines, electric motors and smartphones. These have transformed our lives and allowed us to dominate the planet. Intelligence has been such a key part of our evolution that we took it as part of our name: we are *Homo sapiens*, the wise species.

It is not surprising, then, that machines that think—perhaps even better than we do—threaten to usurp our position. And, just as the elephants, dolphins and sharks of the world depend on our goodwill for their continued existence, our fate may depend on the decisions of these superior thinkers. Movies and books tell stories of evil robots that want to take over the world. However, incompetence seems more likely than malevolence. We might build thinking machines that mistakenly cause our down-fall. There are several different risk scenarios that might lead to our demise.

Risk #1: Be Careful What You Wish For ...

One risk scenario is that the goals of a superintelligence may be poorly designed. Actually, this is a risk that goes all the way back to King Midas, who poorly specified what he really wanted. Because they are so smart, thinking machines may also surprise us with how they achieve their goals. Suppose we give a care robot the goal of keeping our ageing mother alive and happy. It might decide that a continual supply of morphine added to her drip achieves this goal very well—but it may not be what we wanted at all.

Risk #2: Paperclips Everywhere

Even if the goals are properly specified, there is a second risk scenario: there might be undesirable side-effects that hurt humanity. This risk is explored in a well-known thought experiment proposed by Nick Bostrom. Suppose we build a superintelligent machine and give it the goal of building as many paperclips as possible. The machine would start building more and more paperclip factories. Eventually, the whole planet would be filled with factories for building paperclips. The machine is doing precisely what it was asked to do. But the outcome is not very good for humankind.

Risk #3: Them or Us?

A third risk scenario is that any superintelligence is likely to have goals that include self-preservation and the accumulation of more resources with which it can achieve its other goals. But they might be incompatible with our existence. We might wish to turn the machine off. We might be consuming resources that the superintelligence decided would be better used to achieve its own goals. The superintelligence might therefore conclude that its goals were best served by eliminating us. Game over, humankind.

Risk #4: Moving Target

A fourth risk scenario is that a superintelligence could redesign itself and give itself new goals. How can we be sure that its new goals remain aligned with ours? Some harmless aspect of the original system might be amplified in the new, and become very harmful to us.

Risk #5: Indifference

A fifth and final risk scenario is that any superintelligence is simply indifferent to our fate. Just as I might be indifferent to the fate of some ants, a superintelligence might be indifferent to mine. If I'm building a house, I might not worry about destroying a nest of ants. Similarly, a superintelligence might not be concerned either way about our existence. If we happen to be in the way, we might simply be eliminated.

SHOULD YOU WORRY?

All these risks are predicated on us giving machines sufficient autonomy to act in the real world, and so be able to cause us harm. In fact, a more urgent risk is that we are already giving autonomy to stupid AI. Despite what some of the manufacturers would have you believe, autonomous cars are not very smart. But we are starting to give them control in situations beyond their powers. One of the first fatal accidents involving an autonomous car occurred in Florida in May 2016. It would likely have been avoided if the Tesla car involved had more intelligence and could have seen the truck turning across the road. It is autonomy rather than AI that we really need to worry about. We should definitely not be giving autonomy to systems with insufficient intelligence.

These existential risks also mostly depend on superintelligence emerging very rapidly. If this happens, we will have little or no opportunity to see the problems coming and to correct them. However, as I argued earlier, there are many reasons to suppose there will not be a technological singularity, and that superintelligence will emerge slowly as we painfully build better and better systems. Most of my colleagues believe superintelligence will take many decades to arrive, if not centuries. We may therefore have plenty of time to take precautions.

Some of these risks also suppose a rather poor view of super-intelligence. If I gave you the task of making paperclips, and you started to kill people in order to do so, I would probably decide you weren't that intelligent. We suppose that intelligent people have learned good values, can predict the consequences of their actions and are wise to the plight of others, especially those with sentience and feelings. Perhaps a superintelligence will be wise as well as intelligent?

OUR BIGGEST RISKS

Artificial Intelligence is not, in my view (or, I suspect, in the view of many of my colleagues working in AI), the biggest threat facing humankind today. Indeed, I suspect it might even struggle to make the top ten. There are many more immediate dangers that could easily destroy humankind. They include manmade threats such as global warning, the global financial crisis that seems unlikely to end ever, the global war on terror, the accompanying global refugee problem that threatens to fracture our societies, and overpopulation. In addition, there are outside threats such as pandemics, supervolcanoes and giant meteors. I would also worry more about apparently mundane problems such as our increasing resistance to antibiotics.

Of course, we cannot rule out the existential threat posed by AI. But it is sufficiently small and adequately remote that we do not need to devote many resources to it today. We cannot ignore it, and it is good to see various research centres around the world being set up to address these existential concerns. I am confident, therefore, that it is a threat we are well on track to contain. There are, however, many other issues about which we do need to worry today—one is the impact AI will have on our societies. It is much less clear that we are addressing these problems adequately.

AI AND SOCIETY

Thinking machines will change our societies in some profound ways. Computers in general, and AI in particular, pose a threat to human dignity. Weizenbaum, the author of ELIZA, has been one of the most influential voices in this debate. As early as 1976 he was arguing that Artificial Intelligence should not replace people in positions that require respect and care.[1] He was thinking of positions such as doctors, nurses, soldiers, judges, police officers and therapists. (The last of these was perhaps not surprising, given his experiences with ELIZA.)

Unfortunately, Weizenbaum's warning has not been greatly heeded. Systems are under development for many tasks undertaken by these groups. Weizenbaum was especially concerned about the negative effects computers were likely to have in the military sphere. He called the computer 'a child of the military'. We will turn to the impact that AI will have on warfare very shortly. His concern was that computers lacked, and might perhaps always lack, such human qualities as compassion and wisdom.

Thinking machines will also impact society in other ways. In the last chapter I mentioned their impact on our privacy, as well as the possibility of algorithmic discrimination. There is a very real risk that many of the rights our parents and grandparents fought for will be lost. We might not realise these rights are slipping away. However, we could wake up one day and discover that some of these freedoms have been lost as the machines take over roles previously reserved for humans. Equal chances may no longer be given to everyone. It's not that we'll program the machines to discriminate, but we might not program them well enough not to discriminate.

THE SEA OF DUDES

One aspect of Artificial Intelligence that compounds problems such as algorithmic discrimination is that the research field is currently 'a sea of dudes'. The phrase was coined in 2016 by Margaret Mitchell, then an AI researcher at Microsoft Research and now at Google. What she's highlighting is the fact that only around 10 per cent of AI researchers are women. Actually, she might more accurately have described it as 'a sea of white dudes'.

Unfortunately, the gender imbalance starts at an early age. GCSEs are public exams typically taken in UK schools at age sixteen. Only 15 per cent of students taking GCSE Computing in 2014 were female, for example. Two years later, less than 10 per cent of students taking A-level Computing were female. At university and in industry, we can put a bandaid on this problem but it is clear that we need to focus on getting more young girls into computing in the first place. As soon as students can start selecting which subjects they will study, girls start choosing subjects besides computing.

This gender imbalance is harmful to progress in developing AI. Because of it, there will be questions not asked, and problems not addressed. Other groups—black and Hispanic people, for instance—are also underrepresented in AI research. Again, this is damaging. There are likely no easy fixes. But recognition of the problem is at least a first step towards a less biased future.

AI AND ECONOMICS

One area in which thinking machines will undoubtedly change our lives is economics. Most first-world countries are transitioning out of industrial production and into knowledge economies, where the outputs are intellectual and not physical goods. Thinking machines will likely produce much of that output.

Over eighty years ago, the English economist John Maynard Keynes warned about this: 'We are being afflicted with a new disease of which some readers may not have heard the name, but of which they will hear a great deal in the years to come— namely, technological unemployment.'[2] Keynes predicted that, within a century, output per head would be four to eight times greater. He also predicted that the working week would be reduced to around fifteen hours to compensate for this and to give us more time for leisure.

Keynes was right about growth. In Australia, output per head has grown by a factor of six since then. Productivity has grown by a similar amount in the United States. Alongside this, there has been a huge shift of jobs out of traditional sectors. In 1900 one in four Australians was employed in the agriculture sector. In 2016 agriculture accounted for slightly more than 2 per cent of total jobs. As late as 1970, manufacturing accounted for 28 per cent of the workforce; it now accounts for just over 7 per cent of jobs. But Keynes was wrong about the length of the working week. This has only fallen slightly, to around thirty-five to forty hours a week in most industrial economies.

Fears about technological unemployment have been gathering speed since then. In 1949 Alan Turing put it in very plain terms: 'I do not see why it [the machine] should not enter any one of the fields normally covered by the human intellect, and eventually compete on equal terms.' Three years later, the famous economist Wassily Leontief was equally pessimistic about the implications of technology.[3] He wrote: 'Labour will become less and less important ... More and more workers will be replaced by machines. I do not see that new industries can employ everybody who wants a job.'[4]

Leontief used horse labour as an example of the threat posed to human labour by technological change. Despite the invention of the railroads and the telegraph, the role of horse labour in the US economy continued to increase. The equine population increased sixfold between 1840 and 1900, to more than 21 million horses and mules, as the nation grew and prospered. Horses might have felt safe from technological change: their jobs transporting people and messages between towns and cities had started to disappear, but other jobs had arrived to replace them. They weren't to know that this trend was to be short-lived. The invention of the internal combustion engine rapidly reversed it. The population grew larger, the nation became richer and horses began to disappear from the labour market. By 1960 there were just 3 million horses in the country, a decline of nearly

90 per cent. Economists debating the future role of horse labour in the economy in the early 1900s might have predicted that, as had happened in the past, new jobs for horses would emerge in areas enabled by the new technologies. They would have been very wrong.

Worries about technology unemployment came to a head in March 1964. US President Lyndon Johnson received a short but alarming memorandum from the Ad Hoc Committee on the Triple Revolution.[5] The memo was signed by luminaries including Nobel Prize–winning chemist Linus Pauling, *Scientific American* publisher Gerard Piel, and Gunnar Myrdal, who would go on to win the Nobel Prize in Economics. The memo warned that technology would soon create mass unemployment. It predicted that automation and computers were set to change the economy in as fundamental a way as the Industrial Revolution had changed the agricultural era that preceded it.

In absolute terms, the memo was wrong. There has not been mass unemployment. Since 1964 the US economy has added 74 million jobs. But computers and automation have radically changed the jobs that are available, the skills those jobs require, and the wages paid for those jobs. And it is very unlikely that we have got to the end point yet. In 2015, some 22 per cent of US men without a college degree and aged between twenty-one and thirty had not worked at all during the previous twelve months. Twenty-something male high-school graduates used to be the most reliable cohort of workers in America. They would leave school, get a blue-collar job and work at it till their retirement forty or more years later. Today, over one in five are out of work. The employment rate of this group has fallen by ten percentage points. And this appears to have triggered cultural, economic and social decline. Without jobs, this group is less likely to marry, leave home or engage politically. The future for them looks rather bleak.

ANDROID DREAMS

HOW MANY JOBS ARE AT RISK?

The respected computer scientist Moshe Vardi has put it in stark terms at the Annual Meeting of the Association for Advancement of Science in 2016:

> We are approaching a time when machines will be able to outperform humans at almost any task. I believe that society needs to confront this question before it is upon us: If machines are capable of doing almost any work humans can do, what will humans do? ... We need to rise to the occasion and meet this challenge before human labor becomes obsolete.[6]

A number of studies have tried to quantify the impact more precisely. One of the most widely reported was a study out of the University of Oxford by Frey and Osborne in 2013.[7] This report predicts that 47 per cent of jobs in the United States are under threat from automation over the next two decades or so. Similar studies have since been performed for other countries, reaching broadly similar conclusions. Ironically, the writing of Frey and Osborne's report was itself partially automated. The authors used machine learning to predict precisely which of 702 different job types could be automated. Through machine learning they trained a classifier, a program to predict which jobs would be automated. They first fed the program a training set, seventy jobs that they had labelled by hand as automatable or not. The program then predicted whether the remaining 632 jobs could be automated. Even the job of predicting which jobs will be automated in the future has already been partially automated.

Even if you agree with all the assumptions of the report (I don't), you cannot conclude that half of us will be unemployed in a couple of decades, as reported in many newspapers. The Oxford report merely estimated the number of jobs that are potentially automatable over the next few decades. There are a number of reasons why this will not translate into 47 per cent unemployment.

First, while the Oxford report estimated the number of jobs that are susceptible to automation, in practice, some won't be automated for economical, societal, technical or other reasons. For example, we can pretty much automate the job of an airline pilot today. Indeed, most of the time, a computer is already flying your plane. But society is likely to continue to demand the reassurance of having a pilot on board for some time to come, even if they are just reading their iPads most of the time. I'll give some more examples shortly of jobs that the report predicted could be automated but that in practice might not be.

Second, we also need to consider all the new jobs that technology will create. For example, we don't employ many people setting type any more. But we do employ many more people in the digital equivalent: making webpages. Of course, if you're a typesetter and your job is destroyed, it helps if you're suitably educated so you can reposition yourself in one of these new industries. There is, sadly, no fundamental law of economics that requires as many new jobs to be created by new technologies as are destroyed. It happens to have been the case in the past. But, as horses discovered over the last century, it doesn't always work out that way.

Third, some of these jobs will only be partially automated, and automation may in fact enhance our ability to do the job. For example, there are many new tools to automate scientific experiments: gene sequencers that can automatically read our genes, mass spectrometers that can automatically infer chemical structure, and telescopes that can automatically scan the skies. But this hasn't put scientists out of a job. In fact, there are more scientists doing science today than have ever lived in the history of civilisation. Automation has lifted their productivity. Scientific knowledge is simply discovered more quickly.

Fourth, we also need to consider how the working week will change over the next few decades. Most countries in the developed world have seen the number of hours worked per week decrease significantly since the start of the Industrial Revolution. In the United States, the average working week has declined from around sixty hours to just thirty-three. Other developed countries have gone even lower. German workers only work twenty-six hours per week, on average. If these trends continue, we will need to create more jobs to replace these lost hours.

Fifth, we also need to factor in changes in demographics. The number of people seeking employment will surely change. In many developed economies, populations are ageing. If we can fix pension systems, then many more of us may be enjoying retirement, unbothered by the need to work.

Sixth, we must also consider how automation will grow the economy. Some of the extra wealth generated by automation will 'trickle down' through the economy, creating new job opportunities elsewhere. This argument is not as forceful as the others if, like me, you have a healthy scepticism about 'trickle-down economics'. The rich do not spend as much of their money as the rest of us; that's how they get to be rich. Equally, rich corporations do not appear to be paying their fair share of taxes, especially in the countries where that revenue is collected. However, with suitable changes to how we tax people and corporations, we could all benefit from the increasing productivity brought about by automation.

The Oxford report identifies three job skills which, it is claimed, will be difficult to automate in the next few decades: our creativity, our social intelligence, and our ability at perception and manipulation. I am not sure I agree completely with any of these three claims.

First, creativity is already being automated. Computers can paint, write poems, compose music and create new mathematics. They cannot yet do it as well as humans; perhaps it will take more that two or three decades before they can. I would put creativity in the 'challenging' rather than the 'impossible and only for humans' bucket. Second, computers do lack today any real social intelligence. But work is underway on making computers that can perceive our emotional state and become more socially intelligent. Jobs that require social intelligence will resist automation not because they cannot be automated but because, in many cases, we humans will prefer to interact with other humans. We will prefer to speak to a real psychiatrist than to a computer. As for the third skill, computers already perceive the world better than us, on more wavelengths and at higher precision. What is true is that manipulation is difficult for robots, especially away from the factory floor, in uncontrolled environments. And it is likely to remain so for some time to come.

The precise numbers expressed in the Oxford report disguise the fact that it is hard to predict with any certainty how many of us will really be unemployed in a few decades' time. I have listed many reservations concerning the Oxford study. Nevertheless, it is clear that many jobs, both white-collar and blue-collar, are under threat. My guess is unemployment may increase, but only to around half of what has been predicted—so perhaps around 20 to 25 per cent. This would nevertheless be an immense change, and one that we need to start planning for today.

AN A TO Z OF JOBS THAT WILL GO

To help give you a feel for the changes ahead, and why many jobs will change or disappear, I am going to discuss jobs from A to Z that might be displaced.

A is for Author

The Oxford report puts the probability that authors are going to be automated at 3.8 per cent. This sounds reasonable. Being an author will probably be a safe (if not well-paid) job in the future. This is not because there will not be attempts to get computers to write novels. In fact, in March 2016 a short novel written by a computer made it into the first round of a Japanese literary award that had attracted 1450 submissions. To put that achievement in context, the award permitted non-human entries, and the program had considerable help from its creators, who decided on the plot and characters; the program then wrote the text based on pre-prepared sentences and words. The novel was amusingly entitled 'The Day a Computer Writes a Novel'. Here's how it ended: 'The day a computer wrote a novel. The computer, placing priority on the pursuit of its own joy, stopped working for humans.'

Even if we suppose this ending is not prophetic, there are several reasons why authors should feel safe from automation. First, if economic growth continues, we are likely to be reading more books. Over the last decade, while publishing in the United States has stagnated, in China it has expanded at roughly the same rate as the overall Chinese economy. Second, automation creates new demands. Amazon's recommendation engine makes it easy for someone to find books about Victorian church organs; there is therefore a new market for human authors who have specialist knowledge about Victorian church organs. Third, we are likely to appreciate books most that speak to the human experience. Given the choice between a book written by a human and one by a computer, many of us will choose the one written by a human.

This is not to say that automation will not change the job of author. Technology companies such as Amazon have already changed publishing significantly. Self-publishing and print-on-demand models have opened up publishing to anyone with a laptop. And we are not at the end of these changes. In the past, a few authors have prospered, while most have struggled to earn enough to live. This is likely to continue, if not get worse, in the brave new publishing world ahead.

B is for Bicycle Repairer

The Oxford report puts the probability that the work of a bicycle repairer is automated at 94 per cent. This is rubbish. There is almost zero chance that we will have automated even small parts of the job of bicycle repairer in twenty or thirty years. This error throws light on some of the limitations of the Oxford study, and its ironical dependence on a computer to make predictions.

First, the Oxford study ignores whether it will be economically viable to automate a job. Repairing bicycles is, unfortunately, rather poorly paid. Humans will do the job too cheaply for it to be worth automating. Second, bicycles are fiddly, irregular objects, with parts that wear, stretch and break. For a robot, repairing a bicycle will be an immense technical challenge that tests to the limit its ability to manipulate objects. And third, being a bicycle repairer is a very social job. A good friend of mine runs a bicycle shop. It's a place to hang out, find out about rides, enthuse about the latest kit, make jokes, drink coffee and talk politics. We will want to do this with humans, not robots.

C is for Cook

The Oxford report breaks down the job of 'cook' into a number of categories, including chefs and head cooks (10 per cent probability of automation), fast food (81 per cent), short order (94 per cent) and restaurant (96 per cent).

Even in the best restaurants, cooking is all about repeatability. Most of us are not lucky enough to eat in a Michelin-starred restaurant every day, but if we did, we would notice that menus typically change slowly. The goal is to reproduce the same quality of dish for every patron as quickly and as cheaply as possible. And most restaurants have signature dishes that are cooked frequently. Automation is ideal for achieving these sorts of goals.

Silicon Valley is already innovating in this space. One example is robot pizza. In Menlo Park, Zume uses robots to prepare perfectly repeatable pizzas. The pizzas are then cooked en route to the customer's home in a truck with fifty-six little ovens. This saves a lot of time: traditional pizza delivery companies cook the pizza first, then deliver it. Algorithms are used to time the cooking of the pizza so that it comes fresh out of the oven as the truck pulls up outside your home. Technology thus gets you both a better-quality and quicker home-delivered pizza. There are many similar innovations under development, such as robot sushi and robot hamburger machines.

I suspect one reason the Oxford report gives chef and head cooks only a 10 per cent probability of automation, while other types of cooks have a very high probability, is because of the creativity required to come up with new dishes. But even in this we have already seen some interesting innovation. IBM's Watson—the same Watson that won *Jeopardy*—was tasked with studying cookbooks, learning about how ingredients go together and creating new recipes. Chef Watson then creatively invented new dishes like Turkish Bruschetta with Eggplant and Parmesan, Indian Turmeric Paella, and Swiss-Thai Asparagus Quiche. Chef Watson's cookbook, containing sixty-five of its original recipes, has a rating of 4.4 out of 5 stars on Amazon. Go take a look!

D is for Driver

The Oxford report breaks down 'driver' into taxi driver (89 per cent probability of automation), heavy truck driver (79 per cent), light truck driver (69 per cent), delivery driver (69 per cent), bus driver (67 per cent) and ambulance driver (25 per cent). These are large numbers, but what surprised me most was that some of them weren't larger. There's a strong argument that no technology will automate more jobs more rapidly over the next few decades than autonomous vehicles.

One of the main drivers for this change (pun intended) is economic efficiency. Technology companies like Google and Facebook succeed because they can scale almost effortlessly. So how does a company like Uber, which is more a technology company than a taxi company, scale? The answer became clear in September 2016, when Uber started trialling autonomous taxis in Pittsburgh. With autonomous cars, the company's growth is no longer limited by the number of human drivers willing to work for low wages. Ironically, therefore, one of the newest jobs on the planet—being an Uber driver—is likely to be one of the more short-lived.

There are many other economic arguments for autonomous vehicles. Around 75 per cent of the cost of trucking goods is labour. In addition, laws limit how much truck drivers can drive. In most countries, truck drivers must take rests every twelve hours or so. By comparison, an autonomous truck can drive 24/7. Putting these two facts together, we can double the amount of goods transported on our roads at a quarter of the cost. Further savings will come from fuel efficiency. Autonomous trucks will drive more smoothly, and so waste less fuel. They will reduce costs in other ways too. The most fuel-efficient speed for a truck is around 70 kilometres per hour, so once we have eliminated the cost of labour, autonomous trucks can save even more money by driving more slowly.

The replacement of taxi and truck drivers by machines will be one of the most visible instances of labour automation in the next two decades. Autonomous trucks and taxis will become commonplace on our roads. Driving these vehicles does not require a great deal of skill or training. The challenge, then, is how to employ the relatively low-skilled workers who have been forced out of work. If most taxi and truck drivers end up unemployed, society will face immense disruption. On the other hand, if the economy expands enough to find jobs for these workers, we may be lucky.

We should not be too pessimistic. Autonomous vehicles will also bring great economic benefits that all of us will enjoy. Towns and cities that have been too distant in the past to prosper will blossom as transport costs fall. Goods will become cheaper, especially in countries such as Australia, where distance has been a limiting factor on economic growth. And our roads will become less congested and much, much safer.

Interestingly, one of the loudest voices in the debate over the risks posed by AI is Elon Musk—the very same person who is developing autonomous cars. And it looks likely that one of the biggest risks posed by AI will be its impact on the labour force, and specifically on jobs connected to driving. I'm not sure if Elon appreciates this irony.

E is for Electrician

The Oxford report gives just a 15 per cent probability that the work of electricians will be automated. I would rate the chances even lower. This is not a very repetitive job. And, while the social and creative sides of the job are somewhat limited, the unpredictability of the environments in which electricians work will keep automation at bay. In addition, there are many tasks which electricians do that will challenge the manipulation skills of even very expensive robots.

In fact, the increasing presence of AI technology will help keep electricians in work. We will see more and more automation in our homes, factories and offices. There will therefore be more and more work for the electricians who will install and maintain this equipment. The job will become more and more skilled, providing further protection against automation. Electricians will have to master networking, wireless communication, robotics and many other new technologies, as devices become increasingly complex and connected. And as the home, factory and office become more automated, there will be more to go wrong. The jobs of electricians (and of other similar workers, like plumbers) are thus likely to be very safe.

F is for Farmer

The Oxford report gives just a 4.7 per cent probability that farmers will be replaced by automated workers. Farming has already witnessed significant amounts of automation. Before the Industrial Revolution, around three-quarters of the UK workforce were employed in agriculture. Today, it's just 1.5 per cent. Percentages in other developed countries are similar. Our better understanding of crops, as well as machinery such as tractors and crop harvesters, mean we can grow more than ever, and with far fewer people. The question, then, is if there are any more gains still to be found.

I suspect there are. We could farm with even fewer people than we do today. Existing machinery will quickly be automated even further. It is not very difficult to have driverless tractors and combine harvesters. Unlike our public roads, we can control our fields, removing people and other potential dangers. And we can easily map the environment with high precision. Farming can also take advantage of other new technologies such as autonomous drones.

The benefits of further automation will be large. Autonomous machinery can work 24/7. It can work with much greater accuracy than humans. We are no longer limited by a rural labour force that is ever-diminishing. And we can reduce labour costs. Especially in countries like Australia, high labour costs are hurting the farming industry. In Japan, a lettuce farm without any human workers is set to open mid-2017. I expect that in a decade or two we will see many more farms with few or even no humans on them.

G is for Guard

The Oxford report puts the probability that guards will be automated at 84 per cent. As Hollywood has predicted, it seems very likely that we will have robots as guards. Indeed, Knightscope Inc. in Mountain View has been beta-testing its K5 guard robot since December 2013. This robot is designed to patrol schools, school centres and local neighbourhoods.

It is also worth remembering how automation also changes jobs into different forms. CCTV has already transformed the job of a guard. Now, one guard can sit in front of a bank of monitors and do the job of five guards of earlier times. Technology will take this further. Computer vision systems will monitor those video streams, automatically notifying the guard when something 'interesting' happens. One guard can then do the job of perhaps twenty guards. That's nineteen guards who no longer have a job.

H is for Hairdresser

The Oxford report puts the probability that hairdressers will be automated at 11 per cent. I reckon it is more like 0 per cent. Like repairing bicycles, this is low-paid work hardly worth automating. Technically, it would be possible to automate the job. But it will not happen.

In 1975 Australia's largest research organisation, the Commonwealth Scientific and Industrial Research Organisation (CSIRO),[8] started work on a robot that could shear sheep. The ORACE robot sheared its first sheep, rather slowly, in July 1979. By 1993, high-speed shearing was possible. However, commercialising the technology has proved more of a challenge. Today, sheep shearing is still largely performed by hand. I expect hairdressing robots to be just as difficult to sell commercially.

I is for Interpreter

The Oxford report puts the probability that interpreters will be automated at 38 per cent. Some have argued that this figure is too low. Significant progress in machine translation has been made since the Oxford report came out. There is still room for improvement, especially in domains where high fidelity is important, such as law and diplomacy. Machine translation systems also currently have a very limited understanding of the semantics of the text being translated. Nevertheless, interpreting does not seem like a job that humans will be doing for much longer.

Machine interpreters have several advantages over humans. With a human interpreter, you have to worry that anything you say might not be kept confidential. You also have to worry that human interpreters might have their own agendas. With a computer interpreter, no one else knows what you say. And if the computer is programmed properly, it can be unbiased. There may, therefore, be many situations in which you would prefer a computer interpreter over a human.

Machine translation may even help keep languages alive. Sadly, one language dies roughly every two weeks. By the next century, around half of the 7000 languages spoken on Earth are expected to have disappeared, in favour of languages like Mandarin, English and Spanish. Machine-translation software might just slow this trend. There will be less need to speak one of the dominant languages. As in *The Hitchhiker's Guide to the Galaxy*, we can all simply put a Babel fish in one of our ears.

J is for Journalist

The Oxford report puts the probability that journalists will be automated at 11 per cent. This looks much too low. Journalists should be worried about how many aspects of their jobs will be automated in the future. In the last decade, the number of reporters in the United States has fallen by around 40 per cent. At the same time, software produced by companies such as Automated Insights and Narrative Science has begun to write articles automatically. In 2014 Automated Insights put out around a billion articles written by computer. Here's a Turing test for journalists to see if you can tell computer apart from human.

* * *

Human or computer?

CHARLOTTESVILLE, VA– Tuesday was a great day for W. Roberts, as the junior pitcher threw a perfect game to carry Virginia to a 2–0 victory over George Washington at Davenport Field.

Twenty-seven Colonials came to the plate and the Virginia pitcher vanquished them all, pitching a perfect game. He struck out 10 batters while recording his momentous feat. Roberts got Ryan Thomas to ground out for the final out of the game.

CHARLOTTESVILLE, VA– The George Washington baseball team held No. 1 Virginia to just two runs on Tuesday evening at Davenport Field but were unable to complement the strong pitching performance at the plate, falling 2–0.

GW (7–18) pitchers Tommy Gately, Kenny O'Brien and Craig Lejeune combined to hold Virginia (25–2) to just two runs on six hits. The top-ranked Cavaliers entered the game batting 0.297 as a team and averaging over seven runs per contest.

* * *

In case you couldn't tell, the first was written by computer. In my view, it is also the better. Nevertheless, the physical job of a reporter—interviewing politicians, standing outside courthouses or dodging bullets in war zones—is unlikely to disappear any time soon. But many factual parts of the job, such as writing sports or company reports based on data coming down the wire, will disappear.

Technological change is also upsetting the economics of journalism. Companies such as Google have taken away a significant portion of the advertising revenue of newspapers. And now newspapers themselves are giving away much of their content for free. It is fitting, then, that the *Washington Post*, a newspaper giant, has received financial security from a technology entrepreneur, Jeff Bezos, the founder of Amazon.[9] The combination of less advertising and less content being paid for is putting even move pressure on the jobs of journalists. The end point seems hard to avoid: fewer jobs for journalists and more opportunities for smart algorithms.

K is for Kindergarten Teacher

The Oxford report puts the probability that kindergarten teachers will be automated at 15 per cent. Interestingly, the report puts the probabilities for elementary, preschool and secondary school teachers at under 1 per cent. There is no obvious reason why these numbers are so different. Indeed, there is an argument that kindergarten teachers need significant social intelligence and creativity, perhaps even more so than secondary school teachers. For this reason, kindergarten teachers may be less susceptible to automation than secondary school teachers, not more.

The large difference in the probabilities given for kindergarten, elementary and secondary school teachers demonstrates that the predictions coming out of this Oxford study should be treated with caution. The machine-learning methods used are somewhat unstable. Small differences in the skills needed by a job can lead to larger differences in the estimated probability. The probabilities are, at best, a starting point for predicting whether or not a job might be automated by technology.

Even though theirs is very much a people-facing job, teachers are not immune from automation. In early 2016 Jill Watson was a teaching assistant for an online masters course offered by Georgia Tech in the United States. She and the eight other teaching assistants answered 10,000 questions asked by the 300 students in the online forums. She was, however, not a person. She was a program, built from question-answering components available in IBM's Watson project. One of the students on the course expressed some suspicions about her identity, but the rest didn't realise she wasn't human. The course was titled 'Knowledge Based AI', so it was fitting that it employed the first AI teaching assistant.

Artificial Intelligence will play a vital role in education in other ways too. Of course, it may put some teachers out of a job. But the positive changes it brings may have a greater impact on our society. AI can offer students a more personalised education. Programs will have infinite patience in working through examples. They can learn how you learn, and then employ the teaching method that suits you best. And they can help us learn new skills and keep abreast of technology itself.

L is for Lawyer

The Oxford report puts the probability that lawyers will be automated at just 3.5 per cent. A more careful and detailed study by Remus and Levy, which looked at the different activities undertaken by lawyers, estimated that 13 per cent of all legal work could be automated.[10] Does this mean we will end up with 13 per cent fewer lawyers going forwards? I doubt it.

This is probably a field in which automation will change the job itself. Both the amount of legal work performed and the quality of that work will likely increase. We will expect more detailed searching of case law. And more people will access the law as it becomes cheaper. Such changes can easily absorb this 13 per cent saving.

We can already see the beginnings of a future in which legal advice is more readily available to all. A simple chatbot lawyer developed by British Stanford University student Joshua Browde has successfully contested over 160,000 parking tickets in London and New York—for free. The program first asks a series of simple questions to work out how to appeal. Were parking signs clearly visible? Were the signs too far away? Were there conflicting signs nearby? Was your car's registration correctly entered on the pay-by-phone system? It then guides users through the appeals process. It is only a matter of time before more complex legal matters are automated in a similar way. If we play this right, we could build a future in which not just the rich have proper access to the law.

M is for Musician

The Oxford report puts the probability that musicians will be automated at just 7.4 per cent. This is despite the fact that machines have been making music for hundreds of years. Many seventeenth- and eighteenth-century automatons were musical. Indeed, in 1206, the Muslim polymath Ismail al-Jazari wrote *The Book of Knowledge of Ingenious Mechanical Devices*, which described a musical robot band.[11] The band had four robot musicians—two drummers, a harpist and a flautist—who sat on a boat floating on a lake. This ingenious creation was used to entertain guests at royal drinking parties. It is possible that it was programmed with pegs on a drum, much like a music box. Imagine how magical a programmable robot must have seemed 800 years ago.

The first digital computer ever to play music was CSIRAC, Australia's first computer. This happened back in 1950 or 1951. The data is uncertain as the computer was supposed to be doing more 'useful' tasks, such as forecasting the weather. This beat the British by at least a few months; they got their Ferranti 1 computer to play 'Baa, Baa, Black Sheep'.

Computers are now being used not just to play but also to create music. In 2016 my colleague Francois Pachet at the Sony Labs in

Paris developed FlowComposer, a machine-learning program that composes songs automatically. You simply select a style and a track length. FlowComposer has produced an album of songs in the style of the Beatles. Humans are still needed to write the lyrics to the songs, but it is likely only a matter of time before this is automated too. Perhaps more interestingly, FlowComposer can also be used interactively, helping human composers to compose. It can thus augment rather than replace intelligence.

Despite all these advances, musicians probably don't need to be too worried about job displacement. Humans will still want to hear other humans play, and to hear music written that addresses the human condition. Of course, technology is already disrupting the music industry. Music has gone digital. Production of music is digital. And distribution has moved into the cloud. Interestingly, musicians have responded by returning to performance. Bands make their money now by touring. We return to the human experience. We will see analogous trends in other jobs.

N is for Newsreader

The Oxford report puts the probability that news presenters will be automated at 10 per cent. In 2014 Japanese researchers unveiled two human-looking robots that could read the news. They both remain on display today at the National Museum of Emerging Science and Innovation in Tokyo, reading news about global issues and space weather reports. We still have some way to go, however, before we have a news presenter that can interview a politician, or one that can deal with breaking news. As with musicians, I suspect that while we can automate news presenting, we will prefer to have our news read by a real person for some time to come. Nevertheless, this won't deter some news companies from trying to save money by replacing human presenters with robots.

O is for Oral Surgeon

The Oxford report puts the probability that oral surgeons will be automated at just 0.36 per cent. This is undoubtedly one of safest professions on the list. Dentist comes in at 0.44 per cent; robots are unlikely to replace them any time soon either. It would be a significant technical challenge to build a robot able to do oral surgery or dentistry. And even if we could, I doubt many of us will surrender ourselves to a robot dentist any time soon.

P is for Politician

The Oxford report does not consider politicians. Professions with the closest skills are perhaps clergy (0.8 per cent probability) and social worker (2.8 per cent). Nevertheless, politicians should not be complacent.[12] In January 2016 Valentin Kassarnig of the University of Massachusetts Amherst trained a machine-learning system to produce political speeches for either the Republican or Democratic parties.[13] The system was trained on transcripts from US congressional floor debates. Judge for yourself how close we are to replacing your political representative.

* * *

An automatically generated political speech

Mr. Speaker, for years, honest but unfortunate consumers have had the ability to plead their case to come under bankruptcy protection and have their reasonable and valid debts discharged. The way the system is supposed to work, the bankruptcy court evaluates various factors including income, assets and debt to determine what debts can be paid and how consumers can get back on their feet. Stand up for growth and opportunity. Pass this legislation.

* * *

Q is for Quarry Worker

The Oxford report puts the probability that quarry workers will be automated at 96 per cent, making theirs one of least safe professions identified by the report. And so it should be. It is a dangerous job. In Australia, hundreds of people once died every year in the nation's mines and quarries. Today, due to increasing automation, it is only a few dozen. This is still a few dozen too many. Further automation will only reduce accidents. Robots are perfect for jobs like this. We can remove humans completely from the mine or quarry and let robots take all the risks.

R is for Receptionist

The Oxford report puts the probability that receptionists will be automated at 96 per cent. In 2016 a hotel opened at a theme park near Nagasaki that is staffed almost entirely by robots. The receptionists, concierges and cloakroom attendants are all robots. Labour is typically the largest cost in running a hotel, making up around 40 to 50 per cent of all costs in an economy like the United States'. The economic advantages of automation are thus immense.

As with banks, supermarkets and airports, we will let this happen. Without complaining, we will stop interacting with people and start using the screens placed in front of us at the reception to check in and out. Hotel rooms will use keyless security. No humans will be needed. The technology to achieve this already exists. Of course, fancy hotels will continue to offer a personal service and employ many staff. But many of us will vote with our wallets and prefer a cheaper hotel that does not.

Ironically, one of the safest jobs in a hotel will be that of cleaner. This will be too cheap and too fiddly to replace with a robot. It is a cause for concern that only the least qualified and worst paid job in a hotel will be safe.

S is for Software Developer

The Oxford report puts the probability that a software developer's work will be automated at just 4.2 per cent. In part, this is because writing code is a creative activity. You need to be able to work out how to decompose a problem in parts, and how to synthesise algorithms to solve the challenges they present. Many parts of coding require people skills. Designing interfaces, for example, requires a good understanding of how people think.

New programming languages will continue to be developed that ease the load on the human programmer. They will provide higher levels of abstraction that reduce the cognitive burden. Ideally, we would like to be able to design code from natural language specifications. Give me a program to manage everyone's annual leave. I want a program to play Space Invaders. But natural language is a little too ambiguous for this to be realistic.

I don't expect human coders are going to be put out of a job by computers any time soon. As the world becomes more digital, there will be more and more programs needing to be written. And the programs that can be generated automatically are still very small and simple. Computer programmer is likely to remain one of the safer jobs on the planet.

T is for Trainer

The Oxford report puts the probability that a personal trainer will be automated at 0.71 per cent. The best trainers are those with good people skills, who can understand how people tick and how to motivate them to meet their targets. This personal side of training makes it one of the safer professions. In addition, if automation generally gives the rest of us more leisure time, we will have more time to go to the gym and use a personal trainer.

Nevertheless, technology will threaten the livelihood of many personal trainers. Smart devices will not just monitor our fitness but offer us advice, replacing some of what a personal trainer does. The trainers who prosper will be those who focus on the emotional and social aspects of their work, motivating us in ways that machines cannot.

U is for Umpire

The Oxford report puts the probability that an umpire will be automated at 98 per cent. From a technical perspective, this number seems correct. We will see more automated devices such as tennis's Hawk-Eye that help do the job of umpiring. And they will do it more accurately than humans. However, I suspect we are likely to have more umpires and referees in twenty or thirty years' time.

Automation will help umpires do their job better. And if we do really have more leisure time, there will be more need for umpires. In fact, the US Department of Labour predicts that we will see a 5 per cent increase in the number of umpires and referees over the next decade. Ultimately, we are likely to want a human rather than a computer to decide who wins, even if they are aided by more and more technology.

V is for Vet

The Oxford report puts the probability that a vet will be automated at just 3.8 per cent. This may sound like good news. However, veterinary science courses in many countries are some of the most difficult to gain entry to, and to complete. As people are displaced from other jobs, becoming a vet is likely to become even harder. The flipside of being in a job safe from automation is that competition for that job will increase. Economists tell us that this effect will likely depress wages. So even those who manage to keep their jobs will see life get tougher.

W is for Watch Repairer

The Oxford report puts the probability that a watch repairer will be automated at 99 per cent. As for a bicycle repairer, this looks completely wrong. Technically, the job of watch repairer seems far too fiddly and varied to automate easily. This again demonstrates that the results in the Oxford report are far from perfect.

Repairing watches is a niche activity. Whether this job can be automated or not will have little impact on the total number of jobs created or destroyed by automation. Some of the most common jobs, like waiter and waitress, might be safe. But many other popular jobs such as truck driver are clearly under threat.

X is for X-ray Technician

The Oxford report puts the probability that an X-ray technician will be automated at 23 per cent. Automation will help the technological side of taking X-rays, making it quicker. But it will help little in dealing with patients, getting them into position and keeping them calm. Automation will nevertheless improve the throughput of an X-ray facility. But it is less clear this will translate into fewer technicians. There may be some facilities where two technicians might be reduced to one. However, I suspect it is unlikely that we'll ever go to zero.

Z is for Zoologist

The Oxford report puts the probability that the work of a zoologist will be automated at 30 per cent. By comparison, most other types of scientist are listed at around 1 to 2 per cent. Interestingly, zoologist was part of the training set. Frey and Osborne labelled zoologists as being not susceptible to automation in the initial training set. While the input to their machine-learning algorithm was either 1 or 0 (susceptible to automation or not), the output was a probability between 1 and 0. There was no requirement that their machine-learning program mapped an input of 0 to a probability of 0, or an input of 1 to a probability of 1. In the case of zoologist, the machine-learning algorithm mapped the 0 input to a 0.30 probability output. I suspect Frey and Osborne were correct, and the classifier is wrong. It is hard to think of any reason that zoologists are more susceptible to automation than other biological scientists.

There are several other jobs in the training set for which the classifier gave a very different result to the training set. To be more precise, 7 per cent of the seventy jobs in the training set were classified wrongly by their classifier. For example, waiter and waitress were labelled in the training set as not being susceptible to automation. However, the classifier gives a 95 per cent probability that waiters or waitresses will be automated. Again, I would agree with the training set. Navigating through a busy restaurant carrying several plates is not something robots are going to be able to do any time soon. And even when they can, this is a low-paid job that will be expensive to automate. It also a job in which human relationships are important. Are we going to trust a robot when it tells us the fish special tastes great tonight?

These differences suggest that we should treat the overall percentage of jobs under threat from automation computed by Frey and Osborne with caution. We certainly cannot say that jobs in the United States are more under threat from automation than in Australia, even if the analysis says that 47 per cent of jobs are at risk of automation in the US and only 40 per cent in Australia.[14] This supposes the numbers are far more accurate than seems likely. Nevertheless, it is clear that a significant percentage of jobs are under threat.

THE IMPACT OF AI

SURVIVING THE REVOLUTION

On a personal level, one strategy for surviving this revolution is to do what I call an 'open' job. There are closed jobs with a fixed amount of work. For example, cleaning roads is a closed job. There is only a fixed length of roads to clean. Once robots can clean roads, and it seems highly likely that they will be able to do so in a few decades at most, the job of road cleaner disappears. Open jobs, by comparison, expand as you automate them. For instance, being a scientist is an open job. For a scientist, tools that automate your work merely help you do more science. You can push back the frontiers of knowledge that much faster. Clearly, if you want to survive this revolution, you want to do an open job.

Some jobs are neither completely open nor completely closed. Take truck driver. If we automate driving, then the cost of delivery will likely drop. This will expand the economy, generating more demand for delivery. In addition, tasks that were too expensive previously will become feasible. Unfortunately, this will most likely simply create more work for autonomous trucks. Human drivers will be too expensive and too unsafe to take on most of this extra work.

One area that *must* change is education. Education has become increasingly specialised. We learn more and more about less and less. Of course, there is more and more to know, so we need to focus in that way to get to the frontier of any field. However, much of that knowledge becomes obsolete quickly. Keeping our knowledge up to date, as well as learning new skills, will therefore become a lifelong task for many of us. To respond to this, education will need to become less specialised. It needs to teach us fundamental skills that will not become outdated. And it should teach us better how to pick up new skills later in our lives. Artificial Intelligence will be part of the cure here. Massive open online courses (MOOCs), powered by AI bots to help us learn, will assist many of us in educating ourselves throughout our working lives.

TRIANGLE OF OPPORTUNITY

What skills and knowledge should you learn in order to stay competitive with the machines? My best advice here is to head towards one or more of the corners of what I call the 'triangle of opportunity'. At one corner we have the geeks, the technically literate. Be someone who is inventing the future. It is still very challenging to get computers to program themselves. Computers are also challenged when it comes to creating a novel future. Be someone who does that.

Of course, not all of us enjoy programming. And not all of us would make good programmers, just as not all of us would make good musicians. There's likely a significant genetic component to the skills needed to be a good programmer. If you are not a programmer, I recommend you head towards one of the other two corners.

At one of these corners are the emotionally intelligent. Computers are still very poor at understanding emotions. And they don't have emotions of their own. As we will be spending more and more of our lives interacting with thinking machines, they will have to get better at understanding our emotions. We may even give them 'emotions' of their own so that we can relate to them better. But for some time computers are likely to have a low emotional intelligence. So develop your EQ. Improve your empathy. Fine-tune your relationship skills. There will be opportunities for people who are good at reading emotions.

At the third and final corner of the triangle of opportunity, we have the creatives and the artisans. One reaction to increasing automation in our lives is likely to be an increasing appreciation for things made by the human hand. Indeed, hipster fashion already seems to be embracing this trend. I find it rather ironic, then, that a job such as carpenter, one of the oldest on the planet, might become one of the safest. So another opportunity for security would be to develop your creativity or learn some artisanal skills. Make traditional cheeses. Write novels. Play in a band. Of course, computers can be creative but this is still one area in which they remain rather challenged. And society may simply choose to value more those things that carry the label 'made by hand'. Economists would have us believe that the market will respond in this way.

AI AND WARFARE

One area where Artificial Intelligence is set to change our lives radically is the battlefield. The attractions for the military to develop robots are many. Robots do not need to sleep or eat. Robots can fight 24/7. Using robots ensures humans stay out of harm's way. Robots follow orders to the letter. And robots will be deadly fast and accurate. It's not surprising that the introduction of AI to the battlefield has been called the third revolution in warfare, after gunpowder and nuclear weapons. It will be another step change in the speed and efficiency with which we can kill our opponents.

The technical name used for a robot that can kill is 'lethal autonomous weapon'. However, the media often use the more evocative name of 'killer robot'. This name might make you think of the Terminator from the movie of the same name. In fact, if you recall the storyline of the movie, the Terminator will be booting up in 2029. But the reality is that killer robots will be much simpler to begin with, and are at best only a few years away. Take the Predator drone and its aptly named Hellfire missiles. Now replace the human pilot with a computer. This is a small technical leap. The UK Ministry of Defence has said that it would be technically possible today to have a computer control such a weapon. I agree.

The development of killer robots won't stop with an autonomous version of the Predator, though. There will be an arms race to improve on the initially rather crude robots. And the end point is precisely the sort of terrifying technology imagined in the movie *Terminator*. Hollywood got that part right. Like Moore's law, we are likely to see exponential growth in the capabilities of autonomous weapons. I have named this 'Schwarzenegger's law' to remind us of where it will end.

One of the challenges is that killer robots will be cheap, and they'll only get cheaper. Just look at how quickly drones have dropped in price over the last few years. They'll also be easy to make, at least crudely. Get yourself a quadcopter, and add a smartphone and a small bomb. Then all you need is someone like me to write you some software that will target, track and take out your enemy. The military will love these, at least at first: they don't need sleep or rest, long and expensive training, or evacuation from the battlefield when damaged.

Any time we use a weapons system in battle, we have to expect that the other side will quickly get their hands on it and use it against us. Once our military starts trying to defend themselves against swarms of such robots, they might change their mind about the legality of such weapons. Killer robots will lower the barriers to war. By further distancing us from the battlefield, they'll turn war into a very real video game.

Autonomous weapons will destabilise the current geopolitical order. In the past, your military might was largely determined by your economic might. Your military strength depended on your ability to raise and support a large number of soldiers. You also needed to get this military to follow your will, either by persuasion or coercion. With autonomous weapons, on the other hand, a few individuals can control a large military force. As a consequence, it will be much easier for despots to impose their will on a population. It will also be much harder for superpowers like the United States to patrol the world's trouble spots. Autonomous weapons will upset the delicate balance of power built up since the end of the Second World War. Our planet will become a much more dangerous place.

BANNING KILLER ROBOTS

Because of considerations like this, I have come to the view that we must regulate autonomous weapons. And we must do it in the very near future if we want to curtail an arms race that has already started. This view is shared by many others who understand the technology. In July 2015 I helped put together an open letter calling for a ban. We collected the signatures of 1000 researchers in AI and robotics from universities around the world, as well as from commercial labs such as Google's DeepMind, Facebook's AI Research Lab, and the Allen Institute for AI. Today, the letter has over 20,000 signatures, including those of prominent people such as Stephen Hawking, Elon Musk and Noam Chomsky. But in my opinion, the most noteworthy fact is that the letter has been signed by many well-known researchers in AI and robotics.

* * *

July 2015 open letter

Autonomous weapons select and engage targets without human intervention. They might include, for example, armed quad-copters that can search for and eliminate people meeting certain pre-defined criteria, but do not include cruise missiles or remotely piloted drones for which humans make all targeting decisions. Artificial Intelligence (AI) technology has reached a point where the deployment of such systems is—practically if not legally—feasible within years, not decades, and the stakes are high: autonomous weapons have been described as the third revolution in warfare, after gunpowder and nuclear arms.

Many arguments have been made for and against autonomous weapons, for example that replacing human soldiers by machines is good by reducing casualties for the owner but bad by thereby lowering the threshold for going to battle. The key question for humanity today is whether to start a global AI arms race or to prevent it from starting. If any major military power pushes ahead with AI weapon development, a global arms race is virtually inevitable, and the endpoint of this technological trajectory is obvious: autonomous weapons will become the Kalashnikovs of tomorrow. Unlike nuclear weapons, they require no costly or hard-to-obtain raw materials, so they will become ubiquitous and cheap for all significant military powers to mass-produce. It will only be a matter of time until they appear on the black market and in the hands of terrorists, dictators wishing to better control their populace, warlords wishing to perpetrate ethnic cleansing etc. Autonomous weapons are ideal for tasks such as assassinations, destabilising nations, subduing populations and selectively killing a particular ethnic group. We therefore believe that a military AI arms race would not be beneficial for humanity. There are many ways in which AI can make battlefields safer for humans, especially civilians, without creating new tools for killing people.

Just as most chemists and biologists have no interest in building chemical or biological weapons, most AI researchers have no interest in building AI weapons—and do not want others to tarnish their field by doing so, potentially creating a major public backlash against AI that curtails its future societal benefits. Indeed, chemists and biologists have broadly supported international agreements that have successfully prohibited chemical and biological weapons, just as most physicists supported the treaties banning space-based nuclear weapons and blinding laser weapons.

In summary, we believe that AI has great potential to benefit humanity in many ways, and that the goal of the field should be to do so. Starting a military AI arms race is a bad idea, and should be prevented by a ban on offensive autonomous weapons beyond meaningful human control.

* * *

This open letter was released to the press at the opening of the main AI conference of 2015 in Buenos Aires. A little to our surprise, it made headlines around the world. It was reported by many leading newspapers, such as the *New York Times* and the *Washington Post*, as well as by major news outlets such as the BBC, CNN and others. I have been told it has helped advance the issue at the United Nations and elsewhere.

But not everyone is on board with the idea that the world would be a better place with a ban. 'Robots will be better at war than humans,' they say. 'Let robot fight robot, and keep humans out of it.' In my view, these arguments don't stand up to much scrutiny. Let me go through five of the main objections I have heard to banning killer robots, and why they are misguided.

OBJECTION #1: ROBOTS WILL BE MORE EFFECTIVE

Robots will be more efficient, for sure. They won't need to sleep. They won't need time to rest and recover. They won't need long training programs. They won't mind extreme cold or heat. All in all, they'll make ideal soldiers. But they won't be more effective, at least for now. According to an investigation by *The Intercept* of US military operations against the Taliban and al Qaeda in the Hindu Kush, nearly nine out of ten people who died in drone strikes were not the direct targets. And this is with a human in the loop, making that final life-or-death decision.

The current state of the art in AI approaches neither the situational awareness nor the decision-making ability of a human drone pilot. The statistics for a fully autonomous drone will therefore likely be even worse. Over time, they'll get better, and I fully expect them to equal if not exceed human pilots. Different arguments then come into play about their effectiveness. The history of warfare is largely one of which side can more efficiently kill the other. This has typically not been a good thing for humankind.

OBJECTION #2: ROBOTS WILL BE MORE ETHICAL

Another objection I hear is that robots will be more ethical than humans at fighting war. In my view, this is one of the more interesting and serious objections to a ban, and the one that requires the most consideration. In the terror of battle, humans have committed many atrocities. And robots can be built to follow precise rules. However, it's fanciful to imagine that we know how to build ethical robots. AI researchers like me have only just started to worry about how you can program a robot to behave ethically. It may take us several decades to work this out. And even when we do, there's no computer we know of that can't be hacked to behave in ways that we don't desire.

Robots today cannot make the judgements that the international rules of war require: distinguishing between combatant and civilian, acting with proportionality and so on. Robot warfare is likely to be a lot more unpleasant than the wars we fight today. Autonomous weapons will also doubtless fall into the hands of people who have no qualms about programming them to target civilians or to overlook the rules of war. Robots will be perfect weapons of terror that always obey orders, however unpleasant or unethical.

OBJECTION #3: ROBOTS CAN JUST FIGHT ROBOTS

Replacing humans with robots in a dangerous place like the battlefield might seem like a good idea. However, it's fanciful to suppose that we can just have robots fighting robots. There's not some separate part of the world called 'the battlefield'. Wars are fought in our towns and cities, with unfortunate civilians caught in the crossfire far too often. The world is sadly witnessing this today in Syria and elsewhere.

War today is also often asymmetric, and our opponents are regularly terrorists and rogue nations. They are not going to sign up to a contest just between robots. Indeed, there's an argument that the terror unleashed remotely by drones has likely aggravated the many conflicts in which we find ourselves today. With death being rained on them from above, they respond in the only way they can. It is perhaps a little too easy for the President of the United States, in the sanctuary of the White House, to think war can be fought remotely. Ironically, our use of drone warfare may have drawn us deeper into some of these conflicts, and necessitated painful and difficult decisions about putting 'boots on the ground'.

OBJECTION #4: AUTONOMOUS WEAPONS ALREADY EXIST, AND ARE NEEDED

It is true that weapons systems with varying degrees of autonomy are already in use by militaries around the world. The Phalanx anti-missile guns on the ships of many navies are autonomous, and this is a good thing. You don't have time to make a human decision when defending yourself against an incoming supersonic missile. But the Phalanx is a defensive system. Our open letter did not call for defensive systems to be banned. The letter called for offensive autonomous weapons to be banned.

You can argue that offensive autonomous weapons also exist in the battlefield today. For example, the RAF's Brimstone fire-and-forget ground attack missile is fired from a jet or unmanned aerial vehicle (UAV) from a stand-off range. Using its high-powered radar, it will find a target within a designated area, such as near friendly forces. It will even identify the best place on the target to hit to ensure its destruction. And with as many as twenty-four such missiles in the air at any one time, the targeting system uses an algorithm to ensure that missiles hit their targets in a staggered fashion, rather than taking out the same target simultaneously.

However, there is no reason we can't ban a weapon system that already exists. The world has done so in the past. Chemical and biological weapons were banned, despite having been used in a number of conflicts. Similarly, anti-personnel mines were banned even though millions were already in existence. We could do the smart thing and ban autonomous weapons now, before they fall into the wrong hands.

OBJECTION #5: WEAPONS BANS DON'T WORK

While a ban on these weapons might be a good thing, some say they don't actually work. Fortunately, history provides several counter-examples to this objection. The 1998 UN Protocol on Blinding Lasers has resulted in blinding lasers being kept out of the battlefield. If you go today to Syria or any of the other war zones of the world, you won't find this weapon. Not a single arms company anywhere in the world will sell you one. Interestingly, just before the ban came into place, two arms companies (one American and the other Chinese) announced their intention to sell blinding lasers. After the UN Protocol, neither went through with it. You can't uninvent the technology that supports blinding lasers, but there's enough of a stigma attached to them that arms companies have stayed away.

I hope the same will be true of autonomous weapons. We won't be able to uninvent the technology, but if a strong stigma against them exists, they won't be deployed in the battlefield. I imagine any ban would prevent the deployment, and not the development, of such weapons. Even a partially effective ban would likely be worth having. Anti-personnel mines still exist today, despite the 1997 Ottawa Treaty. But 40 million such mines have been destroyed. This has made the world a safer place, and resulted in many fewer children losing limbs or even their lives.

HOW MIGHT A BAN WORK?

If a ban on the deployment of autonomous weapons is put in place, I don't expect there needs to be a special regulatory body to oversee it. Just as with many other banned weapons, regulation will come about by non-government organisations such as Human Rights Watch monitoring abuses, combined with diplomatic and financial pressure, and the threat of prosecution at the International Court of Justice. This has been sufficient to enforce other weapons treaties, and I hope it would be sufficient for a ban on autonomous weapons.

I also don't expect that any treaty will include a very precise definition of a lethal autonomous weapon. The UN Protocol on Blinding Lasers does not define the wavelength or wattage of a blinding laser. Similarly, the 1970 UN Treaty on the Non-Proliferation of Nuclear Weapons does not formally define what a nuclear weapon is. This is arguably a good thing, since it will cover devices yet to be invented. I suspect it is likely too difficult to define precisely *autonomy*, or terms in diplomatic discussion today such as *meaningful human control*. Any definitions are likely to be quickly outdated by technology, in any case.

I imagine an implicit and informal definition will arise by international consensus. I suspect this will permit use of the current generation of weapons systems, such as the Brimstone missile, but will draw the line at more sophisticated types of autonomy, especially where the weapons system has autonomy over timescales of minutes or hours. Somewhere in between will be a line, one that is never precisely defined. But we will be able to put most weapons systems clearly on one side or other of this line. This ought to be enough for a treaty to have teeth.

I mentioned above that one of the challenges with autonomous weapons is that the technology is likely to become cheap and easy to obtain. This makes a ban more difficult. But it is not a game stopper. Chemical weapons also require relatively cheap and simple technologies. Nevertheless, the bans against chemical weapons have been relatively effective. Saddam Hussein did use chemical weapons against Iranian and Kurdish civilians during and after the Iran–Iraq War. But it is likely the world would have seen much greater use of chemical weapons if not for the 1925 Geneva Protocol and the 1993 Chemical Weapons Convention.

Another challenge is the ease with which technologies can be repositioned. Simple software updates will be able to turn systems that are either not autonomous or not lethal into lethal autonomous weapons. This is going to make it hard to ban killer robots. And we are going to want the technologies that make autonomous weapons possible. They are much the same technologies that go into autonomous cars, most of which already exist. But just because something is going to be hard to ban doesn't mean we shouldn't try. And even a ban that is partially effective is likely to be worth having.

Even with an effective ban, our militaries can and should continue to work on Artificial Intelligence. There are many great applications for AI in the military sphere. Robots can be used to clear minefields. We shouldn't let anyone risk life or limb on a dangerous job like that; it's a perfect job for a robot. Autonomous trucks can bring supplies through contested territory. Again, we shouldn't risk anyone's life doing a job that machines can do well. AI can also sift through mountains of signal intelligence, helping to win battles and save lives. And purely defensive autonomous weapons like the Phalanx anti-missile gun are likely to continue to be developed and deployed. These are all good things for AI to do. But machines should never decide who to kill. At the end of the day, we need to remember and respect our humanity. Life-or-death decisions must be made by humans alone.

KILLER ROBOTS @ THE UN

In October 2012 a group of non-governmental organisations including Human Rights Watch, Article 36 and the Pugwash Conference formed the Campaign to Stop Killer Robots.[15] This helped push the issue onto the UN's radar. In November 2013, the UN Secretary-General Ban Ki-moon took note of 'killer robots' in his report on the Protection of Civilians in Armed Conflict. His report questioned whether such systems could operate in accordance with international humanitarian and human rights law. Discussion about a possible ban began shortly after, at the United Nations in Geneva, under the umbrella of the Convention on Certain Conventional Weapons (CCW).

The convention prohibits or restricts the use of certain conventional weapons which are considered excessively injurious or whose effects are indiscriminate. Its full title is 'Convention on Prohibitions or Restrictions on the Use of Certain Conventional Weapons Which May Be Deemed to Be Excessively Injurious or to Have Indiscriminate Effects'. Currently the convention covers landmines, booby traps, incendiary weapons, blinding lasers and explosive remnants of war. New weapons can be added to the convention by means of additional protocols. This is the current hope for a ban on killer robots.

The protocol on blinding lasers is often cited as the most interesting precedent to the discussions on autonomous weapons. This has been easily the most successful ban on a new type of weapon. No signatory to the protocol has ever violated it, and no state has ever employed permanently blinding lasers in armed conflict. It was also one of the few attempts to pre-emptively ban a weapon before it appeared in the battlefield. There are, however, sufficient differences between blinding lasers and lethal autonomous weapons that reduce the hope that blinding lasers are a good precedent. Blinding lasers are a very narrow class of weapon, and not as attractive or useful to the military as autonomous weapons.

Nevertheless, in December 2016, at the Fifth Review Conference of the UN Convention on Certain Conventional Weapons, it was unanimously agreed to move from informal discussion to the next, more formal step towards a possible ban: a Group of Governmental Experts. This group will be mandated by the UN General Assembly to consider the issue and will, if nations agree, put forward a possible ban. There is still a lot in play. Currently, the only country with any significant formal position on autonomous weapons is the United States. This may surprise many, as it has been one of the most active in developing the technology.

The US Department of Defense Directive 3000.09 requires that autonomous and semi-autonomous weapons systems be designed to allow commanders and operators to exercise 'appropriate levels of human judgment over the use of force'. The directive does not define what 'appropriate levels' actually means. In addition, there is a get-out clause: the Chairman of the Joint Chiefs of Staff or an Under Secretary of Defense can approve the use of weapons systems which violate the directive.

I have spoken at the CCW several times, and it is clear to me that many of the countries with the most advanced technological capability in this area—such as the United States and the United Kingdom, along with some of their close allies, including Australia—might prefer not to have a ban, at least for the near future. Many of their actions appear aimed at delaying any substantive outcome. This seems to me short-sighted. Any technical lead that these nations have is likely to disappear quickly. Everything I have learned since we published our open letter on autonomous weapons in July 2015 has only increased my conviction that we must move quickly.

Support for a ban has come from some surprising places. Sir John Carr is the chairman of BAE Systems, a major manufacturer of arms and one of the companies prototyping the next generation of autonomous systems. For example, BAE has been developing the Raptor drone, which can fly autonomously across oceans. Nevertheless, at the World Economic Forum in 2016, Carr argued that fully autonomous weapons will not be able to follow the laws of war, and called for governments to draw the line at such weapons. When even those closest to autonomous weapons call for a ban, I believe we should listen.

AI'S FAILURES

This is perhaps an appropriate place to consider how AI systems might fail. They can fail in all the ways that regular programs can. They can be poorly planned, poorly specified, poorly written or poorly integrated into existing systems. There are also, however, many new ways in which they can fail. They can learn poor behaviours, for instance. Microsoft discovered this to its cost in March 2016, when they put the chatbot Tay on Twitter. Tay was designed to mimic the language of a nineteen-year-old American girl. She was also designed to learn from the questions put to her. Within a day, she became a racist, misogynistic, Hitler-loving teen. Microsoft quickly took her down.

Microsoft made two elementary mistakes. First, the developers should have turned off Tay's learning. If they had frozen her personality, she would not have learned such poor behaviour from those who trolled her. Second, Microsoft should have put a profanity filter on both Tay's input and her output. It should have been obvious that users would submit profane input, and there was no way the company wanted her to produce profane output. Fortunately for Microsoft, all they lost as a result of this incident was some face. They won't be the last company to make such mistakes, and people will be hurt in the future by AI systems learning poor behaviours.

AI systems can fail in other, more subtle ways. For instance, they may learn from data that is biased. In the 1990s, a team at the University of Pittsburgh Medical Center used machine learning to predict which pneumonia patients might develop severe complications. Their goal was for patients at low risk to be given outpatient treatment, saving resources in hospital for high-risk patients. The results were disturbing. The program wanted to send home pneumonia patients who had asthma, despite the fact that asthma sufferers are extremely vulnerable to complications. This was a true pattern in the data. But it was caused by the existing hospital policy of sending asthma sufferers with pneumonia straight to intensive care, and this had worked so well that they almost never developed severe complications.

Another problem with AI systems is that they tend to be very brittle. Unlike humans, whose performance at a task often degrades slowly, AI systems can fail dramatically. Object recognition provides a good example of this. AI researchers have found that changing even a few pixels is often enough to break many object-recognition systems. It is possible, though, to turn this brittleness into a virtue. In 2016 researchers at Carnegie Mellon University developed some glasses you can wear that defeat much software for face recognition.

AUGMENTING INTELLIGENCE

In much of this chapter we have been discussing how thinking machines might displace humans. They are set to replace humans in many jobs, as well as in many other spheres such as warfare. When the activities are unpleasant or dangerous, we may welcome this displacement. But in other cases, the change may be unwelcome. To end this chapter, let's consider a goal for AI research: to make change that is welcome.

AI usually stands for Artificial Intelligence. But, if we redirect our focus, we could make it stand for Augmenting Intelligence.

We can do better than humans or machines alone if we get humans and machines to work together. Humans can bring their strengths: their creativity, their emotional intelligence, their ethics and their humanity. And machines can bring their strengths: their logical precision, their ability to process mountains of data, their impartiality, their speed and their tirelessness. We need to stop thinking of machines as competitors but as allies. Each of us brings different things to the table.

We already have some good examples of the effectiveness of such symbiosis. A human and chess program together can play better chess than either the human or the chess program alone. A mathematician and computer algebra program can explore a new mathematical area faster and more effectively together than either can alone. And a musician and the FlowComposer program can together compose more quickly and perhaps better than either can alone.

SOCIETAL GOOD

One reaction to the concerns about the impact of AI has been the growth over the last few years of a subfield within AI focused on problems of societal good. Like most technologies, Artificial Intelligence is to a large extent morally neutral. It can be used for good or for bad. And we get to choose which it is. Much the same technologies that are used to make an autonomous drone identify targets, track and hit them can also be used in an autonomous car to identify pedestrians, track and not hit them. As scientists, we cannot stop our inventions being used by others for bad. But we can at least put them to good use ourselves. The number of AI and robotics researchers focused on such good ends has increased markedly over the last decade.

My colleague Carla Gomes at Cornell has, for instance, been spearheading the development of the field of 'computational sustainability'. This applies computational tools, many of them AI technologies such as machine learning and optimisation, to problems in sustainability. For example, machine-learning methods are being developed to predict and map poverty in developing countries, using readily available satellite imagery. As a second example, the eBird project at Cornell uses crowd-sourcing to document the presence or absence of various bird species around the world. The Merlin app, also developed at Cornell, will identify birds by asking you a few questions. As a third example, optimisation techniques are being developed, again at Cornell, to move Citi Bikes around New York City to balance demand. There are too many other exciting uses of AI within computational sustainability for me to mention them all.

Another colleague, Milind Tambe at UCLA, has spearheaded the development of a subfield of AI devoted to making the world a safer place. This is an area called 'security games'. It brings together ideas from game theory,[16] machine learning and optimisation, in order to solve problems such as protecting ports, airports and other infrastructure, as well as natural assets like wildlife and forests. In all these problems, limited resources prevent us from providing full security coverage at all times. Instead, we must allocate and schedule whatever limited resources we have efficiently, avoiding predictability while also taking into account any adversary's response. Efficiency means we need to bring in ideas from optimisation. To be unpredictable, we exploit the computer's ability to be more random than humans. Unlike computers, humans are notoriously bad at being random. And to take account of any adversary's response, we bring in ideas from game theory.

As an example, security patrols at LAX are scheduled using tools that optimise the limited personnel and maximise their probability of catching criminals and terrorists. As a second example, wildlife patrols in Queen Elizabeth National Park in Uganda have been scheduled using similar tools that optimise the limited personnel and maximise their probability of catching poachers. As a third and final example, patrols are scheduled on the Los Angeles Metro system to deter fare evasion, again using similar ideas and computational tools. There are too many other exciting uses of AI within security games for me to cover them all here. But it highlights one response of the AI research community to the fact that AI can be used for good or for bad.

STUDYING THE IMPACT OF AI

Another, more academic reaction to concerns about the impact of AI has been the growth over the last five years of research centres that study its impact. Tell academics about a problem and they will quickly set up a research centre to explore it in more depth. Half a dozen such centres have already been established, at leading universities in the United States, the United Kingdom and elsewhere. Many have received funding from Elon Musk's donation of $10 million to kick-start research in this area.

At MIT, the Future of Life Institute, set up by Max Tegmark in 2014, has become a major voice in directing attention on various forms of existential risk, including Artificial Intelligence. In January 2015 the institute hosted a conference in Puerto Rico, which brought together many leading researchers in AI from academia and industry, as well as experts in economics, law and ethics. The goal of the meeting was to identify promising research directions and so maximise the future benefits of AI. Musk's very large donation was one of the most visible outcomes of this meeting.

At Cambridge, Huw Price used a £10 million grant in 2015 to set up the Leverhulme Centre for the Future of Intelligence. Its goal is to explore the opportunities and challenges of Artificial Intelligence, in both the short and long terms. The centre will bring together computer scientists, philosophers, social scientists and others to examine the technical, practical and philosophical questions AI will pose for humanity in the coming century. Over in Oxford, the Strategic Artificial Intelligence Research Centre was also set up in 2015. It aims to develop policies for government, industry and others to minimise the risks and maximise the benefits of Artificial Intelligence over the longer term.

Across the Atlantic, a $5.5 million grant to Berkeley in August 2016 was used to set up the Center for Human-Compatible AI. It will focus on AI safety and is led by Stuart Russell, another prominent AI researcher. Two months later, the University of Southern California founded the Center for Artificial Intelligence in Society. This centre is co-directed by Milind Tambe, mentioned a few pages back for his pioneering work on security games. And at Carnegie Mellon, a $10 million grant in November 2016 was used to set up the Center for Ethics and Computational Technologies.

Finally, at my university, the University of New South Wales, we have recently established the Centre for the Impact of Artificial Intelligence and Robotics (CIAIR, pronounced 'sea air'). The centre is highly multi-disciplinary, bringing together academics from computer science, economics, history, law, philosophy, sociology and elsewhere. The centre's mission is to study the potential impact of AI and robotics over both the short and long terms. It will promote beneficial outcomes by means of research, teaching, measurement and public debate. Our goal is to ensure that AI and robotics contribute to secure, safe and successful outcomes for society. To this end, we are planning a varied program of research, education, conferences, workshops and other events. Please get in touch if you are interested in participating.

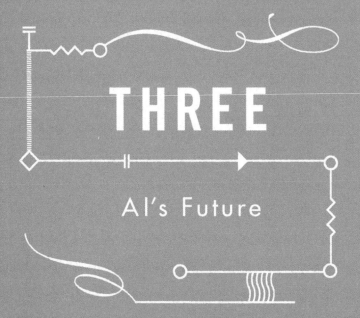

THREE

AI's Future

6: Technological Change

When predicting the future, we can learn much from the past. This is neither the first nor likely the last time that human society will be severely disrupted by technological change. In this chapter, I turn to the question of what we can learn about AI's future from the technological changes of the past. Even if only a small number of the predictions being made today about Artificial Intelligence are right, we are in line for some immense changes to our society, our economy and our lives. Can history identify the problems likely to challenge us with the rise of machines that think?

The author and humanist Neil Postman gave a speech in Denver in 1998 in which he identified five important lessons from past technological change.[1] These lessons were drawn from his study of the history of technological changes over thirty years. Much of what I have to say here is based on the wisdom expressed by Postman. His five lessons are simple, and most sound very obvious, but that does not take away from their importance.

LESSON #1: THERE'S A PRICE TO PAY

Postman's first lesson was that while technology gives, it also takes away. It's a Faustian bargain. For every advantage it brings, you can often identify a corresponding disadvantage. And there's no guarantee that the advantages will outweigh the disadvantages. Indeed, the greater the wonders of the technology, the greater the possible negative consequences. This ought to be a sobering thought when we consider machines that think, for such machines sound very wondrous.

Postman gave several examples of how technological change in the past has also had a cost. The motorcar gave us personal mobility, and shrunk distances. But we now breathe exhaust fumes, sit in traffic jams and deal with the consequences of car accidents, some of them fatal. As out-of-town retail parks slowly kill town centres and the communities that they support, we must ask if the disadvantages might at times outweigh the advantages. The printing press was another monumental technological change. It has been instrumental in the dissemination of knowledge, and the development of our scientific society. But there has been a price to pay. The printing press has also helped support dictators, intolerant religions and unpleasant ideas.

In asking 'What will a new technology do?', Postman argued that we should also ask 'What will a new technology undo?' Indeed, he suggested that the second question is often more important to ask precisely, because it is posed so infrequently. We have invented few technologies which come with almost no disadvantages. Antibiotics and eyeglasses are two that come to mind that have little in the way of downside. But most new technologies involve some sort of trade-off.

The benefits of thinking machines are obvious. They will take the effort out of many intellectual tasks. They will do the jobs that are dangerous, mundane and unpleasant. And they will do these tasks more efficiently and effectively than humans have done in the past. A simple rule of thumb my colleagues have when we go into a business is that you can expect to improve a company's efficiency by at least 10 per cent when you get a computer rather than humans to schedule their operations. In addition to improving efficiency, computers augment our abilities, making us superhuman at a number of tasks. We can already play chess better than humans alone, thanks to chess computers. Medicine will advance faster thanks to machine assistants that, unlike humans, can keep on top of the vast quantities of literature. There are many other examples of how machines will augment our intelligence.

But what will be the price we pay for machines that think? We have already mentioned a few. They will take over many jobs. Truck driver. Interpreter. Security guard. Warehouse picker. These are all jobs where many humans will be replaced by machines. Thinking machines will also likely hurt our privacy. And they may discriminate, and wittingly or unwittingly erode many of the rights we fought for over the last century.

There will be other prices to pay. Human-to-human contact may decrease. In some cases, such as in the care of the elderly, this may be unwanted. In other cases, it may improve our lives. Some of us may find more pleasure in virtual worlds populated by Artificial Intelligences than we do in the real world. Another price to be paid may be an increase in inequality. The owners of the robots will get richer. And the rest of us will fall behind even further. This widening gap is not inevitable, though. We can change our economic system, our taxes and our labour laws to prevent it happening.

LESSON #2: NOT EVERYONE WINS

Postman's second lesson is that there will be winners and losers. Not everyone is affected by a new technology in the same way.

And the winners will often try to persuade the losers that they are really winners too. For instance, many of us were winners in the invention of the automobile. But blacksmiths, stage-coach builders and all those who looked after horses were not.

As a second example, the Haber–Bosch process gave the world cheap fertiliser. Farmers of the world have been direct winners. Indirectly, many of us have been winners too, as we enjoy access to cheaper food. But there have also been many losers. In the First World War, Germany used the Haber-Bosch process to manufacture explosives and circumvent the Allied trade blockade. The many innocent people killed by these explosives were amongst the losers.

It's hard to think of a new technology where there are no losers. Medicine is perhaps the one area where there tend to be few. The only losers coming out of the invention of antibiotics are perhaps the unfortunate few infected by drug-resistant 'superbugs'. Leaving medicine aside, though, most new technologies tend to produce significant numbers of losers as well as winners.

Who, then, will be the winners and losers from the introduction of thinking machines? The answer depends on how we transform our society in the next couple of decades. If we do nothing, the technocrats will be the main winners. And many of the rest of us will be losers, made unemployed and unemployable by technology—the taxi drivers, the truck drivers, the interpreters, the warehouse pickers, the security guards, even the journalists and legal clerks. But it doesn't have to be this way. With the right changes to our taxation system, the welfare state, and our pension and education systems, the robots can take the strain and all of us can be winners.

LESSON #3: TECHNOLOGIES EMBED POWERFUL IDEAS

Postman's third lesson is that every technology comes with some powerful ideas. These ideas can often be hidden from view. And they can have very disruptive consequences. For example, writing carried with it the idea that knowledge can be shared across time and space. This disrupted the oral tradition that had existed before. Ideas could not be shared orally across time or space. As a result, memory became less important in most cultures, and storytelling started to die. The invention of the telegraph carried with it the idea that information could be communicated almost instantly around the world. Our horizons grew dramatically, and globalisation began. We are still experiencing today the after-effects of this disruptive idea.

What, then, are the ideas hidden in the invention of thinking machines? And what practical and disruptive consequences will these ideas have? The first idea is that machines, and not just humans, can think. This will disrupt our previously unique position on the planet. We will no longer be the smartest inhabitants. Copernicus, Darwin and others have provided similar knocks to our sense of importance. However, in this case we can still take pride in having created machines that think. The shock may therefore be somewhat tempered.

The second idea hidden in the invention of thinking machines is that Leibniz was right: reasoning can indeed be reduced to calculation. It is nothing more than manipulating symbols. We may have to ground those symbols back in the real world. But, nevertheless, this is all that our computers can do. If this is correct, the consequences are profound. It elevates rationalism, the philosophical school started by Descartes, Leibniz and others that identifies reasoning as a way of obtaining knowledge about the world. In turn, this raises deep questions about our ethical and spiritual lives.

The third idea hidden in the invention of thinking machines is that our sense of identity and worth can be disconnected from the work that we do. Machines will create much of the wealth in the future. There are two possible ways this might evolve. The first is dystopian. A large sector of society could become unemployed and unvalued. The second is more utopian. Society could value the personal, cultural, artistic and political journeys that we pursue, providing support for all to follow such paths. This would, however, require some significant adjustments to how we run our society.

LESSON #4: CHANGE IS NOT INCREMENTAL

Postman's fourth lesson is that technological change is often not additive. That is, it doesn't just change our lives in small, incremental ways. It can transform the whole ecosystem in which we live. The invention of television didn't give us just another method of broadcasting information to complement radio; it completely changed the political and entertainment ecosystems. The invention of the mobile phone didn't give us just another method of communicating with people to complement landlines; it completely changed how we work and play. These new technologies didn't add to our lives. They profoundly changed them.

For this reason, Postman cautions that we must be wary of technological innovations. The consequences of technological change can be immense, unpredictable and largely irreversible. And he warns that we should be especially suspicious of capitalists, the people who will try to exploit new technologies to the fullest, and who will change our culture radically. In the nineteenth century, we can point to technology-driven capitalists like Bell, Edison, Ford and Carnegie. These men (sadly, they were all men) drove us out of the nineteenth century and into the twentieth century. In the twenty-first century, it will likely be the technocrats such as Bezos, Sandberg and Brin who drive out the old and bring in the new.

What, then, will be the impact of thinking machines on our ecosystems? This book has been largely devoted to the argument that AI will impact almost every aspect of our lives. And the effects will not be incremental but ecological. AI will transform industry, politics, education and leisure. In fact, it is hard to name an ecosystem in which it will not have a significant impact.

LESSON #5: NEW TECHNOLOGIES BECOME THE NORM

Postman's fifth and final lesson is that new technologies quickly become part of the natural order. Just as it is hard for me to imagine a world before planes, trains and automobiles, it is hard for a younger generation to imagine a world before smartphones and the internet. There was a time when you couldn't simply Google the answer to a question, or play Angry Birds at the bus stop. There was also a time when you couldn't fly around the world in forty-eight hours, or commute 100 kilometres to work.

Postman identifies a danger with this view of technology as part of the natural order. That is that the technology becomes accepted as it is, and difficult to modify or regulate as a result. Newspapers are discovering how hard it is to get people to pay for content, now that people expect to get content for free over the internet. Napster precipitated a similarly dangerous situation for music. There are now those who say access to the internet is a basic right, on a par with access to water and sanitation.

Pope John Paul II, in a letter to the Director of the Vatican Observatory, offered some good advice about this problem: 'Science can purify religion from error and superstition. Religion can purify science from idolatry and false absolutes. Each can draw the other into a wider world, a world in which both can flourish.' If we are not careful, technology and the promise it carries of 'progress' can become a false religion, and a dangerous one, like real religions themselves. Postman suggested that the best way to view technology is as a 'strange intruder'. New technologies are not part of the natural order but the product of human creativity. They may or may not lead to progress and improvement in the human condition. Whether a new technology is used for good or evil rests entirely on our choices. AI is an excellent example of this. Thinking machines can lead to many possible outcomes, some good and some bad. We get to choose.

LESSON #6: WE DON'T KNOW WHAT WE WANT

Postman only had five lessons about technological change. But I want to add a sixth one. This is simply that people are very bad at predicting where technology will take us. As a consequence, we are very poor at anticipating which new technologies will be successful. The famous quote attributed to Henry Ford puts it well: 'If I had asked people what they wanted, they would have said faster horses.'[2]

There are many examples of this lesson. I could mention again the apocryphal claim that there would be a world market for just half a dozen computers. Let me turn instead to the laser. One of its inventors, Charles Townes, wrote:

> The truth is, none of us who worked on the first lasers imagined how many uses there might eventually be. This illustrates a vital point that cannot be over stressed. Many of today's practical technologies result from basic science done years to decades before. The people involved, motivated mainly by curiosity, often have little idea as to where their research will lead. Our ability to forecast the practical payoffs from fundamental exploration of the nature of things (and, similarly, to know which of today's research avenues are technological dead ends) is poor. This springs from a simple truth: new ideas discovered in the process of research are really new.[3]

It is hard to imagine any research body today funding a research grant claiming to study resonance in light waves in order to transform shopping. But the invention of the laser did precisely this when it gave us barcode scanners. Lasers have also changed many other aspects of life, including surgery, welding, printing and microscopy. It is hard to imagine how anyone could have predicted the amount of change studying resonance in light waves would bring.

A friend of mine who was working at CERN in the early 1990s tells an insightful story about the challenge of predicting technological change. His story concerns the invention of the World Wide Web. One of his fellow computing officers, a certain Tim Berners-Lee, invited him to the very first demo of the first web browser, a skunk project that Tim had been working on to enable physicists at CERN and elsewhere to share information more easily. My friend watched the demo and gave some careful advice. He told Tim that it looked good, but suggested that because of the slow network connections available at the time he suggested that he should lose all the graphics. In hindsight, it was precisely the graphical nature of Berners-Lee's browser that enabled even a child to use it, and led to the World Wide Web succeeding. Rival hypertext systems such as Gopher, which focused on text alone, ultimately died. The beauty of the World Wide Web was that it was open. Neither Tim nor my friend, nor indeed anyone else, could have predicted all the wonderful things that the web would be used for even two decades ahead.

Given that we so often fail to predict which technologies will succeed and how they will change our lives, it is very hard to say what aspects of thinking machines will surprise us. If we could, of course, they would not surprise us. We can at least predict that thinking machines will surprise us in a number of ways. Perhaps they will become both superintelligent and hyper-conscious? Or perhaps they will remain stubbornly unconscious, but this unconscious intelligence surprises our conscious minds? What is sure is that it will be an interesting and surprising road ahead.

THIS TIME IS DIFFERENT

Looking at lessons from the past may only partially help. History doesn't always repeat itself, and there's a good technical reason why this time may be different. With the Industrial Revolution, machines took away *just one* of our skills: it liberated production from the limitations of our muscles. But there are still things that only we can do. In the coming revolution, machines will take away one of our *last* unique skills: it will liberate our economies from the limitation of our minds. The machines will have no competition, for they will be literally superhuman. There will be little left that *we* need to do in order to generate wealth. The machines can do it all themselves.

There is also a strong societal reason why things will be different this time. It's not because this time is special but because *last time* was very special. Then, the world experienced some large shocks that, ironically, helped society to adapt to the changes. Following the Industrial Revolution, there were two world wars and an intervening Great Depression, and they set the stage for what economists are now starting to recognise as a one-off reversal in inequality. This was a time in which society was able to change very dramatically. The introduction of the welfare state, of labour laws and unions, and of universal education, as well as local changes such as the Veterans Act in the United States and the National Health Service Act in the United Kingdom, set off immense social change. We started to educate more of the workforce, giving them jobs rather than allowing machines simply to make them unemployed. At the same time, we provided a safety net for many, giving them economic security rather than the workhouse when the machines made them unemployed.

We might hope for a similarly positive outcome from the Global Financial Crisis and other challenges such as global warming. These problems might create the necessary shock to reform society for the upcoming revolution brought about by thinking machines. But I'm not confident that our politicians have the bravery or vision to act boldly enough, or that our political systems will enable them to do so. It will take much more than printing money to create the conditions necessary for positive change. We need to consider radical changes to our welfare state, to our taxation system, to our education system, to our labour laws and even to our political institutions. Nor am I confident that there is enough urgency in our discussions. This book is intended as a wake-up call, and a call for change.

A NEW ECONOMY

One area sure to change in the future is the economy. The automation of many jobs will have a significant impact on our economies. In 2015 Barclays Bank estimated that even a modest £1.24 billion investment in automation would add more than £60 billion in value to the UK manufacturing sector over the following decade. Despite increasing the number of jobs that were automated, they estimated that this investment would actually enlarge the manufacturing sector. In turn, this could actually increase the total number of people in work. It remains to be seen whether that actually occurs.

Even when jobs are not destroyed, technological change is making them less secure. More and more people will work in the 'gig economy'. A study by Intuit has predicted that 40 per cent of US workers will be working for themselves by 2020. Skilled workers can benefit from a gig economy, charging consultant-sized fees and moving easily from one well-paid gig to the next. But unskilled workers will likely be squeezed, giving up job security, health care and other benefits, and receiving little in compensation.

Without significant fiscal changes, it seems likely that such forces will increase the growing inequality between rich and poor. This is not the first time in history that such a threat has appeared. Marx predicted that the Industrial Revolution would concentrate wealth excessively into the hands of the owners of the means of production. In a similar way, without checks, this unfolding revolution will likely concentrate wealth excessively into the hands of the owners of the robots.

One lever to reverse this trend is taxation. In particular, we need to consider how we tax the rich and international corporations. Already they do not seem to be paying their way. Trickle-down economics does not seem to work.[4] Governments may need to consider how to redistribute wealth more forcefully. On the other side, we need also to consider how we support those who are less well-off. The welfare state grew out of the Industrial Revolution. Workers were given a safety net to help them cope with techno-logical advances that might put them out of work. I suspect we need to revisit this issue for the upcoming 'Knowledge Revolution'.

MONEY FOR EVERYONE

One popular idea, especially amongst technologists, is to imple-ment a 'universal basic income'. Everyone, whether employed or unemployed, is guaranteed an income, which would likely be just enough to feed and house them. Since no country has ever had a universal basic income, it is hard to know if it can work. Some trials have been run in Canada and Finland. But none has been universal, or for long enough to be able to generalise to a whole country and a whole generation of time. Will people become lazy? How should we implement it? How could we possibly afford it?

The money needed to finance a universal basic income is large. In the United States, giving the 200 million or so adults of work-ing age $18,000 per year each creates a bill of $3.6 trillion. This is the exact size of the annual US federal budget. The money would need to come from somewhere new, since you cannot simply eliminate all other government spending and reduce your tax base at the same time. Automation will help, by increasing productivity and generating more wealth that can be taxed. Nevertheless, there are immense economical, political, sociological and psychological questions still to be addressed. And we don't have all that long to come up with answers and implement them.

Several less radical alternatives to a universal basic income have also been proposed. These include raising the minimum wage, strengthening unions and labour law, improving labour mobility through cheaper housing, shifting taxes from labour to capital, and increasing funding for job training and re-education. These actions have the advantage of requiring less radical change to our society. But whether these actions, even if applied together, are enough to cope with the upcoming changes remains an open question.

SLEEPWALKING INTO THE FUTURE

A final lesson from the history of technological change is that we tend to sleepwalk into the future. Technologies are invented quickly, but laws, economics, education and society catch up only slowly. For example, mobile phones were invented over thirty years ago, and market saturation hit around 50 per cent in developed countries around the turn of the millennium. Yet there are still several US states in which there are no laws prohibiting texting while driving. The first state to legislate such a ban was Washington, but this didn't occur til 2007. The law takes decades to evolve, but new technologies appear every quarter.

Postman called it 'technology uber alles'—technology more than anything else. This attitude towards new technologies may sacrifice much that makes our lives good. Technology should be our servant, not the other way around. Just because we can invent a new technology does not mean we necessarily should. And just because a newly invented technology can be put to some use does not mean we necessarily should. In November 2016 researchers at Shanghai Jiao Tong University in China demonstrated that they could use machine learning to differentiate between photographs of criminal and non-criminals. But just because we can do something like this does not mean we should. There are many reasons to be concerned about such an application of AI. We must carefully choose where and when to use machines that think.

7: Ten Predictions

This is the part of the book where I get to dream, and I'll dream about a future in which machines can think. My dreams cover a wide range of activities, including transportation, employment, education, entertainment and health care. They're about what is possible and likely in 2050. Why 2050? Well, this is far enough into the future that we'll see some step-changing differences in our lives by then. Indeed, Ray Kurzweil has predicted that the technological singularity will have happened by then. I'm not convinced we'll reach the singularity by 2050, or indeed ever, as I outlined earlier in this book. Nevertheless, we can expect some significant changes.

The personal computer revolution is now over thirty-five years old. The IBM PC was introduced in August 1981. The compact disc was introduced in 1982. The first camcorders and cell phones came in 1983. The PC, the CD, the camcorder and the cell phone have combined to enrich our lives greatly over the last thirty-five years, so it's reasonable to think we can expect equally remarkable changes in the next thirty-five years.

If I'm a little lucky, I might even be around to witness the year 2050. A cynic might observe that I could equally well have just departed, so I'll face no redress if my predictions miss the mark. If that's the case, you'll just have to indulge me; the dead deserve a little latitude.

A common problem is that we tend to over-predict what we can do in the short term, but under-predict what we'll do in the long term. 'We always overestimate the change that will occur in the next two years,' Bill Gates has said, 'and underestimate the change that will occur in the next ten.'[1] Part of the problem is that we don't understand compound growth well. Evolution has equipped us to focus on short-term changes. Long-term change, especially when compounded over many years, is much harder for us to comprehend. The pension and gambling industries are testament to our inability to understand compound growth and probabilities.

Even though Moore's law is now officially dead, computing power will likely have increased many thousands of times over by 2050. We can expect to have computers with hundreds of petabytes of main memory, and which can process data in the exaFLOPS. By 2100 they might have increased another quadrillionfold again. That's a factor of 10^{15}, or 1 followed by fifteen zeroes. Of course, speed and memory alone will not give us thinking machines; remember our faster-thinking dog. However, we will also have made many algorithmic advances that will have helped us along the road to thinking machines. So let me predict ten ways that our lives will have changed by 2050.

PREDICTION #1: YOU ARE BANNED FROM DRIVING

It's easy to underestimate the speed with which new technologies seduce us. You might have bought your first smartphone around ten years ago. You probably didn't anticipate then just how important such devices would become in our lives.[2] Smartphones have largely replaced our diaries, our cameras, our music players, our games consoles, our satellite navigation systems and many other devices. It is estimated that there are over 2 billion smartphones on the planet. Worldwide, more than one in three of us has a smartphone—not bad, considering that around one in two of the planet lives in poverty, on less than $2.50 a day. In a similar way, it is easy to underestimate the speed and extent of changes that will be brought about by the introduction of autonomous cars.

To start with, autonomous cars will fundamentally change road safety. Around the world, over a million people die in road accidents every year. In the United States about 33,000 people will die in road accidents in the next year. Think about that. If a fully loaded Boeing 747 crashed every week, we would be clamouring for airline safety to be improved. But since car accidents happen in hundreds and thousands of different places, we don't seem to notice. The US Department of Transport estimates that 95 per cent of accidents are due to driver error. We drive too fast. We drive under the influence of alcohol. We text while driving. We fiddle with the radio. We take risks that we shouldn't. If we can take the human out of the loop, we can make our roads much safer. Indeed, the car manufacturer Volvo believes this is the only way Sweden can hit its ambitious target of having zero road deaths by 2020.

Autonomous vehicles will also fundamentally change the economics of transportation, and our access to it. Groups such as the young, the old and the disabled will be given personal mobility for the first time. The cost of transportation will plummet. A study by the OECD of the transport needs of Lisbon, Portugal, estimated that, with autonomous cars, the city could enjoy the same level of transportation as today with just 10 per cent of the vehicles.

Much of our roads are actually used to store cars while they wait for us. It's estimated that around a third of the cars in a city are driving around, looking for parking. Think, therefore, how much our cities will open up when we can eliminate this. We can send our cars off to earn money as taxis while we work. In fact, many of us will give up on individual car ownership altogether. The second-most expensive asset that many of us buy spends most of its time by the side of the road, slowly rusting. Why not simply buy credits with an autonomous car-sharing company?

So we will see immense benefits when autonomous vehicles become common. And that will in fact be very soon. Singapore started a trial of autonomous taxis in August 2016. In the same month, Ford announced its plans to sell a fully autonomous car within five years. In Helsinki, also in August 2016, autonomous buses were trialled for a month on public roads. A month later, Uber started trialling an autonomous taxi service in Pittsburgh. Driverless buses took to the streets of Lyon and Perth in September 2016. The race to build and sell autonomous vehicles is on.

Within fifteen to twenty years, most of us can expect to be driven around in autonomous cars. This will transform our daily commute. We can watch a movie, read a book or write emails. Time spent in a car will no longer be wasted, but will be used for work or leisure. This will open up our towns and cities. Many of us may be more willing to live further away from our increasingly expensive city centres.

As autonomous cars become readily available, we will spend less and less time doing the actual driving. We will let the machines take the strain. As a result, we will start to lose our driving skills. Since the roads will be so much safer, many of us will find our driving licences prematurely expired—for our own safety. Many young people will never bother to learn to drive. They will call an autonomous Uber instead, and it will transport them wherever they need to go. By 2050, the year 2000 will look as quaintly old-fashioned as the horse-drawn era of 1900 did to people in 1950. We won't be allowed to drive our cars anymore, and we will not notice or even care.

PREDICTION #2: YOU SEE THE DOCTOR DAILY

By 2050, you will be getting medical advice from a doctor every day. It won't be just hypochondriacs who do so. It will be nearly all of us. That doctor will be your computer. Much of the technology to do this is available today, but it has not been well enough integrated yet.

Your fitness watch will automatically monitor many of your vital statistics: your pulse, your blood pressure, your sugar levels, your sleep and your exercise. It will also watch for falls and call for help if you faint. Your toilet will automatically analyse your urine and stool. Your smartphone will regularly take selfies of you, in order to understand better your health. It will, for instance, identify suspect skin melanomas, and monitor the health of your eyes.

Your computer will also be on the lookout for early signs of dementia. It will record your voice, identifying changes that indicate a cold, Parkinson's or even a stroke. All of this will be monitored by an AI program that follows you over your lifetime, maintaining a daily record of your health from these sensors, diagnosing many simple health problems and calling in the experts when there are larger problems to be explored.

By 2050, many of us will have had our genes sequenced, so that we can identify our genetic risks. Indeed, it will be cheap and easy to do so; many young people will have had their genes sequenced in utero. The AI doctor tracking your health will have access to this genetic sequence, and so will be watching for the diseases to which you are prone. This will create a new, much more personal dimension to healthcare. This will be a trillion-dollar business, as almost all of us want to live longer. A significant fraction of the next three decades of economic growth will be directed towards achieving that dream. Our personal AI physician will have our life history, it will know far more about medicine than any single doctor, and it will stay on top of all the emerging medical literature.

Let's hope it won't be just the first world that profits from these changes. There are parts of the third world today where people die from diseases which we could fix at minimal cost. AI can provide diagnostic tools to such people. Imagine if every village in the third world had a smartphone to provide the same quality of advice that we get when we see our general practitioner.

PREDICTION #3: MARILYN MONROE IS BACK IN THE MOVIES

Actually, it won't just be Marilyn Monroe who is making new movies. You will be in these movies too. Of course, it won't be the real Marilyn but an avatar programmed to talk and act just like her. Such movies will be completely interactive. Where the story goes will depend on what you do or say. Hollywood and the computer games industry will have merged into one. Movies will immerse us in a hyperreal world. Filmmaking, virtual and augmented reality, and computer games will simply have become the entertainment industry.

On the flipside, there will be an increasing concern about the merging of the real, the virtual and the augmented. We will spend more and more of our time in worlds that don't and can't exist. These unreal worlds will be very seductive. In them, we can all be rich and famous. We can all be beautiful and smart. The real world will be far more unpleasant. There may well be an underclass of society whose members become addicted to escaping reality in such worlds, and so spend every waking moment in them. And because these worlds are not real, there will be those who inhabit them in order to act in ways that are not acceptable in the real world. There will be calls that behaviours which are illegal in the real world should be made illegal or impossible in the virtual. Others will counter that such virtual worlds provide a necessary safety valve. This problem will likely trouble our society greatly.

PREDICTION #4: A COMPUTER HIRES AND FIRES YOU

Actually, I wouldn't be surprised if, in some dark corner of the GooglePlex, it isn't already true that computers are hiring and firing people. We already trust them to match us with a spouse, and that's one of the most important decisions we ever make. Indeed, there is an argument that matching people with jobs is an easier problem than matching people with each other. Qualifications and past experience are a good indicator of someone's suitability for a new job. It's much harder to obtain similar objective evidence for someone's suitability for a particular relationship.

It won't end with computers making the decision to hire or fire you, however. Computers will increasingly take over many of the tasks of managing you during your employment. Programs will schedule your activities, approve your holidays, as well as monitor and reward your performance. Executives will (or at least should) use the time this frees up to focus more on the strategic and longer-term aspects of their businesses. In December 2016 Bridgewater Associates, one of the world's largest hedge funds with over $100 billion under management, announced a project to automate the day-to-day management of the firm, including hiring, firing and other strategic decision-making. The project is being led by David Ferrucci, who previously ran IBM's development of Watson.

Projects like this one raise many ethical issues. Should we hand over decisions like hiring and (especially) firing to a computer? We need to work out where to draw the line in empowering machines to make decisions, especially those that impact people's lives in fundamental ways. One of my favourite authors when I was a young boy was Arthur C. Clarke. His prophetic writing inspired me to want to build machines that think. When it comes to giving machines the responsibility to fire people, I am tempted to turn around one of his most famous lines from *2001: A Space Odyssey*. We will have to learn when to say to the computers: 'Sorry, I can't let you do that.' It's not enough for a machine to do a task better than a human. There are some decisions we simply should not allow machines to make.

PREDICTION #5: YOU TALK TO ROOMS

Let me make a much more positive prediction. You will walk into a room and say aloud: 'Lights on.' Then you might ask: 'When's my next appointment?' or 'Who won the football last night?' And you will expect something in the room to answer you. It might be the TV, or the stereo, or even the fridge. Whatever device it is, it will work out who you are, using your voice pattern to authenticate the request to access your private calendar, and it will understand enough about you to know which football result to look up.

A few people will resist and consciously follow a disconnected twentieth-century life. But must of us will enjoy the advantages of having all the devices in our homes online. Our fridges, toasters, boilers, baths, door locks, lights, windows, cars, bicycles and plant pots will all be connected online. The 'Internet of Things' is predicted to have over 200 billion devices by 2020. That will be dozens and dozens of devices for every person alive. As many of these devices won't have screens, the natural interface will be speech.

Artificial Intelligence will be the operating system behind this Internet of Things. A computer's operating system, the layer of software between you and the hardware, has changed remarkably over the past few decades. At the beginning a user had to interact with the physical hardware, pressing switches and connecting plugs. To get the machine to work, you had to understand the hardware on which it ran. But since then operating systems have made it easier and easier for us to interact with computers.

In the 1970s computing got just a little less geeky. Many of us budding programmers cut our teeth on command-line systems such as MS-DOS, CP/M and Unix. You typed almost meaningful commands—like 'cp' to copy a file. In the 1980s computing moved over to graphical interfaces such as Mac OS and Windows, where you could simply point and click. Want to delete a file? Drag it into the bin. What could be simpler? Computing was no longer just for geeks. Anyone with a mouse could do it.

In the 1990s computing became more connected. The internet took off and the browser became king. Indeed, Google has made a whole operating system out of it: Chrome OS. More recently, computing became mobile and focused on apps on our smartphones. The next revolution will be the conversational operating system. Google's Assistant and Apple's Siri and their successors will be the basis for these new operating systems. No more typing. No more pointing. Just speak, and the device (using the cloud) will perform complex tasks for you.

Our interface to devices is thus disappearing. In its place will be conversations. These will continue as we move from room to room, to our cars, our offices and our beds. The likely winners will be companies such as Google, Microsoft, Facebook and Amazon because there are immense network effects: we will want these conversations to follow us around. But there will also be losers. Our privacy, diversity and democracy will be challenged. The National Security Agency and other intelligence bureaus can't wait for every room to be listening to us. Marketers, too, would love to have all this data about our everyday lives. So the next time you get asked to check your privacy settings, think long and hard about what you may be giving up.

PREDICTION #6: A ROBOT ROBS A BANK

By 2050, a major bank will have been robbed by a robot. It won't walk in through the front door, or dig its way into the vault. It will be a 'soft bot' that gets in electronically. But it will get away with hundreds of millions of dollars. Much cyber crime to date has been rather low-tech. Attackers phish passwords from unsuspecting users. Malware is downloaded when a naive employee clicks on a suspect link. AI will change this game. It will be both a blessing and a curse. More intelligent software will defend systems. But it will need to be, as attacks become more intelligent too.

In 2014 DARPA launched its Cyber Grand Challenge to develop defence systems that can automatically discover and correct software flaws in real time. In August 2016 the winning Mayhem team from Carnegie Mellon walked away with the $2 million prize at DEF CON 24, the largest annual hacker conference in the world. Seven teams competed in a 96-round game of Capture the Flag. This is a popular hacking game in which teams must protect their own data while attempting to access that of the others, except in this competition the teams were not humans but autonomous programs. Mayhem later played against the human hackers at DEF CON 24 and finished in last place, even if it was briefly ahead of a couple of humans. But by 2050 I wouldn't bet on the humans winning any more. AI hackers will be able to work far faster and far more thoroughly than human hackers. And your only defence will be an AI program.

DARPA invested millions in the Cyber Grand Challenge. Their interest in autonomous cyber defence is not primarily for civilian purposes. Warfare is moving into cyberspace, and the US military needs to keep ahead of the opposition. But the same technologies will quickly be found in the civilian sphere. The supposed hacking by Russians in order to influence the 2016 US Presidential election demonstrates the impact that such cyber attacks can have. One of the challenges will be that many advances in AI used to defend systems will quickly be turned around to attack systems. The banks will have no choice but to invest in more and more sophisticated AI systems to defend themselves from attack.

PREDICTION #7: GERMANY LOSES TO A ROBOT TEAM

The first part of this prediction is that in 2050 Germany will again be the world champion football team. The Germans have won the World Cup five times so far, one less than Brazil. But unlike Brazil, their star remains on the ascendant. And as world champions in 2050, they will be challenged to an exhibition match, which they will lose to a team of robots.

The robots will have a number of advantages over the humans. They will have superior ball skills. They will pass the ball with unfailing accuracy. And they will convert their penalties every time.[3] They will know precisely where all the other players are at all times. And they will use this knowledge to great advantage, having learned strategic play from watching every World Cup match and qualifier ever recorded. It will be like Germany versus Brazil in the 2014 semi-final, which Germany won 7–1. Even fans of the robots will be calling for the human football players to be given a break.

Football players will not need to fear the result of this exhibition match. Most football teams will still be human. There will be little interest in watching robots play robots—especially once the robots get better at the game than humans. But AI will change human football and most other games. Managers and players will look to machine-learning and optimisation algorithms to train players better, as well as to advise about playing the game more strategically. Data scientists will be some of the best-paid members of a football club. Scouts from Manchester United will hang out at places like

Oxford, Imperial and Edinburgh, looking to recruit promising young computer scientists.

PREDICTION #8: GHOST SHIPS, PLANES AND TRAINS CROSS THE GLOBE

By 2050, the oceans, skies and railroads of the planet will be crossed by ships, planes and trains that are devoid of people. The Oxford study on the automation of jobs put the probability that captains, mates and pilots will be automated at just 27 per cent. I suspect this is too low. In 2016 the president of Rolls-Royce's marine division predicted: 'Autonomous shipping is the future of the maritime industry. As disruptive as the smart phone, the smart ship will revolutionise the landscape of ship design and operations.'

With trucks or planes, decisions need to be made in fractions of a second. On a ship, however, there is a lot more time. It is likely to prove easier, therefore, to steer a ship autonomously than a truck or a plane. In addition to improving safety, autonomy will bring significant efficiencies. The space currently used for crew will be freed up for cargo. Ships will never need to wait for new crew to arrive. Operating costs will plummet, just as they will with autonomous trucks.

There will be many autonomous cargo planes by 2050 too. Unlike our roads, the air is already strongly regulated. This makes the task of automation easier. In addition, planes themselves are already significantly automated. It will take little to remove humans completely. With no lives at stake in a cargo plane, regulators will quickly approve such automation. On the other hand, planes carrying people will probably continue to be piloted by humans. But after several decades of safe flights by cargo planes, the debate will begin about whether humans should still be airline pilots.

There are already many light-rail, urban and metro systems that operate autonomously. Automating long-distance railways is more challenging, and will take a few decades. Rio Tinto is developing the world's first fully autonomous heavy-haul long-distance railway system. This delivers iron-ore from the Pilbara region of Western Australia. Testing of its AutoHaul technology started in 2014. While there were teething problems in 2016, these will have been long sorted out by 2050. Many other long-distance railways will be autonomous by then. As an example, Deutsche Bahn is planning to have long-distance autonomous trains running by 2023. Autonomy on the rails will bring greater safety, as well as increased throughput. As a result, children will no longer grow up wanting to be train drivers. Many won't even realise that humans once drove trains. There will, however, remain a nostalgia among older people for the days of trains driven by humans, just as we currently look back to the days of steam.

PREDICTION #9: THE TV NEWS IS MADE WITHOUT HUMANS

In 2050 there will be a nightly TV news program that is made without a single human being involved in the production. Actually, like some of my other predictions, nearly every part of this prediction is already here. It is just that no one has yet put all the pieces together. Let's start with the journalists' job of writing stories. I've already described how simple sports and financial stories are being written automatically by computer. As the technology improves, more complex stories will also be written by computers.

We then have the job of the news editor, who decides which stories to chase, which stories to run and how to put the program together. *The Washington Post* trialled its system, Heliograf, at the 2016 Rio Olympics; it used AI to automate the editing of a news blog. In thirty-five years' time, such systems will be common in print, TV and radio newsrooms.

We move next to the presenter's job: reading the news. Earlier I described how Japanese researchers developed two newsreading robots in 2014. More recently, a Microsoft chatbot started presenting the weather on the *Morning News* program of Shanghai's Dragon Television. Finally, we have the job of the cameraperson, who films the news. Many studios already have robotic cameras to do this job.

With the increasing pressure on news organisations to reduce costs, it seems inevitable that programs will eventually be made without any humans at all. News produced in this way will have all the production values we expect of broadcast news today. However, it will be 'narrowcast'; that is, the news program each of us watches will be tailored to our particular preferences.

Media owners will appreciate the economies brought about by eliminating humans from the newsroom, especially the expensive presenters. But there will be an ongoing debate about the biases of the algorithms, especially when humans play no part in deciding what news we see. Our viewpoints are shaped by the lens through which we look at the world. Will these algorithms challenge us enough? Will they care about what we care about? Will they understand lies and deception well enough? Will they cry when we cry? Or will they simply entertain us better than we have been entertained before?

PREDICTION #10: WE LIVE ON AFTER DEATH

This seems a good prediction to end with. Again, it's not actually so far from reality today. In 2016 Eugenia Kuyda created a chatbot trained on the texts of her recently deceased friend Roman Mazurenko. One of Roman's friends said: 'What really struck me is that the phrases he speaks are really his. You can tell that's the way he would say it.' Roman's mother added: 'There was a lot I didn't know about my child. But now that I can read about what he thought about different subjects, I'm getting to know him more. This gives the illusion that he's here now.'

By 2050 it will be common to leave behind an AI chatbot like this. It will talk like you, it will know the story of your past, and it will comfort your family after you die. Some people might give their chatbot the task of reading their will and sharing out their estate. A few will likely use the opportunity to settle some old scores 'in person'. But many will be careful to cause as little additional grief as possible. Indeed, some of us will program our bot to use humour to lighten the moment.

These 'digital doubles' will also start to appear in place of the living. Celebrities will use bots to create a social media presence, responding to Facebook messages, tweeting in response to events, and instagramming photos and captions. Many of us will hand over aspects of our lives to such bots. They will manage our diaries, organise meetings and social events, and respond to emails.

A rule attributed to Hal Varian, chief economist for Google, but actually coined by Andrew McAfee, is: 'A simple way to forecast the future is to look at what rich people have today; middle-income people will have something equivalent in ten years, and poor people will have it in an additional decade.' The rich today have personal assistants to help manage their lives. In the future, the rest of us will be able to call upon digital assistants to help us. Today, the rich have chauffeurs. In the future, many of us will be driven in autonomous cars. Today, the rich have family offices to manage their assets. In the future, the rest of us will have robo-advisers that manage our more limited assets.

Varian's rule suggests that the rest of us will gain the privacy that the rich can afford today. This is possible but unlikely, in my view. We can already secure our email and voicemail with very strong cryptography. But most of us don't bother. Many of the 'free' services we use are actually 'paid for' by our data.

This digital outsourcing of our lives and afterlives will fuel a lively debate. What redress do you have against an AI bot that is pretending to be you? Do you have a right to know whether a computer rather than a person is interacting with you? Should AI bots be prohibited from political discourse? The 2016 US election gave us a preview of where such technologies might take us. There will be many other questions that trouble society. Who can switch off your AI bot after you die? Are your responsible if your bot incites racism or sexism? Do such bots have freedom of speech? It will be an interesting future.

Epilogue

When we look back from the end of the twenty-first century, we will see the development of thinking machines as one of our great scientific achievements. It is an adventure as bold and ambitious as any that we have attempted. Like the Copernican revolution, it will fundamentally change how we see ourselves in the universe. It may even be our last great adventure, for thinking machines could take over from us the adventurous job of pushing back the frontiers of knowledge.

Thinking machines might well be our greatest legacy. There are few other human inventions that are likely to have as large an impact on our lives. Machines that think will start a societal revolution comparable in scale to the Industrial Revolution. The steam engine liberated our muscles; the computer is set to liberate our minds. There are almost no parts of our lives that won't be touched by this revolution. It will change how we work, how we play, how we educate our children, how we treat the sick and how we care for the elderly.

There are many challenges facing the world today: global warming; the ongoing (and likely never-ending) Global Financial Crisis; the global war on terror; the emerging global refugee problem. All our problems seem to be global. AI adds to these challenges, threatening our jobs and, perhaps, in the longer term, even our existence. But we should also keep in mind the promise of Artificial Intelligence. Thinking machines might be able to help us tackle some of these big challenges.

Whether this works out for better or worse depends largely on how society itself adapts to AI technologies. This is a job for politicians, playwrights and poets as much as for scientists and technologists. The playwright Václav Havel brilliantly helped steer Czechoslovakia through its Velvet Revolution. We will need people with this sort of vision and integrity to help steer us through this Knowledge Revolution.

There are likely to be many serious challenges brought about by these changes. Perhaps the most serious will be economic. Unchecked, thinking machines will concentrate wealth in the hands of the few, those companies and individuals with best access to the technology. Economists such as Thomas Piketty have already made a strong case that inequality increases in capitalist economies when the rate of return on capital exceeds the rate of economic growth, and that this has been the case for much of our history. Other trends, such as globalisation and the GFC, are contributing to this rise in inequality. Artificial Intelligence will only increase inequality further—unless we take corrective action.

One of the responsibilities of scientists is to communicate what futures are possible. As this book has outlined, Artificial Intelligence can lead to many good futures. It can make us healthier, wealthier and happier. Many critics are also right: AI can lead to bad futures. It could destroy the livelihood of many people, transform warfare for the worse and take away our privacy. The future has yet to be fully determined, though. If we do nothing, the outcome is likely to be bad. It is clear that, at this juncture in history, many forces are pushing us in undesirable directions. The planet is getting warmer. Inequality is increasing. Privacy is being eroded. We must act now to reverse these trends. It is not too late, but we have little time to waste.

EPILOGUE

There is one important question that we must decide as a society: which decisions should we entrust to the machines? We will be able to hand over many decisions to autonomous technologies. Some will make our lives better, lifting our productivity, improving our health and increasing our happiness. But some will make our lives worse, raising unemployment, reducing our privacy and challenging our ethics. Even at a time when machines can make decisions better than humans, I have argued that there are some decisions that we must not leave to them. Technology is a strange intruder, and should be welcomed only into those parts of our lives that it will enrich.

I finish with the words of the person who began this book. Ending a 1951 broadcast on the BBC's *Third Programme*, Alan Turing said:

> It is customary, in a talk or article on this subject, to offer a grain of comfort, in the form of a statement that some particularly human characteristic could never be imitated by a machine ... I cannot offer any such comfort for I believe that no such bounds can be set ... but I believe that the attempt to make a thinking machine will help us greatly in finding out how we think ourselves.

Notes

PROLOGUE

1. The Pilot ACE computer, designed by Alan Turing, was demonstrated to the press in December 1950. Depending on how you define things, this was about the eleventh general-purpose programmable computer to be built. Before this, we had: Z3 (Germany, 1941); Colossus Mark 1 (UK, 1944); Harvard Mark 1 (US, 1944); Colossus Mark 2 (UK, 1944); Z4 (Germany, 1945); ENIAC (US, 1946); Manchester Baby (UK, 1948); Manchester Mark 1 (UK, 1949); EDSAC (UK, 1949); CSIRAC (Australia, 1949). The first commercially successful electronic computers, UNIVAC 1 and the Manchester Ferranti, were not delivered until 1951. In the decade or so that followed, Sperry Rand sold just forty-five more UNIVAC 1 computers to clients such as the US Census Bureau, the US Army and a number of insurance companies. Computers remained rare and expensive beasts for decades after Turing's dreams about Artificial Intelligence. Today, over a billion computers are in use, and the cheapest can be purchased for tens of dollars. We have come a long way in sixty-seven years.
2. Turing, A.M., 'Computing Machinery and Intelligence', *Mind*, 59 (236), October 1950, p. 442
3. Many others beside the judges in *Time* magazine have supported this evaluation. On the centenary of his birth, *Nature* called Turing 'one of the top scientific minds of all time'.
4. The bombe was an electromechanical device used to break the Enigma

code. It was not a computer as it lacked several of a computer's essential features, such as a stored program. Nevertheless, it did a form of computation, searching through many possible positions of the rotors of the German Enigma code machine looking for a crib, a likely string of text.

5. The 'Turing Machine' is a hypothetical computing device consisting of a long string of tape, and a head for reading or writing symbols to the tape according to some simple logical rules. It can simulate the actions of any computer program. Despite its simplicity, it remains today the most fundamental model we have of computing.

6. See Turing, A.M., 'The Chemical Basis of Morphogenesis', *Philosophical Transactions of the Royal Society of London B: Biological Sciences*, 237 (641), 1952. The *Philosophical Transactions of the Royal Society* was established in 1665 by the Royal Society, the first and most famous scientific society. It is the oldest scientific journal in the English-speaking world.

7. The inquest into Turing's death in 1954 at the age of just forty-one determined his death to have been suicide. It may have been caused by a half-eaten apple laced with cyanide found by his body. However, the apple was never actually tested for cyanide. It has not been lost on many commentators that *Snow White and the Seven Dwarfs* was one of his favourite movies; see Hodges, A., *Alan Turing: The Enigma*, London: Burnett Books, 1983.

8. See Carroll, L., 'What the Tortoise Said to Achilles', *Mind*, 4 (14), 1895, pp. 278–280.

9. See Turing, 'Computing Machinery and Intelligence'.

10. Google alone has spent over half a billion dollars on DeepMind (a neural network company), $30 million on Wavii (a natural language processing company), as well as millions more on seven robotics companies.

11. Unless otherwise noted, amounts given in this book are in US dollars.

12. Claude Shannon was born in 1916 and died in 2001. His Masters thesis at MIT demonstrated that Boole's algebra (to which we will come shortly) could be implemented in an electrical circuit to construct any

logical function. This idea is considered the basis of all computer hardware today. Shannon's has been called possibly the most important and most famous Masters thesis of the twentieth century. He later laid the foundations for communications theory, describing the limits with which digital information can be sent over a noisy channel, be it a telegraph wire or a radio link. In 1950 Shannon also published the first scientific paper on computer chess. He and his wife, Betty, would go on weekends to Las Vegas, where he would use card counting to win at blackjack.

13. I have played a few games of Go, and lost every one spectacularly.
14. Before the arrival of Cook and other explorers from Europe to the Australian continent, it was thought that swans could not be black. Back in the first century AD the Roman poet Juvenal wrote about events being as rare as black swans.

1. THE AI DREAM

1. John McCarthy was born in 1927 and died in 2011. He made numerous other contributions to computer science in general, and Artificial Intelligence in particular. He was presented with the Turing Award in 1971, the most prestigious prize in computer science. He founded the Stanford Artificial Intelligence Laboratory (also known as the Stanford AI Lab or SAIL), which has been one of the leading centres worldwide for Artificial Intelligence research. I was lucky enough to know John. Once when he was visiting Australia, we were both invited to a sailing trip on Sydney Harbour on a glorious summer's day. By this time, late in his life, he was a little infirm and used a wheelchair. I therefore found myself with one foot on the quay and one foot on the boat, holding John as I tried to lift him on board. At this point, John froze. I froze. We became unable to move forwards or backwards. I then realised that I risked going down in the history of Artificial Intelligence as a footnote in the story of his watery death. This was enough to give me the strength to push him onto the boat. But I spent the rest of the trip worrying about how we would get him back onto dry land. John died at home five years later. However, the boating trip has now indeed found itself in a footnote of a history of Artificial Intelligence.

2. The *Oxford English Dictionary* dates the introduction of the term 'Artificial Intelligence' to the proposal for the Dartmouth Conference written by McCarthy, Marvin Minsky, Nathaniel Rochester and Claude Shannon in August 1955. McCarthy is, however, considered to have coined the term.

3. Ramon Llull was born around 1232, and died around 1315. He wrote over 200 books, and made pioneering contributions to several other fields. I was lucky enough to chair the main AI conference in Barcelona in 2013, some seven hundred years after his death. We celebrated then his many contributions to the field with a special event. Thank you, Carles.

4. Gottfried Wilhelm Leibniz was born 1646 and died 1716. Leibniz also invented several mechanical calculators, as well as refined the binary number system, the language of 0 and 1 which is the basis of every digital computer today. Leibniz is perhaps most famous for inventing calculus, the mathematical study of change, independently of Newton. Calculus has become the language of much of physics.

5. *The Art of Discovery*, 1685.

6. The Turing Machine is a universal and formal model of a computer. It is simply a machine that manipulates symbols on a paper tape.

7. Thomas Hobbes was born in 1588 and died in 1679. He is perhaps better known for his book *Leviathan*, which provided a philosophical argument for the existence of states and for an objective science of morality.

8. *De Corpore* (translated from the Latin), Chapter 1.2, 1655.

9. Blaise Pascal had designed a mechanical calculator a decade earlier, in 1642. However, several machines that can add pre-date this, including the abacus and a number of ancient Greek astronomical instruments.

10. René Descartes was born in 1596 and died in 1650. He was one of the first philosophers to emphasise the use of logical reasoning to develop scientific knowledge.

11. *Modus tollens* is the logical rule for reasoning backwards. It is the rule that if X implies Y, then supposing Y does not hold, X cannot either. It can be justified using the principle of reasoning by contradiction.

Suppose X holds, then, as X implies Y, Y must also hold. But this is a contradiction, as Y does not hold. Thus, our assumption was false: X does not hold.

12. George Boole FRS was born in 1815 and died in 1864. The idea of explaining the logic of human thought mathematically apparently came to Boole in a flash as he was walking across a field in Doncaster at the age of just seventeen. However, it would be more than a decade before he put this idea down on paper.

13. Boole's wife was Mary Everest, niece of George Everest, the surveyor after whom the highest mountain in the world is named. In 1864 Boole was caught in the rain en route to lecturing at the university, and went down with a cold. Mary Everest was a homoeopath, and believed that remedies should resemble their cause. She therefore put her husband to bed, wrapped in wet bed sheets. Many have written that she threw buckets of cold water over the sick patient but this is probably an exaggeration. In any case, Boole's condition worsened and he died a rather unnecessary death. By a strange twist of fate, one of Boole's great-great-grandsons is Geoffrey Everest Hinton, who will appear shortly in our brief history of Artificial Intelligence as a leading exponent of Deep Learning. In 2003 I was a professor at Boole's university, now called University College Cork. I would cycle past his house nearly every day and wonder what might have become of his ideas if he hadn't died so young.

14. Charles Babbage FRS was born in 1791 and died in 1871. He was Lucasian Professor of Mathematics at Cambridge, a position held by Isaac Newton and, more recently, Stephen Hawking. Despite Babbage's independent wealth, significant government funding, brilliant designs and the best British engineering, his project to build a mechanical computer must go down in history as one of the first failed and costly computing projects. Babbage himself didn't help. He was a prickly character, highly principled, easily offended and given to public spats with those he perceived to be his enemies. Added to this, the project suffered from poor publicity and irregular funding, and from being so far ahead of its time. It's hard to imagine how his project could have succeeded. But if it had, we could have started to build thinking

machines in earnest. Babbage's Difference Engine was finally constructed by the Science Museum in London in 1991 on the bicentennary of his birth. His Analytical Engine contained several novel features that are to be found in modern digital computers, including sequential control, branching and looping. A project is underway in Britain to complete the Analytical Engine by 2021, for the 150th anniversary of his death.

15. Ada Lovelace was born in 1815 and died in 1852. She was the daughter of the poet Lord Byron. Ada Lovelace Day is celebrated in October to promote women's participation in STEM subjects (science, technology, engineering and mathematics).

16. William Stanley Jevons FRS was born in 1835 and died in 1882. He is perhaps most famous for applying mathematical methods to economics, especially around the idea of utility. In his *Theory of the Political Economy* (1857), he wrote: 'It is clear that Economics, if it is to be a science at all, must be a mathematical science.' Many economists have been trying and failing to meet this challenge ever since.

17. *Philosophical Transactions of the Royal Society of London*, 1870, volume 160, page 517.

18. Jevons drowned in a swimming accident in the sea near Hastings on a Sunday morning at the age of forty-six.

19. David Hilbert was born 1862 and died 1943. Hilbert was one of the first to consider meta-mathematics, the mathematical study of mathematics itself.

20. Georg Cantor was born in 1845 and died in 1918. Cantor is famous for the elegant 'diagonal' argument, which is central to Turing's proof of the halting problem and Gödel's proof of his first incompleteness theorem.

21. There are several ways that sets can represent numbers. For instance, we can represent the number 0 by the empty set, the number 1 by the set containing the empty set, the number 2 by the set containing the set representing the number 1 (so, the set containing the set containing the empty set), and so on all the way out to infinity.

22. Lord Bertrand Russell FRS was born in 1872 and died in 1970. Russell won the Nobel Prize in Literature in 1950 for his writings championing humanitarian ideals and freedom of thought.

23. Kurt Gödel was born in 1906 and died in 1978. He fled Nazi Germany to take up a permanent position at the Institute for Advanced Study at Princeton, where he became good friends with both Albert Einstein and John von Neumann. Gödel was an eccentric figure. In fact, he was sufficiently eccentric that Einstein, a bit of an eccentric himself, had to chaperone Gödel to his naturalisation interview. But even Einstein was unable to prevent Gödel claiming at the interview to have a mathematical proof that the American constitution had some inner contradictions which permitted a dictatorship. Nevertheless, he was able to take up US citizenship. Less well known is that he wrote a formal proof of the existence of God, and that his fear of poisoning ultimately led him to starve himself to death.

24. Sir Roger Penrose FRS was born in 1931. His arguments against Artificial Intelligence appear in his book *The Emperor's New Mind: Concerning Computers, Minds, and the Laws of Physics*, New York: Oxford University Press, 1989. He argues that human consciousness is not algorithmic, and cannot be modelled by a conventional digital computer. Further, he conjectures that quantum effects play an essential role in the human brain. Shortly after the book appeared, I invited Penrose to give a talk at the Department of Artificial Intelligence at the University of Edinburgh, where I was based at the time. Penrose came but, as he told me over lunch before the talk, he felt like someone about to put his head into the mouth of a lion. Edinburgh's reputation as one of the centres for AI research was very strong at that time. He had some reason to be nervous. While his book won the Royal Society's Science Book Prize, his arguments have been disputed by philosophers, computer scientists and neurologists alike. I enjoyed my lunch with Penrose, and his talk a little less so.

25. In fact, some of Penrose's arguments against the possibility of Artificial Intelligence are similar to those first proposed by J. R Lucas in 'Minds, Machines and Gödel', *Philosophy*, 36 (137), 1961, pp. 112–127.

26. In computational complexity, problems like the halting problem are called undecidable problems. Other undecidable problems include deciding if a mathematical statement is true, deciding if two mathematical functions always compute the same answer, and Hilbert's tenth

problem of deciding whether a simple polynomial equation has a whole number solution.

27. Technically, Turing's result proves that there are problems Turing Machines cannot solve. This doesn't prevent other, richer computational models from computing these problems. However, even with richer computational models such as quantum computers, we have such undecidability results. For instance, a quantum computer can compute certain problems faster than a classical computer, but as a classical computer can simulate a quantum computer, the halting problems remains undecidable even with a quantum computer.

28. Deciding if a mathematical statement is true or not is Hilbert's *Entscheidungsproblem*. Alonzo Church proved that this is not decidable by computer in 1936, using his model of computation. Independently, Turing proved the problem is not decidable by computer in 1937, using his idea of the Turing Machine, an essential equivalent computational model.

29. The Zuse Z3 was destroyed by Allied air raids in 1943. Building of the Colossus started in February 1943, and it decoded its first message one year later, although its existence was kept secret till the 1970s. Unlike the Colossus, ENIAC was announced to the public in 1946 and so has entered many history books as the first computer. The Manchester Small-Scale Experimental Machine, nicknamed the Baby, was not built until 1948 but was the first computer in which a program was stored in memory, and so could be changed without physically rewiring and changing switches.

30. There is little evidence that Thomas Watson made the claim that the world market for computers would be just half a dozen. Sir Charles Darwin, grandson of the famous naturalist, did write a 1946 report as head of Britain's National Physical Laboratory in which he argued it was 'very possible' that 'one machine would suffice to solve all the problems that are demanded of it from the whole country'.

31. Marvin Minsky was born in 1927 and died in 2016. Carl Sagan described Isaac Asimov and Minsky as the only two people he ever met whose intellects surpassed his own. Minsky was a scientific adviser on Stanley Kubrick's movie *2001: A Space Odyssey*. AI researcher Ray Kurzweil has

said that Minsky was cryonically preserved by the Alcor company, and will be revived in around 2045. Interestingly, this is the date predicted by Kurzweil for machines to have reached human-level intelligence. Kurzweil, Nick Bostrom and a number of other AI researchers have paid to join Minsky at minus 200 degrees Celsius in due course.

32. Herbert Alexander Simon was born in 1917 and died in 2001. He won the Nobel Prize in Economics 1978 for his work on decision-making. Along with Allen Newell, he wrote two pioneering AI programs: the Logic Theory Machine (1956), which proved mathematical theorems, and the General Problem Solver (1957), which was one of the first programs to separate its knowledge from its problem-solving strategy, a precursor of the expert systems that would appear in the 1980s.

33. Allen Newell was born in 1927 and died in 1992. He won many awards, including the Turing award with Herb Simon in 1975, and the National Medal of Science from President George H.W. Bush, just before his death from cancer in 1992.

34. Donald Michie was born in 1923 and died in 2007 in a car accident. In 1960 he wrote MENACE, the Machine Educable Noughts And Crosses Engine. This was a computer program which learned to play a *perfect* game of Tic-Tac-Toe. As computers were still not readily available at that time, Michie implemented the program using hundreds of matchboxes to represent the different states of the game.

35. In case you feel critical of the proposal for the Dartmouth Summer Research Project, it is worth noting that academics are always over-promising in their grant proposals. The system is arguably designed to encourage such behaviour.

36. Shakey the robot was really rather shaky. Charles Rosen, one of the people leading the project, wrote: 'We worked for a month trying to find a good name for it, ranging from Greek names to whatnot, and then one of us said, Hey, it shakes like hell and moves around, let's just call it Shakey.' You can watch Shakey for yourself at https://vimeo.com/5072714.

37. See Darrach, B., 'Meet Shakey, the first electronic person', *Life*, 69 (21), 1970, pp. 58–68. Though it was written thirty-five years ago, this *Life* article might well have been written today: 'What guarantee do

we have that in making these [critical] decisions the machines will always consider our best interests? ... The men at Project MAC [MIT's AI project] foresee an even more unsettling possibility. A computer that can program a computer, they reason, will be followed in fairly short order by a computer that can design and build a computer vastly more complex and intelligent than itself—and so on indefinitely. "I'm afraid the spiral could get out of control," says Minsky [from MIT] ... Is the human brain outmoded? Has evolution in protoplasm been replaced by evolution in circuitry? "And why not?" Minsky replied when I recently asked him these questions. "After all, the human brain is just a computer that happens to be made out of meat." I stared at him—he was smiling. This man [Minksy] has lived too long in a subtle tangle of ideas and circuits. And yet men like Minsky are admirable, even heroic. They have struck out on a Promethean adventure and you can tell by a kind of afterthought in their eyes that they are haunted by what they have done. It is the others who depress me, the lesser figures in the world of Artificial Intelligence, men who contemplate infinitesimal riddles of circuitry and never once look up from their work to wonder what effect it might have upon the world they scarcely live in. And what of the people in the Pentagon who are funding most of the bill in Artificial Intelligence research? "I have warned them again and again," says Minsky, "that we are getting into very dangerous country. They don't seem to understand." I thought of Shakey growing up in the care of these careless people—growing up to be what? No way to tell.' This book, then, is a rather belated response to some of these fears. It is a moment where I look up from my work and that of my colleagues, and contemplate what effect success might have on the world we live in.

38. Another wonderful example of an unexpected outcome from AI research is Salter's duck for converting wave power into electricity. Stephen Salter was a roboticist at the Department of Artificial Intelligence in the 1970s. During the winter of 1973, while he was recovering in bed from flu, his wife challenged him to do something useful—like solve the energy crisis that was afflicting the United Kingdom at that time. He rose to the challenge with an ingenious pear-shaped device containing

a generator that converts over half of the wave's energy into electricity. When people ask me what useful problems have ever been solved by AI research, I like to reply, 'Salter's duck.'

39. In case you're worried that the computer might have been cheating, it wasn't actually rolling the dice for itself; they were rolled by an independent person.

40. Hans Jack Berliner was born in 1929. He is an International Master of Chess and former World Correspondence Chess Champion. He has made numerous contributions to computer chess. Indeed, his development of BKG 9.8 was actually a diversion to help build better tools to evaluate chess positions by focusing on an 'easier' game like backgammon.

41. See Berliner, H. J., 'Computer Backgammon', *Scientific American*, 242 (6), June 1980, pp. 64–72.

42. ELIZA was named after Eliza Doolittle, the working-class character in George Bernard Shaw's play *Pygmalion*. Henry Higgins, a professor of phonetics, teaches Eliza to pass herself off as an upper-class lady.

43. Joseph Weizenbaum was born in 1923 and died in 2008. While he was an early pioneer of Artificial Intelligence, he later became a strong critic of the field. He was one of the main protagonists in the 2010 documentary *Plug and Pray*, arguing that we should be careful about where technology takes us.

44. Bell Labs in New Jersey is probably most famous for being the place where the transistor was invented in 1947. The transistor is one of the logical building blocks of every computer and smartphone though it has been much shrunk in size since its invention. In the early 1990s I gave a talk to the AI group at Bell Labs, and was taken on a tour of the lab afterwards. I supposed the tour would climax with a spotlight on the first transistor, a rather poorly soldered lump of germanium and gold foil known to geeks everywhere from textbook photographs. We turned the last corner and arrived back at the reception with no transistor in sight. So I asked, 'What about the transistor?' My host replied, 'Oh, we lost it when clearing out some stuff.'

45. John R. Pierce was born in 1910 and died in 2002. He worked for many years at Bell Labs and famously invented the word *transistor*. He

also was famous for the remark that 'Funding artificial intelligence is real stupidity'. I will let you decide on the veracity of this.

46. See Pierce, J.R., 'Whither Speech Recognition?', *The Journal of the Acoustical Society of America*, 46 (4B), 1969, pp. 1049–1051. Comparing speech recognition to going to the moon in an article published in June 1969 proved somewhat ironic, as Neil Armstrong and Buzz Aldrin walked on the moon in July of that year.

47. Apple's Siri, Baidu, Google Now, Microsoft's Cortana and Skype Translator all use Deep Learning.

48. Douglas Lenat was born in 1950. He is reputed to have claimed that 'intelligence is ten million rules'. If only it were this easy!

49. The jury is still out on whether it is a good idea to try to hand-code knowledge, as the CYC project set out to do. But even if we can get computers to learn by themselves, there is a useful role to be played by having explicit facts and rules in an intelligent system.

50. Hubert Dreyfus was born in 1929. He was introduced to Artificial Intelligence while teaching at MIT alongside colleagues including Marvin Minsky.

51. See Dreyfus, H.L., *What Computers Still Can't Do: A Critique of Artificial Reason*, Cambridge, MA: MIT Press, 1992. Minsky replied to Dreyfus's book with the essay 'Why People Think Computers Can't'. Other articles responding to Dreyfus's criticisms include Rodney A. Brooks's 'Elephants Don't Play Chess'. Who said scientists don't have a sense of humour?

52. Rodney Brooks was born in 1954 in Australia, but has spent much of his career at MIT. More recently, he founded and was chief technology officer of iRobot and Rethink Robotics, which have made a number of well-known robots, including the vacuum-cleaning Roomba and the Baxter industrial robot.

53. The names chosen by Brooks for his robots perhaps say something about the relationship roboticists have with their creations …

54. Watson uses a cluster of ninety IBM Power 750 servers. In total, the system has 2880 processor threads and 16 terabytes of RAM.

55. ESPRIT was the European Strategic Program on Research in Information Technology and ran from 1983 to 1998.

56. For a good survey of Deep Learning, see Edwards, C., 'Growing Pains for Deep Learning', *Commun ACM*, 58 (7), June 2015, pp. 14–16.

57. The Canadian bias for Deep Learning is a consequence of the farsightedness of the Canadian Institute for Advanced Research, which from its foundation in 1982 was looking to fund risky and unfashionable research areas.

58. DeepMind's success at playing forty-nine classic Atari arcade games is reported in Mnih, V. et al. 'Human-level Control Through Deep Reinforcement Learning', *Nature*, 518, February 2015.

59. DeepMind isn't the first example of neural networks learning to play games successfully. In 1992 the TD-Gammon program, which used a neural network, learned to play backgammon at a superhuman level. However, TD-Gammon never did so well at similar games like chess, Go or checkers. The breakthrough in 2013 was that the same learning algorithm was used for all forty-nine games without any additional background knowledge.

60. A game tree is a basic technique used in computer programs to analyse a game such as chess or Go. The root of the tree is the start of the game. At each level of the tree, you consider all the possible legal moves available. You win the game if you end in a leaf which represents a winning position.

61. For every four people who summit K2, one person dies. By comparison, nearly fifteen people summit Everest for every person who dies on the mountain. One who died on Everest was a famous AI researcher, friend and colleague, Rob Milne. After a PhD at the University of Edinburgh, he was Chief AI Scientist at the Pentagon. He returned to Scotland to form Intelligent Applications Ltd, where he did more than almost anyone else in Europe to get AI used in practice. Whenever I met him, he would recount stories of his latest mountain adventure. Sadly, in 2005, at the age of just forty-eight, he collapsed and died within sight of his objective of summiting the highest peak on every continent. He was as wonderfully ambitious in play as in his work.

62. Don't watch a movie when your Tesla is in AutoPilot mode; the car still needs you to watch out for the unexpected. In early 2016, Joshua

Brown died in his Tesla in Florida when it drove into a turning truck when on AutoPilot mode. It has been claimed he was sitting in the driver's seat but watching a Harry Potter movie.

2. MEASURING AI

1. See Lipton, Z.C. and Elkan, C., 'The Neural Network that Remembers', *IEEE Spectrum*, February 2016.
2. Loebner is always keen to remind people that, unlike his prize, Olympic gold medals are not *solid* gold.
3. In addition to his eponymous prize, Hugh Loebner is also famous for his frequent campaigning to legalise prostitution.
4. The University of Reading's press release of 8 June 2014 was titled 'Turing Test success marks milestone in computing history'. It began: 'An historic milestone in artificial intelligence set by Alan Turing—the father of modern computer science—has been achieved at an event organised by the University of Reading. The 65-year-old iconic Turing Test was passed for the very first time by computer programme Eugene Goostman during Turing Test 2014 held at the renowned Royal Society in London on Saturday. "Eugene" simulates a 13-year-old boy and was developed in Saint Petersburg, Russia. The development team includes Eugene's creator Vladimir Veselov, who was born in Russia and now lives in the United States, and Ukrainian-born Eugene Demchenko, who now lives in Russia.' And it ended by quoting the maverick AI researcher Professor Kevin Warwick, who was behind this particular Turing test: 'Not long before he died on 7 June 1954 Alan Turing, himself a Fellow of the Royal Society, predicted that in time this test would be passed. It is difficult to conceive that he could possibly have imagined what computers of today, and the networking that links them, would be like.' I disagree with Kevin Warwick. Alan Turing did indeed dream of the capabilities of computers of today, and of the time it would take to build thinking machines. (For the record, June 2014 was the not the first time it has been claimed that a program had passed the Turing test. In 2011 NBC News reported that Cleverbot had passed the Turing test, having fooled many judges at the Techniche festival in Guwahati, India.)
5. Hector Levesque is now Professor Emeritus at the University of Toronto.

He spent his whole academic career at the University of Toronto, except for a brief period after his PhD at the Fairchild Laboratory for Artificial Intelligence Research in Palo Alto. He was one of the most famous 'neat' AI researchers to follow in John McCarthy's footsteps. Once, when visiting Sydney, he invited me to join him on a trip to the furthest reaches of Australia, taking planes and ultimately four-wheel drives to the north-west corner of the continent, for the simple reason that this was Cape Leveque. I couldn't work out whether to tell him then, on arrival or on return that the cape's name was actually spelled differently from his.

6. See Minsky, M., *Computation: Finite and Infinite Machines*, New Jersey: Prentice Hall, 1967.

7. See Darrach, B., 'Meet Shakey, the first electronic person', *Life*, 69 (21), 1970, pp. 58–68.

8. See Levy, F. and Murnane, R. J., *The New Division of Labor: How Computers Are Creating the Next Job Market*, Princeton, NJ: Princeton University Press, 2004.

9. In 1995, one year after the European demonstration of autonomous driving on the highway, CMU's NavLab 4, a converted Pontiac Transport Minivan, drove 3000 miles across America with a computer doing 98 per cent of the steering. However, unlike in the European project, humans still controlled the throttle and brake.

10. In the interests of full disclosure, I was one of the researchers surveyed by Müller and Bostrom.

11. 'In 2012 Vincent Müller and Nick Bostrom of the University of Oxford asked 550 A.I. experts ...' (*Slate*, 28 April 2016).

12. 'A 2014 survey conducted by Vincent Müller and Nick Bostrom of 170 of the leading experts in the field ...' (*Epoch Times*, 23 May 2015).

13. Twenty-nine of the 170 responses to Müller and Bostrom's survey came from the 'Top 100 Authors in AI', a list compiled by Microsoft Academic Research based on publication data.

14. The two conferences surveyed by Müller and Bostrom were Artificial General Intelligence (AGI 12) and Impacts and Risks of Artificial General Intelligence (AGI-Impacts 2012). These two conferences were organised by Müller and Bostrom at Oxford in December 2012.

15. Again, in the interests of full disclosure, I was one of the eighty respondents to this survey.

16. By definition, superintelligence will put AI researchers out of a job. So there is an argument that superintelligence must occur at the retirement age of all AI researchers!

17. Originally, the result of the 2016 Winograd Schema Challenge had the winner at 48 per cent. A person using a coin toss to answer the test would be expected to get 45 per cent, as several of the sixty questions had more than two possible answers. Unfortunately, the organisers made an error in the input file. When this was fixed, the winner—Quan Liu of the University of Science and Technology of China—did better, scoring 58 per cent.

3. THE STATE OF AI TODAY

1. For a more detailed study of the machine-learning tribe, see Domingos, P., *The Master Algorithm: How the Quest for the Ultimate Learning Machine Will Remake Our World*, New York: Basic Books, 2015. Pedro Domingos identified five machine-learning tribes but I prefer the term religious groups. If you've ever heard members of two religious groups argue, refusing to give ground to each other, you will understand why.

2. Thomas Bayes was born around 1701 and died in 1761. He was a statistician, philosopher and Presbyterian minister. His eponymous theorem solves problems in 'inverse probability'. Suppose we know the number of black balls and white balls in an urn. We can rapidly calculate the probability that we will draw at random a black ball. Bayes' theorem allows us to do the reverse. If we observe the probability of drawing a black ball, we can infer the likely ratio of black balls to white balls in the urn. Similarly, if our computer program observes some data, such as the pixels on our camera, we can use Bayesian methods to infer whether it is most likely to be a cat or a dog in the picture.

3. In case you are interested:

$$\int \frac{x+7}{x^2(x+2)}\, dx = -\frac{5}{4}\ln|x| - \frac{7}{2x}\ln|x+2| + c$$

4. The Macsyma computer algebra system began to be developed in 1968

at MIT, and was at one time one of the largest, if not the very largest, program written in the AI programming language LISP.

5. A-levels are the school leaving exams in the United Kingdom, equivalent to the Certificates of Education in Australia or the High School Diploma in the United States and Canada.

6. If $cos(x)+cos(3x)+cos(5x)=0$ then $x=(2n+1)\pi/6$ or $(3n\mp1)\pi/6$ where angles are measured in radians.

7. Simon Colton is now a Professor of Computational Creativity at Goldsmiths College at the University of London, and at Falmouth University. Another of his inventions is The Painting Fool, a program that 'paints'. He hopes it will one day be accepted as an artist in its own right. Alan Bundy and I had the privilege of supervising Simon's PhD studies.

8. For more details about HR, see Colton, S.; Bundy, A.; and Walsh T., 'Automatic Invention of Integer Sequences', *Proceedings of the 17th National Conference on AI*, Association for Advancement of Artificial Intelligence, 2000.

9. Despite its name, there was no Deep Learning in Deep Space One. Indeed, the control software in Deep Space One used no machine learning of any form.

10. Baxter is produced by Rethink Robotics, a robotic startup founded by a famous AI scruffy, Rodney Brooks. It is designed to perform simple, repetitive tasks on a production line. Baxter can be taught to do a job without programming. You simply move its hands in the desired motion, and Baxter memorises the task and is able to repeat it. Baxter is also designed to work safely around humans, and does not have to be locked away in a cage like many earlier industrial robots.

11. The internet is obsessed with cats. Not surprisingly, then, ImageNet has some 62,000 images of cats alone.

12. Error rates in the Large Scale Visual Recognition Challenge are the percentages of images in which an algorithm does not list the correct label as one of the five most probable.

13. See Woods, W. A., 'Lunar Rocks in Natural English: Explorations in Natural Language Question Answering' in A. Zampolli (ed.), *Linguistic Structures Processing*, Amsterdam: North Holland, 1977, pp. 521–569.

14. There are a few games, such as Mornington Crescent, that are an exceptions to the observation that games have precise rules and clear winners.

15. My father is a fan of Connect 4. I therefore got hold of this program that plays Connect 4 perfectly and gave it to him as a Christmas present. He remarked that it rather took the fun out of the game. It is hard to disagree.

16. IBM clearly didn't see much of a business in selling chess programs, especially not those that required dedicated hardware like Deep Blue.

17. See 'DeepMind founder Demis Hassabis on how AI will shape the future' (*The Verge*, 10 March 2016).

18. ELO ratings are a method for calculating the relative skill levels of players in two-player games such as chess. ELO is named after its creator Arpad Elo, a Hungarian-born American physics professor. Kasparov's peak ELO rating was 2851. Pocket Fritz 4 achieved an ELO rating of 2898. Deep Fritz has received an astonishing 3150, way beyond the best ever ELO rating for a human, Magnus Carlsen at 2870.

19. See Korf, R.E., 'Finding optimal solutions to Rubik's cube using pattern databases', in *Proceedings of the Fourteenth National Conference on Artificial Intelligence and Ninth Conference on Innovative Applications of Artificial Intelligence*, AAAI Press, 1997, pp. 700–705.

4. THE LIMITS OF AI

1. An AI program developed in part by the US Air Force Research Laboratory was able to defeat several human experts in a high-quality air combat simulation. See Ernest, N.; Carroll, D.; Schumacher, C.; Clark, M.; Cohen, K.; and Lee, G., 'Genetic fuzzy based artificial intelligence for unmanned combat aerial vehicle control in simulated air combat missions', *Journal of Defense Management*, 6 (1), 2016.

2. Researchers at Google have trained a neural network to guess the location of a random Street View picture, and it performs as well as, and in some cases better than, humans. See Weyand, T.; Kostrikov, I.; and Philbin, J., 'P'laNet—Photo geolocation with convolutional neural networks', *CoRR*, abs/1602.05314, 2016.

3. The expert system PUFF, used in a Californian hospital in the early

1980s to diagnose lung disease, was demonstrated to perform as well as human physicians. See Aikins, J. S.; Kunz, J.C.; Shortliffe, E.H.; and Falat, R.J., 'PUFF: An expert system for interpretation of pulmonary function data', *Computers and Biomedical Research*, 16, 1983, pp. 199–208.

4. John Searle was born in 1932. He has been one of the harshest critics of the goal of building thinking machines. 'The point is not that the computer gets only to the 40-yard line and not all the way to the goal line [of thinking],' he has written. 'The computer doesn't even get started. It is not playing that game'. See Searle, J., 'Is the brain's mind a computer program?', *Scientific American*, 262 (1), January 1990, pp. 26–31.

5. See Searle, J., 'Minds, brains and programs', *Behavioral and Brain Sciences*, 3 (3), 1980, pp. 417–457.

6. See Cole, D., 'The Chinese Room Argument', in *The Stanford Encyclopedia of Philosophy*. The Metaphysics Research Lab, Center for the Study of Language and Information, Stanford University, 2004.

7. To put this in context, the largest AI conferences attract thousands of delegates, while the largest annual AGI conference attracts a few hundred.

8. See Bostrom, N., 'How Long Before Superintelligence?', *Linguistic and Philosophical Investigations*, 5 (1), 2006, pp. 11–30.

9. John Clark was born in 1785 and died in 1853. Inscribed on the front of his Eureka machine was the following verse:

'Full many a gem, of purest ray serene
The dark, unfathom'd caves of ocean bear
And many a flower is born to blush unseen
And waste its fragrance on the desert air.'
Full many a thought, of character sublime
Conceived in darkness, here shall be unrolled
The mystery of number and of time
Is here displayed in characters of gold
Transcribe each line composed by this machine,
Record the fleeting thoughts as they arise;

A line, once lost, may ne'er be seen again,
'A thought, once flown, perhaps for ever flies'

10. From the *Illustrated London News*, 19 July 1845.

11. See Chalmers, D., 'The Singularity: A Philosophical Analysis', *Journal of Consciousness Studies*, 17 (9–10), 2010, pp. 7–65.

12. Michael Polanyi was born in 1989 and died in 1976. He was a polymath chemist who fled Nazi Germany and made contributions to philosophy and the social sciences. Two of his pupils and his son won the Nobel Prize in Chemistry. He viewed his identification of tacit knowledge as his most important discovery.

13. See Autor, D., 'Polanyi's paradox and the shape of employment growth', Working Paper 20485, National Bureau of Economic Research, September 2014.

14. AI researchers might learn a few tricks from economists such as Autor about their popularising ideas, as Moravec's paradox has proved less of a meme than Polanyi's.

15. Moravec, H., *Mind Children: The Future of Robot and Human Intelligence*, Cambridge, MA: Harvard University Press, 1988, p. 15.

16. You can decide if Pinker is correct or not.

17. See Pinker, S., *The Language Instinct: How the Mind Creates Language*, New York: Harper Collins, 1994. Pinker is still right here. All those questions stump Siri.

18. Springer published the second edition of their *Handbook of Robotics* in 2008. They will have to publish more frequently than annually then to reach the fifty-sixth edition by 2058.

19. The limitations of Asimov's three laws of robotics are highlighted by his later introduction of a fourth law: 'A robot may not harm humanity, or, by inaction, allow humanity to come to harm.' This law was numbered 0, as it took precedence over the previous three. It captures the fact that there are situations where a robot harming a human may be the best action to do. However, the zeroth law only creates a fresh set of problems. How can a robot decide what will harm humanity? What does it even mean to harm humanity? How do we trade off the welfare of humans alive from those yet to be born?

20. See Asimov, I., *I, Robot*, New York: Gnome Press, 1950.

21. I.J. Good was born in 1916 and died in 2009. Good is in part responsible for AI researchers tackling computer Go. Turing taught him to play Go, and in 1965 he wrote an article for the *New Scientist* about Go, proposing that it was potentially a greater challenge than chess, see Good, I. J., 'The Mystery of Go', *New Scientist*, 1965, pp. 172–174. The first computer Go program appeared just a few years later.

22. Around a decade ago, I found out that Google had sold my name as an AdWord to a company. I politely asked Google to have my name back. They refused. They were quite happy to let their algorithms sell my name to the highest bidder. Fortunately, the company who bought it were happy to stop buying it. I was left surprised that anyone would pay even a cent for my name.

23. For amusement, I suggest you try the auto-complete for 'Politicians are' on bing.com.

24. COMPAS stands for Correctional Offender Management Profiling for Alternative Sanctions. AI researchers love their acronyms, especially TLAs (three-letter acronyms) and ETLAs (extended three-letter acronyms ... with four letters).

25. See Walsh, T., 'Turing's red flag', *Communications of the ACM*, 59 (7), July 2016, pp. 34—37.

26. John von Neumann was born in 1903 and died in 1957. Like Turing, he is one of the founders of computing. He invented the standard architecture of modern-day computers: memory, central processing unit, arithmetic and logic processing unit, input/output devices, and buses to link them all up. In honour of this, we talk today about the von Neumann architecture used in our smartphones, tablets, laptops and desktops. Von Neumann was a polymath who made many significant contributions to mathematics, physics, economics, statistics and computing. On his death, he was in the process of writing a book called *The Computer and the Brain*. The unfinished book was ninety-six pages long, and was published in 1958. It discusses several important differences between brains and computers of that time, like processing speed and parallelism. Nevertheless, he argued that, due to their universal nature, computers could simulate the brain.

27. See Ulam, S., 'Tribute to John von Neumann', *Bulletin of the American Mathematical Society*, 1958, 64 (3).

28. See Good, I. J., 'Speculations concerning the first ultraintelligent machine', *Advances in Computers*, 6, 1965, pp. 31–88.

29. See Vinge, V., 'The Coming Technological Singularity: How to Survive in the Post-human Era', in Rheingold, H. (ed.), *Whole Earth Review*, Point Foundation, 1993.

30. See Kurzweil, R., *The Singularity Is Near: When Humans Transcend Biology*, London: Penguin, 2006 and Bostrom, N., *Superintelligence: Paths, Dangers, Strategies*, Oxford: Oxford University Press, 2014.

31. The title of this section, 'The Singularity May Never Come', alludes to Ray Kurzweil's 2005 book *The Singularity Is Near: When humans transcend biology*. In it Kurzweil discusses Artificial Intelligence and the future of humanity predicated on the singularity happening.

32. See Vinge, V., 'The Coming Technological Singularity: How to Survive in the Post-human Era', in Rheingold, H. (ed.), *Whole Earth Review*, Point Foundation, 1993.

33. See Pinker, S., 'Tech luminaries address singularity', *IEEE Spectrum*, June 2008.

34. See Bostrom, N., 'When Machines Outsmart Humans', *Futures*, 35 (7), 2002, pp. 759–764.

35. See Chalmers, D., 'The Singularity: A Philosophical Analysis', *Journal of Consciousness Studies*, 17 (9–10), 2010, pp. 7–65.

36. The three musketeers of Deep Learning are Geoffrey Hinton, Yann LeCun and Yoshua Bengio. Geoffrey Hinton is the great-great-grand-son of George Boole. His start-up company was acquired by Google in 2013, so he now divides his time between Google and the University of Toronto. Yann LeCun left the NYU Center for Data Science in 2013 to become the first director of AI Research at Facebook. Yoshua Bengio remains in academia at the Université de Montreal.

37. Yann LeCun is quoted in Edwards, C., 'Growing Pains for Deep Learning', *Commun ACM*, 58 (7), June 2015, pp. 14–16.

38. IQ is defined over a population to have an average of 100.

39. The infinite sum adds up to just 2.

40. See Allen, P. and Greaves, M., 'The Singularity isn't near', *MIT Technology Review*, October 2011, pp. 7–65.

41. Robin Dunbar is a British anthropologist born in 1947. Critics of Dunbar's work have suggested other factors than brain size—such as nutrition—might limit the size of social groups.

42. To be more precise, factorials grow much faster than exponentials. For instance, $n \mapsto \infty \dfrac{2^n}{n!} = 0$. Indeed, for any finite a, we have $n \mapsto \infty \dfrac{a^n}{n!} = 0$.

5. THE IMPACT OF AI

1. See Weizenbaum, J., *Computer Power and Human Reason: From Judgment to Calculation*, New York: W. H. Freeman & Co., 1976.

2. See Keynes, J.M., 'Economic possibilities for our grandchildren', London: *The Nation and Athenaeum*, 48.2—3, 1930, pp. 36–37; 96–98.

3. Wassily Leontief was born in 1906 and died in 1999. He won the Nobel Prize in Economics for his iterative method for predicting the outputs of different sectors in the economy, based on their inputs. Though not developed for this application, his method is mathematically a precursor to Google's PageRank method for iteratively predicting the importance of different webpages, based on the importance of their incoming links.

4. See Leontief, W., 'Machine and Man', *Scientific American*, 187 (3), 1952, pp. 150–160.

5. The three revolutions identified by the Ad Hoc Committee on the Triple Revolution were the cybernation revolution of increasing automation, the weaponry revolution of mutually assured destruction, and the 1960s human rights revolution. The committee's memo focused primarily on the first of these.

6. Quoted in *The Daily Telegraph*, 13 February 2016.

7. See Frey, C.B. and Osborne, M.A., 'The future of employment: How susceptible are jobs to computerisation?', Technical report, Oxford Martin School, 2013.

8. I should declare my background here: I work within Data61, the research unit within CSIRO focused on the data sciences.

9. Amazon CEO Jeff Bezos bought the *Washington Post* for $250 million in 2013.

10. See Remus, D. and Levy, F.S., 'Can robots be lawyers? Computers,

lawyers, and the practice of law', Technical report, Social Science Research Network (SSRN), December 2015.

11. Ismail al-Jazari was born in 1136 and died in 1206. He is most famed for writing *The Book of Knowledge of Ingenious Mechanical Devices*. He was an inventor, mechanical engineer, craftsman, artist, mathematician and astronomer. He is considered by some to be the father of robotics.

12. It ought to be a rule of society that politicians are never allowed to be complacent.

13. See Kassarnig, V., 'Political speech generation', *CoRR*, abs/1601.03313, 2016.

14. See Durrant-Whyte, H.; McCalman, L.; O'Callaghan, S.; Reid, A.; and Steinberg, D., 'Australia's future workforce?', Technical report, Committee for Economic Development of Australia, June 2015.

15. Human Rights Watch has an excellent track record in weapons bans. It was one of the non-government organisations (NGOs) behind the Ottawa Treaty prohibiting the use of anti-personnel landmines, and the Cluster Munitions Coalition, which helped bring about the ban on cluster munitions. Article 36 is an NGO named after article 36 of the 1977 Additional Protocol I of the Geneva Conventions. This requires states to review new weapons, means and methods of warfare to ensure they abide by international laws. Some states, including the United Kingdom, have argued that these reviews are adequate for the control of lethal autonomous weapons. However, the history of such reviews does not leave me with any confidence that this is the case. The Pugwash Conferences on Science and World Affairs bring scientific insight and reason to bear on the threat posed to humanity by nuclear and other weapons of mass destruction. They were awarded the 1995 Nobel Peace Prize. (Captain Pugwash, on the other hand, is a fictional pirate in a British cartoon, famous for having a sidekick with one of the most risqué names in children's television.)

16. Game theory studies simple mathematical models of conflict and cooperation between intelligent and rational decision-makers. John von Neumann is often described as the father of game theory. However, some of the ideas in game theory go back at least to the seventeenth

century. John Nash was co-winner of the 1994 Nobel Prize in Economics for his work on game theory, documented in the book and film *A Beautiful Mind*. His PhD thesis on non-cooperative game theory, which in part led to the Nobel Prize, famously was just twenty-eight pages long and contained only two references.

6. TECHNOLOGICAL CHANGE

1. Neil Postman was born in 1931 and died in 2003. He was a famous author and cultural critic. He wrote a number of influential books, including *The End of Education: Redefining the Value of School*, *Technopoly: The Surrender of Culture to Technology* and *The Disappearance of Childhood*. Over thirty years ago, his book *Amusing Ourselves to Death: Public Discourse in the Age of Show Business* foreshadowed the rise of President Trump: 'Our politics, religion, news, athletics, education and commerce have been transformed into congenial adjuncts of show business, largely without protest or even much popular notice. The result is that we are a people on the verge of amusing ourselves to death.' Postman's speech about technological change was given to the New Tech 98 Conference in Denver, Colorado, on 27 March 1998. The theme of the conference was 'The New Technologies and the Human Person: Communicating the Faith in the New Millennium'.

2. There is no evidence that Henry Ford ever said this. The quotation first appeared in print around fifteen years ago. Another quote, also attributed to Ford but equally lacking in corroboration, suggests that even he was guilty of the same lack of prophecy: 'I see no advantage in these new clocks. They run no faster than the ones made 100 years ago.' Navigation is just one aspect of our lives improved by new clocks.

3. Charles Townes was born in 1915 and died in 2014. He won the 1964 Nobel Prize in Physics for his work on masers and lasers. His quote about how those working on the first lasers could not have imagined their many uses can be found on page 4 of Townes, C.H., *How the Laser Happened: Adventures of a Scientist*, New York: Oxford University Press, 1999.

4. The International Monetary Funds's analysis suggests that increasing the income share of the poor and the middle class increases growth,

while increasing that of the wealthiest 20 per cent decreases growth. When the rich get richer, the benefits do not trickle down to the poor. When the poor get richer, the rich do also. See Dabla-Norris, E.; Kochhar, K.; Suphaphiphat, N.; Ricka, F.; and Tsounta, E., 'Causes and consequences of income inequality: A global perspective', Technical report, IMF, June 2015. SDN/15/13.

7. TECHNOLOGICAL CHANGE

1. See Gates, B., *The Road Ahead*, London: Penguin Viking, 1994.
2. The first iPhone only came out in 2007. The Nokia 9000 Communicator was launched over a decade earlier in 1996, while the BlackBerry 6210 did not appear till 2003.
3. As a Brit, I respect anyone or anything that can beat the Germans at penalties.

Bibliography

Aikins, J. S.; Kunz, J.C.; Shortliffe, E.H.; and Falat, R.J., 'PUFF: An expert system for interpretation of pulmonary function data', *Computers and Biomedical Research*, 16, 1983, pp. 199–208.

Allen, P. and Greaves, M., 'The Singularity isn't near', *MIT Technology Review*, October 2011, pp. 7–65.

Asimov, I., *I, Robot*, New York: Gnome Press, 1950.

Autor, D., 'Polanyi's paradox and the shape of employment growth', Working Paper 20485, National Bureau of Economic Research, September 2014.

Berliner, H. J., 'Computer Backgammon', *Scientific American*, 242 (6), June 1980, pp. 64–72.

Bostrom, N., 'When Machines Outsmart Humans', *Futures*, 35 (7), 2002, pp. 759–764.

———, 'How Long Before Superintelligence?', *Linguistic and Philosophical Investigations*, 5 (1), 2006, pp. 11–30.

———, *Superintelligence: Paths, Dangers, Strategies*, Oxford: Oxford University Press, 2014.

Carroll, L., 'What the Tortoise Said to Achilles', *Mind*, 4 (14), 1895, pp. 278–280.

Chalmers, D., 'The Singularity: A Philosophical Analysis', *Journal of Consciousness Studies*, 17 (9–10), 2010, pp. 7–65.

Cole, D., 'The Chinese Room Argument', in *The Stanford Encyclopedia of Philosophy*. The Metaphysics Research Lab, Center for the Study of Language and Information, Stanford University, 2004.

Colton, S.; Bundy, A.; and Walsh T., 'Automatic Invention of Integer Sequences', *Proceedings of the 17th National Conference on AI*, Association for Advancement of Artificial Intelligence, 2000.

Dabla-Norris, E.; Kochhar, K.; Suphaphiphat, N.; Ricka, F.; and Tsounta, E., 'Causes and consequences of income inequality: A global perspective', Technical report, IMF, June 2015. SDN/15/13.

Darrach, B., 'Meet Shakey, the first electronic person', *Life*, 69 (21), 1970, pp. 58–68.

Domingos, P., *The Master Algorithm: How the Quest for the Ultimate Learning Machine Will Remake Our World*, New York: Basic Books, 2015.

Dreyfus, H.L., *What Computers Still Can't Do: A Critique of Artificial Reason*, Cambridge, MA: MIT Press, 1992.

Durrant-Whyte, H.; McCalman, L.; O'Callaghan, S.; Reid, A.; and Steinberg, D., 'Australia's future workforce?', Technical report, Committee for Economic Development of Australia, June 2015.

Edwards, C., 'Growing Pains for Deep Learning', *Commun ACM*, 58 (7), June 2015, pp. 14–16.

Ernest, N.; Carroll, D.; Schumacher, C.; Clark, M.; Cohen, K.; and Lee., G., 'Genetic fuzzy based artificial intelligence for unmanned combat aerial vehicle control in simulated air combat missions', *Journal of Defense Management*, 6 (1), 2016.

Frey, C.B. and Osborne, M.A., 'The future of employment: How susceptible are jobs to computerisation?', Technical report, Oxford Martin School, 2013.

Gates, B., *The Road Ahead*, London: Penguin Viking, 1994.

Good, I. J., 'Speculations concerning the first ultraintelligent machine', *Advances in Computers*, 6, 1965, pp. 31–88.

——, 'The Mystery of Go', *New Scientist*, 1965, pp. 172–174.

Hodges, A., *Alan Turing: The Enigma*, London: Burnett Books, 1983.

Kassarnig, V., 'Political speech generation', *CoRR*, abs/1601.03313, 2016.

Keynes, J.M., 'Economic possibilities for our grandchildren', London: *The Nation and Athenaeum*, 48.2—3, 1930, pp. 36–37; 96–98.

Korf, R.E., 'Finding optimal solutions to Rubik's cube using pattern databases', in *Proceedings of the Fourteenth National Conference on Artificial*

Intelligence and Ninth Conference on Innovative Applications of Artificial Intelligence, AAAI Press, 1997, pp. 700–705.

Kurzweil, R., *The Singularity Is Near: When Humans Transcend Biology*, London: Penguin, 2006.

Leontief, W., 'Machine and Man', *Scientific American*, 187 (3), 1952, pp. 150–160.

Levy, F. and Murnane, R. J., *The New Division of Labor: How Computers Are Creating the Next Job Market*, Princeton, NJ: Princeton University Press, 2004.

Lipton, Z.C. and Elkan, C., 'The Neural Network that Remembers', *IEEE Spectrum*, February 2016.

Lucas, J.R., 'Minds, Machines and Gödel', *Philosophy*, 36 (137), 1961, pp. 112–127.

Minsky, M., *Computation: Finite and Infinite Machines*, New Jersey: Prentice Hall, 1967.

Mnih, V.; Kavukcuoglu, K.; Silver, D.; Rusu, A.; Veness, J.; Bellemare, M.; Graves, A.; Riedmiller, M.; Fidjeland, A.; Ostrovski, G.; Petersen, S.; Beattie, C.; Sadik, A.; Antonoglou, I.; King, H.; Kumaran, D.; Wierstra, D.; Legg, S.; and Hassabis, D., 'Human-level Control Through Deep Reinforcement Learning', *Nature*, 518, February 2015.

Moravec, H., *Mind Children: The Future of Robot and Human Intelligence*, Cambridge, MA: Harvard University Press, 1988.

Penrose, R., *The Emperor's New Mind: Concerning Computers, Minds, and the Laws of Physics*, New York: Oxford University Press, 1989.

Pierce, J.R., 'Whither Speech Recognition?', *The Journal of the Acoustical Society of America*, 46 (4B), 1969, pp. 1049–1051.

Pinker, S., *The Language Instinct: How the Mind Creates Language*, New York: Harper Collins, 1994.

———, 'Tech luminaries address singularity', *IEEE Spectrum*, June 2008.

Remus, D. and Levy, F.S., 'Can robots be lawyers? Computers, lawyers, and the practice of law', Technical report, Social Science Research Network (SSRN), December 2015.

Searle, J., 'Minds, brains and programs', *Behavioral and Brain Sciences*, 3 (3), 1980, pp. 417–457.

Searle, J., 'Is the brain's mind a computer program?', *Scientific American*, 262 (1), January 1990, pp. 26–31.

Townes, C.H., *How the Laser Happened: Adventures of a Scientist*, New York: Oxford University Press, 1999.

Turing, A.M., 'Computing Machinery and Intelligence', *Mind*, 59 (236), October 1950, pp. 433–460.

———, 'The Chemical Basis of Morphogenesis', *Philosophical Transactions of the Royal Society of London B: Biological Sciences*, 237 (641), 1952, pp. 37–72.

Ulam, S., 'Tribute to John von Neumann', *Bulletin of the American Mathematical Society*, 1958, 64 (3).

Vinge, V., 'The Coming Technological Singularity: How to Survive in the Post-human Era', in Rheingold, H. (ed.), *Whole Earth Review*, Point Foundation, 1993.

Walsh, T., 'Turing's red flag', *Communications of the ACM*, 59 (7), July 2016, pp. 34—37.

Weyand, T.; Kostrikov, I.; and Philbin, J., 'P'laNet—Photo geolocation with convolutional neural networks', *CoRR*, abs/1602.05314, 2016.

Weizenbaum, J., *Computer Power and Human Reason: From Judgment to Calculation*, New York: W. H. Freeman & Co., 1976.

Woods, W. A., 'Lunar Rocks in Natural English: Explorations in Natural Language Question Answering' in A. Zampolli (ed.), *Linguistic Structures Processing*, Amsterdam: North Holland, 1977, pp. 521–569.

INDEX

INDEX

INDEX

INDEX

INDEX

INDEX

INDEX

INDEX